# Effective Classroom Management

## Models and Strategies for Today's Classrooms

### THIRD EDITION

## Carlette Jackson Hardin

*Austin Peay State University*

PEARSON

Boston   Columbus   Indianapolis   New York   San Francisco   Upper Saddle River
Amsterdam   Cape Town   Dubai   London   Madrid   Milan   Munich   Paris   Montreal   Toronto
Delhi   Mexico City   São Paulo   Sydney   Hong Kong   Seoul   Singapore   Taipei   Tokyo

*Vice President/Publisher:* Kevin M. Davis
*Managing Editor:* Shannon Steed
*Editorial Assistant:* Lauren Carlson
*Marketing Manager:* Joanna Sabella
*Production Editor:* Paula Carroll
*Production Manager:* Laura Messerly
*Photo Researcher:* Annie Pickert
*Senior Art Director:* Jayne Conte
*Cover Designer:* Suzanne Behnke
*Cover Image:* Sean Locke/iStockPhoto
*Full-Service Project Management:* Manish Sharma/Aptara®, Inc.
*Composition:* Aptara®, Inc.
*Printer/Binder:* Courier/Westford
*Cover Printer:* Lehigh-Phoenix Color Corporation
*Text Font:* Minion 10/12

Credits and acknowledgments borrowed from other sources and reproduced, with permission, in this textbook appear on appropriate page within text.

**Photo credits:** Shutterstock pp. 1, 51, 71, 112, 198, 253; Annie Pickert/Pearson pp. 3, 19, 27, 41, 139, 214, 271; Bob Daemmrich Photography pp. 61, 80, 93, 99, 117, 119, 146, 155, 163, 181, 188, 204, 223, 263, 275; Thinkstock pp. 231, 235.

**Library of Congress Cataloging-in-Publication Data**

Hardin, Carlette Jackson.
   Effective classroom management : models and strategies for today's classrooms / Carlette Jackson Hardin. — 3rd ed.
   p. cm.
ISBN-13: 978-0-13-705503-6 (alk. paper)
ISBN-10: 0-13-705503-X (alk. paper)
1. Classroom management. I. Title.
LB3013.H343 2012
371.102'4—dc22

                                                           2011004469

4 5 6 7 8 9 10  V092  16 15 14 13 12

www.pearsonhighered.com

ISBN-10:     0-13-705503-X
ISBN-13: 978-0-13-705503-6

*For my sister and friend, Martha Jackson Barnes, who lovingly shared the wisdom gleaned from thirty years of teaching.*

*For my grandchildren, Andrew William Hardin and Avery Reese Hardin, in hopes that school will always be a place where they feel safe and loved.*

# About the Author

Carlette Jackson Hardin is Professor of Education at Austin Peay State University, Clarksville, Tennessee. She currently serves as Dean for the College of Education. Dr. Hardin has degrees from Austin Peay State University (B.S. and M.S.) and Vanderbilt (Ed.D.). Dr. Hardin has been active in professional organizations at the state and national level, having served as President of the National Association for Developmental Education. Dr. Hardin has given over 100 keynote addresses, presentations, and workshops at state, regional, and national conferences.

Since 1981, Dr. Hardin has had numerous professional publications and funded grants. Dr. Hardin and Dr. Ann Harris have written a Fastback for Phi Delta Kappa, *Managing Classroom Crises*, which was published Spring 2000. An orientation textbook for adult students, *100 Things Every Adult Student Ought to Know,* was published in February 2000 by Cambridge Press. She co-authored *Capturing Change: Globalizing the Curriculum through Technology,* published by Rowman and Littlefield Education. Her most recent publication is a monograph published by Phi Delta Kappa, *Making the Most of Student Teaching*.

# Brief Contents

# Contents

## Chapter 3
# Assertive Discipline   41

## Chapter 4
# Positive Classroom Discipline   61

## Chapter 5
## Logical Consequences   80

## Part II   Classroom Management as a System   97

## Chapter 6
## Discipline with Dignity   99

## Chapter 9
## Discipline without Stress® Punishments or Rewards    155

## Part III  Classroom Management as Instruction  179

## Chapter 10
## Inner Discipline  181

## Chapter 11
## Positive Behavior Support  198

## Part IV   Developing a Personal System   251

### Chapter 14
### Research-Based Best Practices in Classroom Management   253

## Chapter 15
# Creating Your Own System   271

# Preface

When I was writing the first edition of *Effective Classroom Management: Models and Strategies for Today's Classrooms,* a friend shared a textbook used by her aunt when she was training to be a teacher in the 1930s. The text, *Classroom Organization and Control* by Jesse Sears, was published in 1928 and left little doubt about the role of the teacher, with chapters devoted to order, discipline, and punishments. The text was a reminder of how much classroom management has changed in the past eighty years. The text from the 1930s is a far cry from many current classroom-management texts that focus less on teacher-centered control and punishment and more on building communities and creating safe learning environments.

The goal of the first and second editions was to provide a synthesis of these changing views of classroom management. This is the goal of the third edition as well. The text presents twelve models of classroom management that fall into three distinct categories: Classroom Management as Discipline, Classroom Management as a System, and Classroom Management as Instruction. The book is a scholarly review of the research based on classroom management. However, it is written and formatted in a way that is easy for students to read, understand, and apply.

This edition retains the practical orientation of the first and second editions while providing an updated view of classroom-management models and research. The revisions include the following:

- The addition of Positive Behavior Support as a model of classroom management. In 1997 Positive Behavior Support (PBS) became an important aspect of most schools' classroom-management system when the amendments to the Individuals with Disabilities Education Act (IDEA) became law and required that schools use positive behavioral support and functional behavioral assessment with students with significant behavioral disabilities. Since then, over 7,000 schools have adopted PBS as their primary management plan.

- The addition of a chapter that focuses on research-based best practices in classroom management. This chapter provides nine proven strategies for managing the classroom.

- The addition of a new feature called Strategies for Dealing with Difficult Students. Many readers have asked for specific strategies for working with students whose behavior is not changed by the strategies that work for the majority of students. Each model now provides more specific information on how to deal with these difficult students.

- The addition or revision of seven tables and figures within the text that are designed to give more practical suggestions for using the models.

- Seven new *Tips from the Field* provided by state teachers of the year.

## INTENDED AUDIENCE

*Effective Classroom Management: Models and Strategies for Today's Classrooms* is especially appropriate as the core text for an undergraduate or graduate course on classroom management. In addition, it may be used for staff-development programs for inservice teachers. This text provides a foundation for selecting a model to follow or for developing an individual classroom-management plan. The content is applicable for teachers and preservice teachers at all levels—elementary, middle, and high school.

## ORGANIZATION

Chapter 1 provides the theoretical framework of the text, in which a rationale is given for considering classroom management as discipline, as a system, or as instruction. The chapter presents a brief review of the major contributors to the field and ends with a discussion of how individual management plans are developed.

*Part I*, Classroom Management as Discipline, presents four models of classroom management. Chapter 2 presents basic behavioral concepts, including a review of B. F. Skinner's theory of operant conditioning. Lee and Marlene Canter's model, Assertive Discipline, is presented in Chapter 3. Chapter 4 provides a different approach to using behavioral theory in Fredric Jones's model, Positive Classroom Discipline. Chapter 5 presents the concept of logical consequences through the work of Linda Albert, Jane Nelsen, Lynn Lott, and H. Stephen Glenn.

*Part II*, Classroom Management as a System, highlights four models that are systematic in approach. Chapter 6 presents Richard Curwin and Allen Mendler's model, Discipline with Dignity. The research of Carolyn Evertson is the foundation of her model, Classroom Organization and Management Program (COMP), which is presented in Chapter 7. Chapter 8 focuses on building communities and discusses the theory of Alfie Kohn. Chapter 9 presents a theory that is being adopted by schools across the United States, Marvin Marshall's Discipline without Stress® Punishments or Rewards.

*Part III*, Classroom Management as Instruction, provides four models that have the teaching of prosocial skills as their central focus. The first model, presented in Chapter 10, is Barbara Coloroso's Inner Discipline. Chapter 11 provides a review of Positive Behavior Support. Several approaches to teaching conflict resolution and peer mediation are presented in Chapter 12. Finally, Forrest Gathercoal's model, Judicious Discipline, is the focus of Chapter 13.

*Part IV*, Developing a Personal System, provides information to assist the teacher in designing a personal system of classroom management. Chapter 14 provides research-based best practices in classroom management. Chapter 15 helps the individual teacher combine all elements of classroom management into a comprehensive program.

## SPECIAL FEATURES

The following features make this text both instructor- and reader-friendly:

- Information and chapter activities are directly tied to Interstate New Teacher Assessment and Support Consortium (INTASC) standards. The table on the inside back cover provides the INTASC standards and the chapters in which these standards are addressed.

- *Tips from the Field* appear throughout the text. These tips offer sage advice from practicing teachers.

- Each chapter contains case studies and scenarios that illustrate the concepts presented. Although most of the case studies and scenarios are based on actual events that occurred in typical classrooms, the names of teachers and students are fictitious.

- Chapter Activities are designed to help readers reflect on the model presented, develop portfolio material, and develop a personal philosophy of classroom management.

- A glossary of the Key Terms presented in each chapter appears at the end of the text.

## ACKNOWLEDGMENTS

Many people provided support and guidance as I prepared the third edition. I would like to thank the reviewers of the new edition for their helpful comments: James Dick, University of Nebraska at Omaha; Karen Roadruck, Lourdes College; Keith Whinnery, University of West Florida; and Sherie Williams, Grand Valley State University.

A very special thanks goes to my husband, William, whose patience and encouragement enabled me to complete the project. The faculty of the College of Education at Austin Peay State University provided daily encouragement and support. My sister, Martha Jackson Barnes, lovingly read each word of this text. I must thank all the teachers who graciously provided *Tips from the Field,* and I encourage readers of the text to submit tips for the next edition.

# Changing Views of Classroom Management

## Objectives

Chapter 1 prepares preservice teachers to meet Interstate New Teacher Assessment and Support Consortium (INTASC) standards #2 (Student Development), #5 (Motivation and Management), and #9 (Reflective Practitioner) by helping them to

■ evaluate different classroom-management approaches.

■ select or create the classroom-management model that best fits their needs.

■ analyze classroom environments and interactions.

■ understand the theoretical background of different approaches to classroom management.

■ reflect on personal skills and philosophy about teaching and classroom management.

## Scenario

For the past week, Marcus Holmes has been going to sleep during Ms. Salerno's math class. Today, one of his classmates reaches over and pokes Marcus while he sleeps. Startled, Marcus jumps from his seat and curses the other student. Before Ms. Salerno can react, Marcus runs from the room.

## INTRODUCTION

Ms. Salerno has only seconds to react to the situation that just occurred. She must deal with a student who has left the classroom, a classroom in uproar, and several violations of the school's and her classroom rules. What she will do in the next few minutes and in the days that follow will be determined by many factors. Marcus's age and grade level will play a major role in her handling of the situation. If a fellow teacher or teacher's aide is available, she may elect to leave the classroom to find Marcus. If she doesn't have such assistance, she must weigh the consequences of searching for Marcus with the cost of leaving the other students unsupervised. How well Ms. Salerno can predict where Marcus may have gone will influence her decision regarding whether to search for Marcus or stay with her students. She will need to consider whether Marcus has a disability that may have contributed to his behavior. She must be cognizant of school policies regarding such situations. She must decide if Marcus will be punished for his cursing or for his leaving the classroom. Eventually, she must decide what should happen to the student who poked Marcus and set the events in motion. This incident, which occurred in less than a minute, will require Ms. Salerno to make a multitude of decisions.

If Ms. Salerno were teaching in the first part of the twentieth century instead of in the first part of the twenty-first century, the answer to this classroom-management situation would be simple: Marcus and the student who poked him would be headed to the woodshed for a spanking. In 1949, Dorothy Walter Baruch in *New Ways in Discipline* suggested that the days of corporal punishment and taking students to the woodshed were over. Many parents, teachers, and legislators lament the end of such trips to the woodshed and suggest that teachers no longer have options when handling classroom-management issues. Nothing could be further from the truth, however, because teachers now have more options in managing students' behavior than in any other period in history.

Each year hundreds of books and articles are written that provide advice on the best way to handle situations like the one facing Ms. Salerno. Theoretically, the vast amount of research available about the nature of students and effective classroom-management practices makes teachers more thoughtful and less reactive in their handling of classroom situations. Unfortunately, the research fails to provide all of the answers teachers need to effectively manage their classrooms. Teachers like Ms. Salerno have learned that there is no *one* answer to discipline or effective classroom management, and ultimately teachers are left to do what they think is best for their students.

## CHANGING VIEWS OF CLASSROOM MANAGEMENT

Teachers have entered a new age of classroom management. Faced with new challenges during the first part of the twenty-first century, teachers, teacher educators, and school administrators have searched for alternate ways to manage classrooms. Finding answers to classroom-management situations, however, is difficult because there is disagreement about what constitutes effective classroom-management approaches.

Some administrators and teachers think of classroom management and discipline as being synonymous terms. Vasa (1984) describes classroom management as behaviors related to maintenance of on-task student behaviors and the reduction of off-task or disruptive behaviors. Those educators who share his view define effective classroom management as the process of controlling students' behaviors.

Others take the opposite view and contend that classroom management is not discipline. Wong (as cited in Starr, 2006) states that teachers need to think less about discipline and more about the practices and procedures that allow students to learn and teachers to teach. Freiberg and Lapointe (2006) expand this vision of classroom management by defining classroom management as "the ability of teachers and students to agree upon and carry forward a common framework for social and academic interactions, by creating an ethos of effort within a social fabric that is built over time, and ultimately leads to student self-discipline" (p. 737). This definition of classroom management expands the view of management as influencing every aspect of the classroom.

*Managing classrooms has become more challenging as instructional methods have changed.*

Educators with a more student-centered approach view classroom management as a way of preparing students for life. They focus not on controlling students' behaviors today, but on preparing students for the world they will live in tomorrow. Teachers and administrators who approach classroom management from this perspective define effective classroom management as the process of creating a positive social and emotional climate in the classroom (Morris, 1996).

How teachers and administrators define effective classroom management depends on their focus and goals. These conflicting views are the basis for classroom models that vary in approach and philosophy.

## Classroom Management as Discipline

In the 1970s and 1980s, the emphasis of classroom management was on making the classroom safe, establishing the rules of behavior, and maintaining discipline. For teachers, discipline was viewed as both a noun and a verb (Hoover & Kindsvatter, 1997). As a noun, *discipline* was defined as the rules established to maintain classroom order. As a verb, *discipline* was defined as what teachers do to help students behave acceptably in school. Both definitions tie discipline to misbehavior, because if there is no misbehavior, no discipline is required (Edwards, 1999). As Doyle (1990) notes, preventing misbehavior has been the dominant theme in classroom management, because the need for management and discipline is most evident when students are misbehaving.

Those who viewed classroom management as discipline turned to psychological theories in counseling, mental health, and behavior modification for answers to classroom-management problems. Most of these theories were developed outside classroom settings and dealt with individual students rather than with groups of students (Brophy, 1983). However, studies in behavior management were the first to show experimentally that teacher behavior could shape and maintain student misbehavior (Freiberg, 1999). Since the 1960s, behavior management has been the most common approach to classroom management. Schools throughout the United States quickly adopted these early models, because they were simple to use and allowed teachers to meet the need to stop inappropriate behavior immediately. For these same reasons, they continue to be used today.

This text contains four models that have discipline as their major focus. Although different in approach, they share the following principles:

- The teacher is responsible for maintaining classroom control.
- Discipline comes before instruction.
- Consequences must exist for inappropriate behavior.

The four models presented are Skinner's *Behavioral Management*, Canter's *Assertive Discipline*, Jones's *Positive Classroom Discipline*, and Albert's *Logical Consequences*.

## Classroom Management as a System

In the late 1970s, teachers began to reject earlier models that focused on discipline. Many found that earlier models did not adequately serve teachers who sought to create calm and

## Tips from the Field

In my first year of teaching, I started teaching academics the first day of school and handled problems as they developed. Needless to say, my first year was a learning process. I now spend the first week of class teaching procedures and rules. Students are given jobs for the year, and everyone accepts a role. I have found that if students are kept busy and know the rules and procedures, I rarely have distractions. Students come to my class expecting to learn and are really surprised if another student disrupts that process.

Grant Bell
Greenbrier Middle School
Greenbrier, Tennessee

safe learning environments for all their students (McEwan, 2000). For these teachers, classroom management and instruction are interdependent rather than separate functions. Therefore, effective classroom management is not seen as a few isolated techniques or learned gimmicks, but rather as a system of management skills (Brophy, 1983; Evertson & Harris, 1992). Kohn (1995) notes that many educators reject discipline models, because they have found punishment and threats to be counterproductive in that they produced temporary compliance at best. Others stress that it is better to have a plan to *prevent* misbehavior than to have a response plan when misbehavior occurs. Doyle (1990) stresses that the new focus on prevention has transformed both research and theory in classroom management.

For these reasons, many teachers have come to believe that the best approach to classroom management is one that is systematic, beginning with preparation before the school year begins and continuing throughout the academic year. Such an approach includes planning and conducting activities in an orderly fashion, keeping students actively engaged in lessons and seatwork activities, and minimizing disruptions and discipline problems (Brophy & Evertson, 1976).

Management programs that use a systematic approach provide solid instruction and create a purposeful learning climate (Hoover & Kindsvatter, 1997). Kohn (1995) suggests that many discipline problems are the result of the teacher asking students to do uninteresting, inappropriate, or unreasonable tasks. When teachers change their instructional strategies, behaviors improve. Carolyn Evertson (as cited in Marchant & Newman, 1996) stresses that classroom management based on control and discipline is not compatible with building the kinds of learning communities in which students have a stake in their own learning and their own school community. Rather, systematic approaches create a positive social and emotional climate stemming from good interpersonal relationships between students and teacher, as well as among students.

This text includes four models that emphasize a systematic approach to classroom management. They include Curwin and Mendler's *Discipline with Dignity,* Evertson's *Classroom Organization and Management Program (COMP),* Kohn's *Building Community,* and Marshall's *Discipline without Stress® Punishments or Rewards.*

These models view classroom management and instruction as interwoven, with the focus being on *preventing* problems rather than *responding* to problems. Each model emphasizes that effective management begins before the first child arrives for the first day of school. Recognizing that each child is unique, the creators of these models reject one-size-fits-all approaches to maintaining classroom control. Instead, these approaches are based on the belief that when students' basic needs are met, misbehavior can be avoided.

## Classroom Management as Instruction

There are those who argue that classroom-management models focusing on rewards, rules, consequences, and procedures overlook the needs of individual students. The necessity to meet individual needs has become more critical as classrooms have become more diverse and as students' needs have become more intense. Wolfgang and Kelsay (1992) contend that childhood has changed, and traditional discipline methods do not work for children who grow up in nontraditional circumstances. Therefore, as Weinstein (1999) notes, "a major change is occurring in our thinking about classroom management—this change can be characterized as a shift from a paradigm that emphasized the creating and application of rules to regulate student behavior to one that also attends to students' need for nurturing relationships and opportunities for self-regulation" (p. 151). Many schools are accepting this philosophy and are replacing rule-bound discipline programs with instruction that helps the student make ethical judgments and decisions.

These new classroom-management models focus on teaching prosocial skills to students. Peterson (1997) stresses that the teaching of some form of conflict mediation, negotiation procedures, and conflict-resolution skills should be included in the curriculum of every classroom. In addition, some teachers use conflict resolution as part of their classroom-management practices. Many schools have adopted schoolwide programs in which participation, support, and resources extend beyond a single classroom. Girard (1995) found that there were approximately fifty school-based conflict-resolution programs in 1984. By 1995, the number of such programs had risen to 5,000 and continues to increase. Because the goal is for students to learn self-discipline, these methods take longer to develop and implement but invite more risk taking on the part of the teacher. However, Curwin and Mendler (1988) feel that these models may be more effective, because they encourage improved teaching as well as improved learning.

Many of these models advance a violence-prevention approach. As Gold and Chamberlin (1996) note, all children who are eventually identified as juvenile delinquents can reliably be identified by age eight. Therefore, effective violence-prevention programming begins in the early grades, in which the habits of peacemaking are first being learned, and continues throughout middle school and high school, with the hope that if violence is learned, it can be unlearned. Remboldt (1998) states that "the key to preventing violence lies in shaping children's beliefs, attitudes, and behaviors before violence becomes an automatic manifestation of their anger" (p. 33).

This text presents four models that have the teaching of prosocial skills as their central focus. The models presented include Coloroso's *Inner Discipline, Positive Behavior Support,* Bodine and Crawford's *Conflict Resolution and Peer Mediation,* and Gathercoal's *Judicious Discipline.* The purpose of these programs is to teach appropriate behavior and social skills,

**Table 1.1** Three Views of Classroom Management

|  | Concepts | Chapters |
|---|---|---|
| **Classroom Management as Discipline** | The teacher is responsible for maintaining classroom control. Discipline comes before instruction. Consequences must exist for inappropriate behavior. | Chapter 2—Behavioral Approaches to Classroom Management Chapter 3—Assertive Discipline Chapter 4—Positive Classroom Discipline Chapter 5—Logical Consequences |
| **Classroom Management as a System** | Classroom management is systematic. Management and instruction are interwoven. There is a focus on the building of learning communities. Planning is essential. | Chapter 6—Discipline with Dignity Chapter 7—Classroom Organization and Management Program (COMP) Chapter 8—Building Community Chapter 9—Discipline without Stress® Punishments or Rewards |
| **Classroom Management as Instruction** | There is a focus on teaching prosocial skills. The goal is to establish habits of peacemaking. Schoolwide programs teach skills of conflict resolution and peer mediation. Teachers help students make ethical judgments and decisions. | Chapter 10—Inner Discipline Chapter 11— Positive Behavior Support Chapter 12—Conflict Resolution and Peer Mediation Chapter 13—Judicious Discipline |

with the focus being on helping students develop positive interactions throughout their lifetime rather than on behavior at a particular moment. Table 1.1 presents the three views of classroom management covered in this book, outlines their basic concepts, and lists the chapters that discuss them.

# CRITICAL INFLUENCES ON CLASSROOM MANAGEMENT

Ms. Salerno's reaction to Marcus's behavior in the opening scenario may also be influenced by her own philosophy of classroom management or that of six major theorists in the field of classroom management: Fritz Redl, William Wattenberg, Jacob Kounin, Rudolf Dreikurs, William Glasser, and Haim Ginott. The philosophical tenets behind these theories have withstood the test of time and continue to be applied to the modern view of classroom management. Each focuses on psychological aspects of human behavior and the interactions between students and teachers. They require teachers to review their own actions and their contributions to the events that occur in discipline situations. Each would suggest that Ms. Salerno review her contribution to Marcus's behavior before reacting to the current situation.

## Fritz Redl and William Wattenberg

Fritz Redl and William Wattenberg were the first researchers to examine the interactions between teachers and students and the impact of those interactions on student behavior. Researching in the 1950s, Redl and Wattenberg suggested that group behaviors differ from individual behaviors and that the influence of group dynamics must be considered in creating an effective classroom-management plan. Before Redl and Wattenberg, much of the focus of classroom management had been on the individual "problem" student, not on the interactions of a class of thirty or more students that might include several "problem" students. Redl and Wattenberg (1959) also noted that each classroom had what they described as "key students" who influenced the other students in the classroom. They emphasized that it is important for classroom teachers to understand the influence of class leaders, class clowns, and instigators in creating or destroying a positive classroom environment. Therefore, teachers were encouraged to anticipate certain behaviors, to be aware of group interactions, and to handle problems from a group perspective.

Redl and Wattenberg (1959) identified four types of interactions that were effective in dealing with difficult students. The first was for the teacher to provide support for self-control. They note that much misbehavior by students is the result of a temporary lapse of the student's ability to apply self-control. Teachers' behaviors that promote self-control include giving signals to cue behavior appropriate in the situation, moving into the student's space, showing interest in the student's work or opinions, or joking with the student to reduce the student's anxiety. In the second type of interaction, the teacher provides situational or task assistance by helping students in getting past temporary frustrations, restructuring or changing the activity, and using situational routines to minimize confusion. The third interaction recommended by Redl and Wattenberg was for the teacher to provide reality or value appraisal. In twenty-first-century terms this would be viewed as a "reality check." The goal is to help students recognize the effects of their behavior on themselves and others. Finally, teachers apply what Redl and Wattenberg called the pleasure-pain principle. This principle is routed in behavioral theory as students are rewarded for appropriate behavior and provided consequences for negative behavior. Redl and Wattenberg felt that if the first three interactions are appropriately utilized, the need for applying the pleasure-pain principle will be reduced.

## Jacob Kounin

Most experts in the field of classroom management agree that the work of Jacob Kounin in the 1970s was pivotal and continues to influence the development of classroom-management approaches. Kounin investigated the effects of teacher-developed classroom procedures and activities on students' on-task behaviors. Like Redl and Wattenberg, Kounin designed his research to gain knowledge about group-management techniques, emphasizing that classrooms are made up of more than one student, and to support the idea that it is the management of group behavior that identifies a successful classroom manager. He identified successful classroom managers as those teachers who "produced a

---

### Tips from the Field

My drama class produced a videotape of class rules and behavior. I assigned each group of two or three students a different rule. The groups had to write, practice, and perform a skit demonstrating appropriate and inappropriate behavior. My drama students had a great time producing the skits, and the video will be a fun way to review the rules in all of my classes.

*In Memory of*
Barbara Keihle
Language Arts Teacher
Nestucca High School
Cloverdale, Oregon

---

high rate of work involvement and a low rate of deviancy in the academic setting" (Kounin, 1970, p. 63). Therefore, his work focused on both classroom management and lesson management. Through his research, Kounin identified the following valid management techniques:

**Desists:** the teacher's actions and words used to stop misbehavior. Kounin found that the clarity, firmness, intensity, and focus of the desist greatly influenced the behavior of the student disciplined and the other students in the classroom.

**Ripple Effect:** the teacher's method of handling misbehavior by one student, which influences the behavior of other students in the classroom. Kounin found that the ripple effect for high school students was related to the students' degree of motivation to learn the material and to their positive feelings toward the teacher.

**Withitness:** the teacher's ability to know everything that is happening in the classroom and an awareness of the verbal and nonverbal interactions of students with the teacher and their classmates. The withitness quality was measured by the following criteria:

- The ability to stop misbehavior before it spreads.
- The ability to stop misbehavior before it increases in seriousness.
- The ability to correct a child who is misbehaving rather than correcting the wrong child.
- The ability to stop serious misbehavior rather than focusing on a less-serious misbehavior (Vasa, 1984).

**Overlapping:** the teacher's ability to manage two issues simultaneously. This involves managing multiple groups or assignments. In more modern language this would be known as multitasking.

**Transition Smoothness:** the teacher's management of various activities throughout the day. Because the teacher must initiate, sustain, and terminate many activities throughout the day, transitions are constant. The ability to make such transitions in a smooth and orderly fashion influences the teacher's management effectiveness.

As Brophy (1999) notes, the results of Kounin's research stressed the point that effective classroom managers were not effective merely because they could handle disruptions when they occurred; they were effective because they prevented disruptions from occurring in the first place by establishing the classroom as an effective learning environment, preparing and teaching good lessons, and monitoring students as they worked. Kounin's research changed the way teachers thought about classroom management by moving the focus on disciplining students to creating and maintaining classroom environments that support learning.

## Rudolf Dreikurs

Working from a theoretical base in Adlerian psychology, Rudolf Dreikurs advises teachers to interpret the goal of a student's problem behavior and react based on an assessment of the reasons for the behavior (Dreikurs & Loren, 1968). He stresses that every student views the world differently and teachers cannot change student behavior until the reasons for the behavior is understood. He also stresses that understanding the reasons for misbehavior must be the guiding principle for teachers as they communicate with students.

Dreikurs suggests that students who are compensating for feelings of inferiority or lacking a secure sense of belonging in the classroom or peer group often misbehave in order to get attention, gain power, exact revenge, or gain sympathy or special treatment by appearing helpless. Dreikurs advises teachers to determine which of these goals the student is trying to achieve before addressing the behavior. He believes that the students would become willing to abandon self-defeating goals and make commitments to more productive goals once they have developed insight into their behavior and its meanings.

Dreikurs also questions the use of traditional punishment techniques by teachers, stressing that such punishment does little to change behavior. Instead, he proposes that teachers should impose consequences that are logically related to the misbehavior. By doing so, students understand the connection between their behavior and the consequences of their behavior. His model promotes communication and respect between teacher and student and allows students to take responsibility for actions. Dreikurs's concepts continue to influence modern classroom-management theory. A more current version of his theory has been adapted and appears in Chapter 5.

## William Glasser

The psychiatrist William Glasser has numerous books and articles on classroom and school management. In 1965, Glasser wrote *Reality Therapy* in which he challenged the widely accepted perception of behavior as externally driven and contended that all behavior is internally motivated. Reality therapy is driven by the following principles:

- Individuals are responsible for their own behavior. Behavior is not seen as a by-product of society, heredity, or an individual's past.

- Individuals can change and live more effective lives when given guidance and support.

- Individuals behave in certain ways in order to mold their environment to match their own inner pictures of what they want.

## Tips from the Field

Most research indicates that classroom lecturing is the least effective method of instruction. What has proven effective is hands-on, teacher-guided, student-centered learning and exploration. Furthermore, when people are busy, they tend to stay focused on the tasks at hand. Therefore, when students are actively engaged in an enjoyable activity that employs a variety of learning styles, the chances of students disengaging from learning significantly decreases, and classroom-management problems virtually disappear.

David McKay,
9–12 English Teacher
Aberdeen High School
Aberdeen, WA
2002 Washington State
Teacher of the Year

In 1969, Glasser's *Schools Without Failure* outlined the application of reality therapy to school situations. School failure, Glasser contends, is the result of students and teachers accepting the notion that behavior is externally manipulated and therefore outside the student's control. This results in teachers spending too much of their time trying to control and manipulate students and students refusing to take responsibility for their own behaviors. However, Glasser stresses that students will feel safe to make these choices only if school is seen as a "good place" where all people—students, faculty, and staff—are treated with respect and caring.

This "good place" is provided in what Glasser calls a "quality school" (Glasser, 1992). In a quality school, students satisfy four psychological needs: the need to belong, the need for power, the need for freedom, and the need for fun. According to Glasser, teachers must teach and manage in a way that helps students meet these four psychological needs and by doing so, add quality to students' lives.

Focused on helping people look at present conditions to find solutions to problems, Glasser opposes coercion, either through reward or punishment. He calls for schools to transform into caring places that students enjoy, and where they feel a sense of belonging. Once teachers and schools meet these needs, he contends that students will behave appropriately and traditional discipline methods are unnecessary. Marvin Marshall's model, Discipline without Stress® Punishments or Rewards, adapts many of Glasser's ideas and is the focus of Chapter 9.

## Haim Ginott

As an elementary teacher in Israel, Haim Ginott wanted to discipline without humiliating, judging, hurting, or destroying the self-worth of his students. When he evaluated his own behaviors and interactions with students, he observed:

> I have come to a frightening conclusion. I am the decisive element in the classroom. It is my personal approach that creates the climate. It is my daily mood that makes the weather. As a teacher, I possess tremendous power to make a child's life

miserable or joyous. I can be a tool of torture or an instrument of inspiration. I can humiliate or humor, hurt or heal. In all situations it is my response that decides whether a crisis will be escalated or de-escalated, and a child humanized or de-humanized. (Ginott, 1972, p. 16)

This quote has influenced the way teachers view themselves and interact with students for over forty years.

In 1972, Ginott wrote *Teacher and Child* in which he questioned traditional behavioral approaches to classroom management and suggested that communication, not rewards and punishments, is the key to effective classroom discipline. Ginott stresses that teachers set the tone of the classroom through positive communication. He maintained that through caring, supportive interactions with students, a teacher builds a community of learners. Alfie Kohn (1995) builds on Ginott's ideas and stresses that the ultimate goal of classroom management should not be on simple obedience but on having students behave appropriately because they know it's the right thing to do, and because they can understand how their actions affect other people. Kohn's model, Building Community, appears in Chapter 8.

## DEVELOPING A PERSONAL CLASSROOM-MANAGEMENT PLAN

McEwan (2000) notes that the issues associated with classroom management are as complex as the time in which we live and as diverse as the students we teach. Different children, and even the same children at different levels of development, require different treatment for optimal results. Therefore, there are no easy answers to discipline problems, nor is there one most effective classroom-management plan. Figure 1.1 describes factors that should be considered in formulating a personal classroom-management plan.

### Figure 1.1

Developing a Personal Classroom-Management Plan

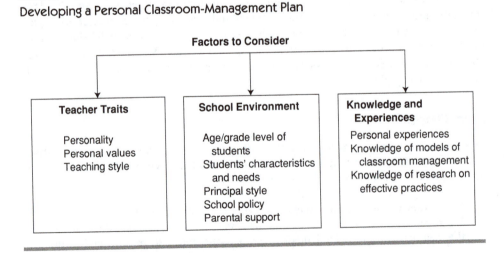

Ultimately, the best classroom-management plan is the one developed by an individual teacher, designed to meet the needs of his or her students. The last two chapters of this text provide information to assist in the design of a personal system. Chapter 14 provides a synopsis of research on classroom management and a description of the best practices identified through this research. Chapter 15 helps the individual teacher put together all elements of classroom management into a comprehensive program.

There is not one perfect discipline approach. Teachers must discover what works best for themselves, their students, and their specific situations. The goal of this text is to provide theories and research from which individual teachers can select, blend, and create the best classroom-management plan to meet their needs.

## Key Terminology

Definitions for these terms appear in the glossary.

| | |
|---|---|
| Desists   9 | Transition smoothness   9 |
| Overlapping   9 | Withitness   9 |
| Ripple effect   9 | |

## Chapter Activities

### Reflecting on the Material

1. Consider the situation with Marcus described at the beginning of this chapter.

   a. What additional information would you want to consider in deciding how to handle this situation?
   b. What strategies could Ms. Salerno have used to prevent the situation from occurring?
   c. In what ways could Ms. Salerno's instructional strategies have created or prevented the situation?
   d. Does the motivation of the student who poked Marcus play into your decision making?
   e. How would you have handled the situation?

2. Kounin's research identified "withitness" as a skill of effective classroom managers. Describe a teacher you have observed who has "withitness." How did the teacher's "withitness" prevent discipline problems or help the teacher in correcting inappropriate behavior?

### Developing Artifacts for Your Portfolio

1. The research on classroom management speaks to the importance of classroom rules. List the rules you are considering for your classroom. What is your rationale for selecting these rules?

### Developing Your Personal Philosophy of Classroom Management

1. This chapter provides several definitions of classroom management. Which definition most closely reflects your personal definition of classroom management? Why?

2. This chapter describes classroom management as discipline, a system, and instruction. Which of these models most closely fits your philosophy of classroom management? Why?

3. One of the most famous quotes about teaching is the statement by Ginott that begins, "I have come to a frightening conclusion." Review the entire quote. Do you agree or disagree with Ginott's statement? Why?

## Chapter References

Baruch, D. W. (1949). *New ways in discipline.* New York: Whittlesey House.

Brophy, J. E. (1983). Classroom organization and management. *Elementary School Journal, 83,* 275–285.

Brophy, J. (1999). Beyond behaviorism. In H. Jerome Freiberg (Ed.), *Beyond behaviorism: Changing the classroom management paradigm.* Boston: Allyn & Bacon.

Brophy, J. E., & Evertson, C. M. (1976). *Learning from teaching: A developmental perspective.* Boston: Allyn & Bacon.

Curwin, R. L., & Mendler, A. N. (1988). Packaged discipline programs: Let the buyer beware. *Educational Leadership, 46,* 68–73.

Doyle, W. (1990). Classroom management techniques. In O. C. Moles (Ed.), *Student discipline strategies: Research and practice.* Albany: State University of New York Press.

Dreikurs, R., & Loren, G. (1968). *The new approach to discipline: Logical consequences.* New York: Hawthorn Books.

Edwards, C. H. (1999). *Building classroom discipline* (3rd ed.). New York: Longman.

Evertson, C. M., & Harris, A. H. (1992). What we know about managing classrooms. *Educational Leadership, 49,* 74–78.

Freiberg, H. J. (1999). Beyond behaviorism. In H. Jerome Freiberg (Ed.), *Beyond behaviorism: Changing the classroom management paradigm.* Boston: Allyn & Bacon.

Freiberg, H. J., & Lapointe, J. (2006). Research-based programs for preventing and solving discipline problems. In C. Evertson & C. Weinstein (Eds.), *Handbook of classroom management: Research, practice, and contemporary issues.* Mahwah, NJ: Lawrence Erlbaum Associates.

Ginott, H. G. (1972). *Teacher and child: A book for parents and teachers.* New York: Collier Books.

Girard, K. (1995). Preparing teachers for conflict resolution in the schools. *ERIC Digest, 94.*

Glasser, W. (1965). *Reality therapy: A new approach to psychiatry.* New York: Harper and Row.

Glasser, W. (1969). *Schools without failure.* New York: Harper and Row.

Glasser, W. (1992). *The quality school: Managing students without coercion* (2nd ed.). New York: HarperCollins.

Gold, V. E., & Chamberlin, L. J. (1996). School/student violence: A primer. *American Secondary Education, 24,* 27–32.

Hoover, R. L., & Kindsvatter, R. (1997). *Democratic discipline: Foundation and practice.* Upper Saddle River, NJ: Merrill/Prentice Hall.

Kohn, A. (1995). Discipline is the problem—not the solution. *Learning, 24,* 34.

Kounin, J. S. (1970). *Discipline and group management in classrooms.* New York: Holt, Rinehart & Winston.

Marchant, G. J., & Newman, I. (1996). Mentoring education: An interview with Carolyn M. Evertson. *Mid-Western Educational Researcher, 9,* 26–28.

McEwan, B. (2000). *The art of classroom management.* Upper Saddle River, NJ: Merrill/Prentice Hall.

Morris, R. C. (1996). Contrasting disciplinary models in education. *Thresholds in Education, 22,* 7–13.

Peterson, G. J. (1997). Looking at the big picture: School administrators and violence reduction. *Journal of School Leadership, 7,* 456–479.

Redl, F., & Wattenberg, W. W. (1959). *Mental hygiene in teaching.* New York: Harcourt.

Remboldt, C. (1998). Making violence unacceptable. *Educational Leadership, 56,* 32–38.

Starr, L. (2006). Harry K. Wong and the real meaning of classroom management. Educational World. Retrieved October 15, 2009, from http://www.educationworld.com/a_issues/chat/chat008.shtml.

Vasa, S. (1984). Classroom management: A selected review of the literature. In R. Egbert & M. Kluender (Eds.), *Using research to improve teacher education.* The Nebraska Consortium. Teacher Education Monograph No. 1. (ERIC Document Reproduction Services No. 246 026).

Weinstein, C. S. (1999). Reflections on best practices and promising programs: Beyond assertive classroom discipline. In H. Jerome Freiberg (Ed.), *Beyond behaviorism: Changing the classroom management paradigm.* Boston: Allyn & Bacon.

Wolfgang, C. H., & Kelsay, K. L. (1992). Problem students in class: Disobedient—or just "devalued"? *Education Digest, 57,* 58–60.

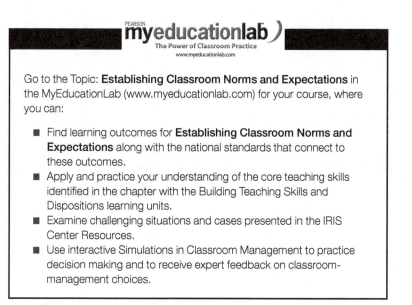

# PART I
# Classroom Management as Discipline

Four models of classroom management are presented in Part I: Classroom Management as Discipline. Chapter 2 presents basic behavioral concepts with a review of B. F. Skinner's theory of operant conditioning. Lee and Marlene Canter's model, Assertive Discipline, is presented in Chapter 3. Chapter 4 provides a different approach to using behavioral theory in Fredric Jones's model, Positive Classroom Discipline. Chapter 5 introduces the concept of Logical Consequences and is based on the work of Linda Albert, Jane Nelsen, Lynn Lott, and H. Stephen Glenn. Although different in approach, the models presented in these four chapters share the following principles:

- The teacher is in control and responsible for all decisions concerning classroom management.

- Discipline is separate from instruction and comes before instruction.

- Consequences must exist for inappropriate behavior and are the same for all students.

- Rules are developed by the teacher and are clearly defined.

- Strategies are reactive, not proactive.

- Students choose to misbehave and must face the consequences of their decisions.

- Rewards are extrinsic rather than intrinsic.

- Strategies are based on behavioral theory.

# Behavioral Approaches to Classroom Management

CHAPTER 2

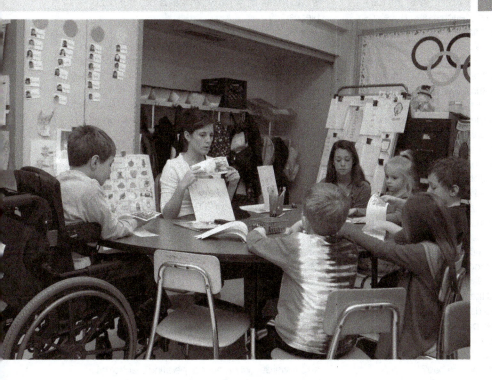

## Objectives

Chapter 2 prepares preservice teachers to meet INTASC standards #2 (Student Development), #5 (Motivation and Management), and #9 (Reflective Practitioner) by helping them to

- use knowledge about human behavior drawn from the research of Pavlov, Thorndike, Watson, and Skinner to develop strategies for classroom management.

- understand the basic principles behind a behavioral approach to classroom management.

- evaluate research concerning the impact of reinforcement and punishment on learning and behavior.

- evaluate the role of extrinsic rewards on students' behaviors.

**19**

- learn techniques for applying behavioral techniques in the classroom.

- determine whether they will incorporate behavioral strategies into their classrooms.

- use behavior theory to deal with problem behavior.

## Scenario

Student teacher Tennill Johnson is nervous about her ability to control the classroom. With the permission of her cooperating teacher, she develops a plan to reward her students for good behavior. Addressing the class, she unveils a twenty-four-inch-square jigsaw puzzle. The puzzle features balloons and confetti, and the word "Party" appears several times on the picture. Getting the children's attention, she removes all the pieces of the puzzle and places them in a basket. She explains that each day the class can earn puzzle pieces when they display excellent behavior. At the end of each day, they will discuss the behavior of the class during the day and Ms. Johnson will determine whether they have earned a piece of the puzzle. Placing a piece of the puzzle back on the board, she demonstrates how the pieces will be placed on the board. "When the puzzle is complete," she explains, "you will get what the puzzle says—a party. I will provide the food and drinks, and we will watch a video you select."

Hands go up around the room. "Can we earn more than one piece in a day?"

"Yes," Ms. Johnson explains. "If I am pleased with how you act during a certain activity, I might put an extra piece on for that day."

"Can we lose pieces if we are bad?"

"No, I will never remove pieces. They are your rewards. I won't take them back."

Carmen raises her hand. "What about David? He is bad all the time. He will make us lose our puzzle pieces."

Ms. Johnson takes a deep breath. "First, I would never assume David will be bad, and neither should you, Carmen." She looked at David. "I am confident David will help the class earn the party." Then, looking back at Carmen, she continues, "This is a class reward, so no individual student will prevent you from getting a puzzle piece. Now, if there are no more questions, it is time to work on our spelling."

When the class returns from lunch, Ms. Johnson explains that she is very pleased with their behavior in the lunchroom. Taking a puzzle piece, she fills in the first piece of the puzzle. At the end of the day, she spens a few minutes talking about the overall behavior of the class for that day. Pleased with their behavior, she puts another piece on the puzzle. The second day, the students aren't as attentive, and Ms. Johnson has to correct several students throughout the day. At the end of the day, she explains that no puzzle pieces have been earned that day and that she hopes the following day will be a better one.

Four days before the end of her teaching assignment, the puzzle is complete, and the students are rewarded with the promised party. Ms. Johnson is also rewarded when her cooperating teacher gives her an excellent evaluation for her student-teaching experience.

## INTRODUCTION

Whether the result of training, good teaching skills, or logic, the approach Ms. Johnson used is one of the oldest classroom-management techniques in existence. The practice of providing consequences for both good and bad behaviors has been used in classrooms since the first cave teacher taught the first cave student to make fire. It is only during the past fifty years, however, that the process of systematically applying rewards (reinforcements) and punishment has been part of classroom-management training. This model of classroom management is known by many terms, including behaviorism, behavioral techniques, behavior modification, and social-learning theory. For the purpose of this chapter, the term **behavioral techniques** will refer to the practices used to modify classroom behaviors, and the term **behavior modification** will be used for the programs developed for individual students.

This behavioral approach to classroom management has its roots in the work of Ivan Pavlov (1849–1936), John Watson (1878–1958), Edward Thorndike (1874–1949), and B. F. Skinner (1904–1990). Focusing on how organisms learn, the behavioral model is concerned with the scientific modification of observable behaviors. Pavlov, considered the father of classical conditioning, began the behaviorist movement with his discovery that when a conditioned stimulus is applied with an unconditional response, the result is a conditioned response. He is best remembered for his conditioning of dogs to salivate (unconditioned response) at the sound of a bell (conditioned stimulus). Thus the concept that learning and behavior can be controlled and manipulated was developed. Watson, who called himself a behaviorist, found that learning was the process of conditioning responses through the substitution of one stimulus for another. Learning, according to Watson, could explain most behaviors. Thorndike was one of the first researchers to apply operant conditions. He developed the concept known as the **Law of Effect,** which states that a rewarded behavior will be repeated, and an unrewarded behavior will cease. Skinner developed operant conditioning as a theory and concentrated on the observation and manipulation of behaviors. Operant conditioning describes the relationship between behavior and environmental events and focuses on the use of reinforcement to obtain desired behaviors (Zirpoli & Melloy, 1997). Classroom management was never the goal of these researchers; however, their research changed the concept of classroom management because their studies demonstrated experimentally how a teacher's behavior could shape and maintain students' behaviors.

## Step-by-Step Behavioral Approaches

To increase desired behaviors:

1. Reinforce desired behavior when it occurs. Begin with continuous reinforcement until behavior is established, and then move to an intermittent schedule.

2. Shape desired behavior by reinforcing approximations of the desired behavior until desired behavior is achieved.

To decrease undesired behaviors:

1. Evaluate your own behavior to make sure you are positively reinforcing desired behavior rather than reinforcing undesired behavior.

2. Ignore undesired behavior until extinction occurs.

3. Apply negative reinforcement until desired behavior occurs. When desired behavior occurs, remove the aversive stimulus.

4. Use functional behavioral assessment to systematically change the behavior.

5. Use punishment as a last alternative.

In 1954, Skinner stressed that "special techniques have been designed to arrange what are called 'contingencies of reinforcement'—the relation which prevails between behavior on the one hand and the consequences of that behavior on the other—with the result that a much more effective control of behavior has been achieved" (p. 86). Through reinforcements, Skinner suggested, the behavior of an individual—student, spouse, employee—could be shaped almost at will. Although some behaviors required successive stages to change behaviors, other behaviors could be changed in a single reinforcement.

Therefore, according to behaviorists, all behaviors (good and bad, appropriate and inappropriate) are learned and maintained by reinforcement. Behavior is conditioned by its consequences: strengthened if followed immediately by reinforcement, weakened if not reinforced. Drawing upon the findings of operant conditioning is the belief that the causes of behavioral problems are not in individual personality variables or emotional well-being, but in the interactions among the child, his or her peers, the parents, and the teacher (Skiba, 1983). Consider the following situations:

> Every day seventh-grader Jacob manages to disrupt the class to the point that he is eventually sent to the office or to in-school suspension. Twice he has been suspended from school. Jacob's teacher, his principal, and his parents are confused about what to do with Jacob and fail to understand the reasons that none of the punishments imposed on Jacob have been effective. Unfortunately, they have not consulted with Jacob's bus driver. He could explain that each day Jacob gets in trouble, Jacob is greeted with high fives from the other kids on the bus who have bets that Jacob can get more suspensions in one year than any other student in the history of his school.

> Because Timothy is always off-task, Ms. Sloan often walks by his desk and stands beside Timothy until he returns to work. Timothy, who is being raised by his father, likes having Ms. Sloan beside him because he thinks she smells good and reminds him of his mom. So, as soon as Ms. Sloan walks away, Timothy puts his pencil down and stares into space. In a few seconds, Ms. Sloan is beside him again.

> Kindergartner Latisha clung to her mother's skirt and cried when her mother attempted to leave the room. Trying to console Latisha, her mother agreed to stay a few minutes longer. Unfortunately, the crying became louder and stronger as weeks went by, and now Latisha's mother is spending most of her day in the kindergarten classroom. She agrees with Latisha's teacher that she needs to leave but can't bring herself to abandon her crying child.

> Whenever Ms. Carter asks a question, Carla raises her hand. If Ms. Carter doesn't call on her immediately, Carla waves her hand wildly. Eventually, Ms. Carter always calls on Carla.

> Mr. Reynolds controls his tenth-grade basic science class by yelling and screaming. The students have learned that when he is especially angry he will begin to stutter and spit. Mr. Reynolds's loss of control is the source of much lunchroom laughter, and eventually most of his classes are pushing him to the point where he is constantly red faced, stuttering, and spitting.

In all the situations described, behavior was modified because of reinforcement. Unfortunately, the modified behavior was not always the behavior desired. In some cases, the adults had *their* behavior modified. To be used effectively in the classroom, the following basic assumptions about behavioral theory must be understood:

- Behaviors are learned. Individuals tend to exhibit behaviors that are reinforced and avoid behaviors that have not been previously reinforced or have been punished.

- Behaviors are stimulus specific—that is, individuals behave differently in different environments. This is because each environment contains its own sets of cues (antecedents) and consequences (reinforcers or punishments) for the behavior exhibited. Behaviors have environmental, situational, and social roots. Therefore, teachers should never question when parents say, "He never acts that way at home," because it may be the school environment that creates the behavior.

- Behaviors can be taught, changed, or modified. Because behaviors are learned, teachers and parents can teach new behaviors and modify current behavior.

- Behavioral change should focus on the here and now. Behaviorists are not concerned with past events; instead, they concentrate on current events within a student's environment, in order to identify the influences on current behaviors (Walker & Shea, 1999; Zirpoli & Melloy, 1997).

## ELEMENTS OF BEHAVIOR MANAGEMENT

The relationship between behaviors and consequences represents the heart of behavior-management strategies. **Consequences** are events or changes in the environment following a behavior. There are three basic consequences of behavior:

1. Behavior followed immediately by a reward (reinforcement) will occur more frequently.

2. Behavior followed closely by a punishing consequence will occur less often.

3. Behavior will be extinguished (stopped) when it is no longer reinforced.

Landrum and Kauffman (2006) note that virtually all classroom-management applications of behavioral theory involve one or a combination of the following basic operations: positive reinforcement, negative reinforcement, extinction, presentation punishment, or removal punishment. Reinforcement is the most powerful of these tools and is used not only to teach new behaviors and change current behaviors but also is the foundation of Skinner's operant conditioning (Zirpoli & Melloy, 1997). Reinforcement leads to an increase in behavior. Extinction is the cessation of a particular behavior resulting from a lack of reinforcement (Colvin, 2009). Reinforcement and extinction are opposite phenomena but should not be confused with punishment. Whereas extinction consists of withholding a reinforcer after a behavior is displayed, punishment involves the application of negative consequences for inappropriate behavior. Thus, when confronted with inappropriate behavior, a teacher has three choices:

- Rewarding appropriate behavior in order to increase the chances the desired behavior will occur again.

- Ignoring the inappropriate behavior in hopes of extinction.

- Punishing the student for inappropriate behavior.

## Consequences of Behavior

Reinforcement involves the use of consequences to *strengthen* the behavior. **Reinforcement** following a behavior operates on the likelihood that the desired behavior will be repeated under the same or similar circumstances. Reinforcement can be both positive and negative, and both positive and negative reinforcement increase behavior. **Positive reinforcement** is the presentation of a reinforcer wanted by the student after the desired behavior has been exhibited. Typically, the student will repeat this behavior in order to get another reward. Positive reinforcement can come in many forms. Examples are

> Jennifer's high school English teacher writes a note at the bottom of the first assignment that reads, "I really enjoyed your writing. I can't wait to read your next paper." Jennifer is so pleased, she spends hours making sure her next paper is perfect.

> Julio's principal stops him on his way back from lunch and tells him that she is proud of the way he helped a classmate who had dropped her lunch tray. She gives Julio a good citizenship slip that qualifies him for a drawing for a prize at the end of the six weeks.

> Brian's teacher places a peppermint on his desk because he is working hard on his math problems.

> Ms. Foster announces that the class will get fifteen extra minutes on the playground because they acted so well during assembly.

> Mr. Bader's principal names him Teacher of the Month because of his work with the debate club. Along with the title comes free lunch in the cafeteria for a month.

### Tips from the Field

For the past four years I've taught grades seven through twelve and GED English in an alternative school. I found the following strategies effective with this group of students.

1. Give students respect. Most young men hate the words "boy" and "son." Call them by their names, or even better, call them Mr. X (last name).

2. Tell the truth as you see it. Make sure they understand that the truth is a form of respect.

3. Teach what a sincere, honest apology is and when it is acceptable. Be sure to offer one every time you mess up, and do it in public before the wronged student.

4. Train students how to handle themselves when a principal, security officer, or teacher is upset with them (this is a wonderful skill and helps at-risk students to get out of trouble).

5. Defend, congratulate, and apologize to students in public. Counsel, irritate, and castigate in private.

Marjory W. Thrash,
East Central Alternative School
Union, Mississippi

Unfortunately, positive reinforcement does not always have the desired effect. Walker and Shea (1999) stress that reinforcement is most effective in maintaining or increasing a behavior when

- reinforcement is given only if the student exhibits the desired behavior. If students are rewarded when they haven't earned the reward, there is little chance of getting the desired behavior in the future.

- reinforcement is individualized for a particular child. Some reinforcements are more effective with some children than others. By asking the student and testing different reinforcers, teachers can generate a reinforcement menu. Brian, in the example given earlier, would not find the peppermint rewarding if he hated peppermint candy.

- the desired behavior is reinforced immediately after it is exhibited. As the interval between the behavior and reinforcement increases, the relative effectiveness of the reinforcer decreases. Initially, an effective reinforcement program reinforces immediately after the desired behavior. Later, the time between the behavior and reinforcement can be increased.

- verbal praise is combined with the reinforcement. It is important to remind the child of the connection between the desired behavior and the reinforcement.

- the target behavior is reinforced each time it is exhibited. When the target behavior becomes routine for the student, it can be reinforced intermittently. However, if all reinforcement ceases, the behavior may end as well.

- the reinforcement is given by someone the child loves, likes, or respects.

**Negative reinforcement** also strengthens the behavior. In fact, the term *negative reinforcement* refers to the same effect observed with positive reinforcement: A behavior is strengthened and is more likely to reoccur. Unlike positive reinforcement, however, it involves the removal of an aversive stimulus following a desired behavior. There are two keywords or phrases in this definition. The first is *removal;* rather than presenting something to the student, as in positive reinforcement, something aversive is removed. The second key phrase is *desired behavior.* In negative reinforcement, the aversive stimulus continues until the desired behavior is achieved. Because there is relief when the aversive stimulus is removed, the student is rewarded, and the likelihood increases that the desired behavior will occur again. There are fewer examples of negative reinforcement in the classroom because most teachers prefer to avoid introducing aversive stimuli into the learning environment. Examples of negative reinforcement include the following:

When Ms. Evans's class becomes too loud, she blows a whistle until the noise level drops. The students find the sound of the whistle aversive and stop talking so Ms. Evans will stop blowing the whistle.

Simone and Dana like to whisper to each other during class. When Mr. Morris notices that they are whispering, he stands behind the girls until they stop whispering and return to their work.

Because the class is too loud as they line up for lunch, Ms. Harris tells the class that they will not go to lunch until their work is put away and they are quietly in line. The students remain in the classroom until all work is put away and every student is standing quietly in line.

Because negative reinforcement requires the use of aversive stimuli, teachers must be careful in its application. If in the earlier example Ms. Harris had kept the students in the classroom throughout the lunch period and the children had had no lunch that day, she would have found that using effective negative reinforcement practices resulted in her having to deal with angry parents and administrators.

It is important to remember that negative reinforcement is not punishment. The main difference between the two is that reinforcement *strengthens* behavior, whereas punishment *suppresses* behavior (Morris, 1996). For example, if Ms. Smith tells Michael he has to miss recess because he failed to complete his work, Ms. Smith has punished Michael. Ms. Smith has no guarantee that Michael will now finish his work. In fact, Michael may reason that because he already missed recess, there is no need for him to finish his work. On the other hand, if Ms. Smith tells Michael that he must miss recess (something Michael finds aversive) *until* he has finished his work (the desired behavior), Michael will realize he must finish the assigned work before he can have recess. It may take Michael five minutes to finish, and he can then join his classmates on the playground, or it may mean that Michael misses several days of recess until he completes the assigned work.

**Punishment** is the application of an unpleasant stimulus or the withdrawal of a pleasant reward in an attempt to weaken a response. It differs from negative reinforcement in that the student may *never* display the desired behavior. Punishment comes in many forms and typically falls into two categories. The first type is **presentation punishment,** which involves the presentation of an aversive stimulus in order to decrease inappropriate behavior. A few examples follow:

> The lunchroom monitor at the school cafeteria tells Ms. Henderson that her class left the tables messy when they finished eating. Ms. Henderson returned the class to the cafeteria where they had to clean all the tables.

> Grandpa tells Phillip that when he was a boy, he was whipped for sassing the teacher.

> Ms. Nelson's principal feels that Ms. Nelson mishandled a situation with a parent and placed a letter of reprimand in her file.

The second type of punishment is removal punishment. In **removal punishment,** a pleasant stimulus or the eligibility to receive a positive reinforcement is taken away. Following are several examples:

> Two of Adams High School's best football players are caught cutting class so they can go to lunch at the local McDonald's. Both the coach and the principal agree that, as punishment for skipping class, they should not be allowed to play in the next game.

> Ms. Richards allows her students thirty minutes of computer time each week. During that time they can play computer games or search the Internet. Daniel loses his time because he shot a rubber band at a fellow student.

> Each day, Ms. Smith's students wear two clothespin bumble bees (the school mascot) clipped to their clothes. One reads, "I'm a busy bee." The other reads, "I will always bee a good citizen." Students who are still wearing the pins at the end of the day get to pick a prize from the treasure box. When students misbehave, they must remove a pin and place it in a box. Students who lose both pins lose the opportunity to receive a prize.

Detention, in-school suspension, and time-out are examples of removal punishments, because they prevent students from receiving positive stimuli from their classmates (Eggen & Kauchak, 2001). As Alberto and Troutman (2002) explain, time-out is a shortened term for time-out from positive reinforcement. During time-out, students are denied the opportunity to earn reinforcement, such as participation in an activity. There are three types of time-out:

1. **nonseclusionary**: The student remains in the classroom but must be completely silent or is required to put his or her head on the desk.

2. **exclusionary**: A disruptive child is removed from the immediate instructional area to another part of the room.

3. **seclusionary**: The disruptive student is removed from the classroom (Smith & Misra, 1992).

Skinner (1968) cautioned against the use of punishment; he stressed that the main lesson learned from punishment is how to avoid or escape punishment in the future. As Skinner explained, children do not learn to tie their shoestrings by being punished when they cannot. In addition, Biehler and Snowman (1990) stress that the results of punishment are neither predictable nor dependable for the following reasons:

- Mild punishment does not eliminate undesirable behaviors permanently. To be effective, punishment must be much more harsh than desired when working with children.

- Punished behaviors may continue when the punishers are not present.

*Desired behavior, such as raising one's hand, will be repeated if reinforced.*

- The punishment itself may be reinforcing. Sometimes the attention given to the student is rewarding, and the behavior will increase rather than decrease.

- The punishment may produce undesirable emotional side effects such as fear, trauma, or hatred of school.

- Punishers model a type of behavior that they would find unacceptable if exhibited by the student who is punished. If the teacher's goal is to produce students who are not aggressive and who can settle differences in a peaceful manner, the teacher must not demonstrate behavior that is counter to this goal.

When reinforcement is no longer forthcoming, a response becomes less and less frequent. This process of ending undesired behaviors by withholding reinforcement is known as **extinction.** Teachers can use extinction to stop undesired behavior by ignoring behavior. For example, had the teacher in the example given earlier in this chapter ignored Carla's waving hand and refused to call on Carla unless she was holding up her hand in an appropriate manner, Carla's hand waving would have stopped. Unfortunately, desired behaviors can also be extinguished if they are never rewarded. If Carla's classmate Joe is never called on, even though he is holding up his hand and waiting quietly to be called on, he will soon stop behaving appropriately and begin the hand waving that seems to work for Carla.

Extinction is also useful when the behavior is one that the teacher wishes to discourage but does not consider punishable. For example, if Chris often uses baby talk when he is tired, ignoring the behavior would be a more appropriate way of handling the situation than punishing Chris for his baby talk.

Extinction does not occur quickly and will take longer when there has been a long history of reinforcement. Although there is no simple relation between the number of reinforced and nonreinforced responses necessary for extinction, disruptive behavior can be extinguished if it is ignored. Unfortunately, the teacher is not the only person in the classroom, and misbehavior may still be maintained by peer attention or other elements outside the teacher's control. If Chris's parents think his baby talk is sweet and reinforce the behavior at home, it will be difficult for the teacher to stop the behavior. Figure 2.1 gives additional examples of positive reinforcement, negative reinforcement, punishment, and extinction.

Traditionally, behavioral techniques have relied on a teacher, parent, or therapist to apply the reinforcement or punishment. The focus has been on the external control of behavior. Contemporary behaviorists are including techniques such as self-reinforcement, self-reprimands, self-instruction, and self-evaluation. These interventions place heavy emphasis on self-regulation and little or no external reinforcement, so they overlap considerably with strategies that promote personal responsibility for behavior (Brophy, 2006).

## Schedules of Reinforcement

A schedule of reinforcement is essential when a teacher uses reinforcement as part of the discipline plan. A reinforcement schedule refers to the frequency or timing of the delivery of reinforcement. Reinforcement schedules are important in developing positive behavior patterns. Reinforcement may occur on a continuous or intermittent schedule.

## Figure 2.1

Elements of Behavior Management

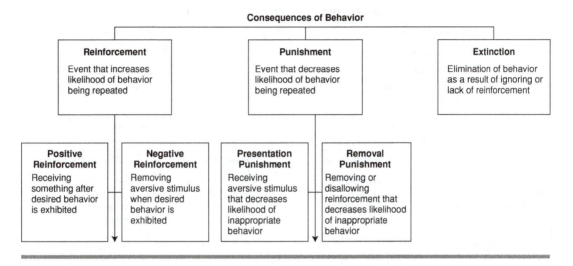

When children are reinforced every time they respond, a **continuous schedule** is being used. A continuous schedule is important until an association is made between the desired behavior and the reinforcement.

When a child is reinforced after some occurrences of the desired behavior, but not each time, an **intermittent schedule** is being used. There are two types of intermittent schedules. **Interval schedules of reinforcement** distribute reinforcement based on time. For example, if after five minutes of seat work by the students a teacher moves through the room and places a reward (gold star, candy, or token) on the student's desk, the teacher would be rewarding the students on an interval schedule. A **ratio schedule of reinforcement** is based on the number of responses rather than the passage of time. If the teacher in the earlier example moved throughout the room placing the reward on the desk of students who have successfully completed five questions, the teacher would be using a ratio schedule. Both interval and ratio schedules can be given on a fixed schedule. In a fixed schedule, students know when the reward will occur because it is predictable. Report cards are based on a fixed-interval schedule because students know exactly when grades will be given. Of course, some students would argue that the issuing of report cards is not reinforcement but punishment!

The last type of reinforcement is a **variable schedule,** in which the giving of the reward is varied so that no patterns can be established. A variable-interval schedule would be one in which students do not know how much time must pass before they will be rewarded. In a variable-ratio schedule, the reward may come after the student has completed five problems or it may not come until the student has completed twenty questions (Zirpoli & Melloy, 1997). The unpredictability of the schedule keeps the student focused and on-task. Figure 2.2 provides an illustration of the types of schedules of reinforcement.

## Figure 2.2

Schedules of Reinforcement

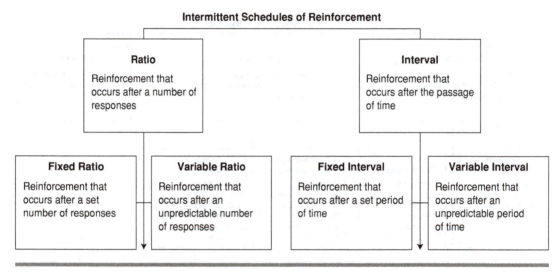

## Types of Reinforcement

One of the criticisms of behavioral strategies is the emphasis on extrinsic reward, because many people believe that children should behave in appropriate ways just for the intrinsic value of the behavior. Kazdin (1975) suggests that with extrinsic reinforcers, "there is no 'real' change in the behavior of the person who is reinforced. The person is just being 'bought' or 'bribed' to perform a particular behavior" (p. 49). Advocates of behavioral strategies counter by suggesting that extrinsic reinforcement is the primary reason for *all* behavior and that those who criticize behavior-modification techniques are being extrinsically rewarded for their criticism!

There are two categories of extrinsic reinforcers: primary (unconditioned) and secondary (conditioned). **Primary reinforcements** satisfy the biological needs or drives of a student, and their reinforcing value does not have to be explained (Kazdin, 1975). They include such things as food, water, and sleep. However, primary reinforcers may not be reinforcing in all situations. A student who has just had a nap will not find sleep reinforcing. Because primary reinforcers are essential to the well-being of students, many would argue they should not be given or withheld as part of classroom management.

The reinforcements used most often in the classroom are **secondary reinforcements.** Not reinforcing in themselves, secondary reinforcements get their power from the significance attached to them by students. A secondary reinforcement can be in the form of a tangible object, approval or attention from another, or being allowed to participate in a preferred activity. A tangible reinforcer can be any object coveted by the student, such as money, certificates, stickers, pencils, games, and personal items. The type of tangible reinforcers

### Tips from the Field

At the beginning of each school year, I present my students with an expected classroom behavior contract. The contract lists all the classroom rules along with the sequence of consequences if the rules are broken. The contract also includes rewards that the student and class can earn if the expected behavior is maintained. The contract has a place for the student and parent to sign. The contracts are filed in each student's notebook for the remainder of the year. I have found this technique to be an effective classroom-management tool.

Jason E. Hughes
9–12 Agri-Science Teacher
St. Marys High School
St. Marys, West Virginia
2005 West Virginia Teacher of the Year

selected is important because what will work for young children (stickers, trinkets, toys) may have little reinforcing value for middle school students or high school students. In many classrooms, tangible reinforcements are earned through the collections of tokens. A **token reinforcer** has no intrinsic reinforcing properties; its value is based on the tangible object or desired activity for which it can be exchanged. Through tokens, students receive immediate reinforcement in the form of a check, chip, or voucher that can be traded for reinforcement at a future date. The use of token economy and other forms of tangible reinforcers have been studied extensively in their relation to student behavior and have been found to modify student behavior (Skiba, 1983). However, as Colvin (2009) stresses, a token economy will not work if the child is too young to understand the exchange value or if the child has a zero token balance at the exchange period.

**Social reinforcers** are the behaviors of other people (teachers, parents, peers, and administrators) that increase desired behaviors. They include compliments, praise, facial expressions, physical contact, and attention. Skiba (1983) notes that for social reinforcers to be effective they must be given only when the desired behavior is exhibited, they must vary, and they must be spontaneous. The advantages of using social reinforcers are that they are easy to use, inexpensive, readily available, and do not interrupt the flow of instruction.

**Activity reinforcers** offer rewards by allowing the student to participate in preferred activities and are another natural and easily dispensable reward for desirable behavior. Appropriate activity reinforcers include extra time on the computer, leadership roles in class activities or sports, and eligibility to operate audiovisual equipment. David Premack's (1959) extensive research on the concept revealed that participation in preferred activities can be used to reinforce participation in less-desired activities. This concept is known as the **Premack Principle.** Activity reinforcers carry many of the same advantages as social reinforcers. Because they must often be delayed and not presented immediately to the student, however, the delay in timing may mean that a student does not understand the connection between behavior and activity. This is especially true for young children.

### Tips from the Field

The Good Behavior Game (Barrish, Saunders, & Wold, 1969) can be used to manage classroom behaviors by rewarding students for displaying appropriate on-task behaviors. The game is useful when students are expected to work quietly or during independent seat work. The class is divided into two teams and a point is given for any inappropriate behavior displayed by one of its members. The team with the fewest points at the game's conclusion wins a group reward. Rewards can be allowing the winning team to line up for lunch first, leave the classroom first when the period has ended, or to have time at the end of the week for a fun, educationally related activity. It is important that the game be scheduled for a maximum of one to two hours a day so as not to overdo the effectiveness of the game and allow students to have some time to relax, socialize, and "be kids."

Jim Wright
School Psychologist
Syracuse, New York

## WORKING WITH INDIVIDUAL STUDENTS

When behaviorists began researching the connection between behavior and reinforcement, the research focused on individuals rather than on groups of people. Behavioral strategies are most effective with individuals. Two strategies, shaping and behavior modification, are especially useful in helping teachers to change the behavior of individual students.

**Shaping** is used to teach new behaviors and skills and refers to the reinforcement of successive approximations of a terminal behavior. For example, if a child were learning the alphabet, one would not wait until the child could recite the entire alphabet before reinforcing the child. Instead, parents and teachers clap their hands when a young child manages to remember the first few letters. As the child becomes more confident, the reward is withheld until more letters are recited. Eventually, reinforcement (cheers, hugs, smiley faces, or applause) is withheld until the entire alphabet is recited. Just as rewarding approximate behaviors can work with learning the alphabet, it can also work as a child learns new behaviors. If Min Lee has never managed to spend an hour in class without leaving her seat, it may be necessary for the teacher to praise Min Lee when she has managed to remain in her seat for ten minutes. Later, the reinforcement should be withheld until Min Lee can stay in her seat for a longer period of time. Eventually, through shaping, Min Lee's behavior should match that of her classmates.

**Behavior modification** involves systematically applying behavioral principles in an effort to change specific behaviors in an individual. Eggen and Kauchak (2001) note that because the term *behavior modification* may have a negative connotation, the term **applied behavior analysis** is often used instead. Both terms refer to a systematic approach to changing behaviors in positive ways through the application of behavioral principles, with strict reliance on the frequent, repeated assessment of observable and measurable behavior and the goal of establishing a functional relationship between dependent and independent variables (Landrum & Kauffman, 2006). The goal of applied behavior analysis is to make long-term changes in the behavior of students. The initial goal is to change the immediate behavior with the ultimate goal of maintaining the change after the program is terminated.

## STRATEGIES FOR DEALING WITH DIFFICULT STUDENTS

Constantly dealing with difficult students can be the bane of the teacher's life. Students with problem behaviors disrupt instruction, prevent classmates from learning, contribute to teacher burnout, and cause tension for everyone in the classroom. It is for these reasons that there are countless discussions occurring in teacher chat rooms with teachers asking for assistance in dealing with such students. Colvin (2009) points out that most teachers are seeking a "silver bullet" that will instantly solve the problem. However, Colvin stresses that there are no silver bullets and to understand and rectify problem behavior, a detailed assessment of the behavior is necessary. This assessment is known as a **functional behavioral assessment.** The good news is that research shows that interventions based on functional behavior assessments are more likely to be effective in changing behaviors than interventions developed without the use of a functional behavioral assessment (Scheuermann & Hall, 2008).

In its 1997 reauthorization of the Individuals with Disabilities Education Act (IDEA), the U.S. Congress demanded that educators conduct a functional behavioral assessment for all students served under the act (Landrum & Kauffman, 2006). Clearly, such an assessment can also be used by classroom teachers to improve the behavior of students with chronic, disruptive behaviors in general classrooms.

Wheeler and Richey (2005) describe functional behavior assessment as a "multistep process that is designed to identify causal factors associated with challenging behaviors and to generate plausible hypotheses about the functions of problem behaviors and also to develop possible interventions aimed at replacing such behaviors" (p. 174). A functional behavioral assessment is designed to gather information about all factors that may contribute to a problem behavior. The ultimate goal is to develop hypotheses for a student's inappropriate behavior and interventions to change this behavior. If the interventions are not effective, then the process begins again with the collection of additional data followed by a new hypothesis. Formats for the functional behavioral assessment vary but traditionally determine the following:

- What is the specific behavior that must be changed? It is this behavior that is targeted for observation, measurement, or modification. This requires careful analysis of the behavior through rating scales, interview, and observations (Robinson & Ricord Griesemer, 2006). A baseline rate of the current behavior is determined and becomes the standard against which the success of interventions will be judged and allows for goal setting by the teacher and the student.

- What are the setting events for the inappropriate behaviors? Setting events may have occurred the day before or much earlier or in a different context (Colvin, 2009). Setting events might be issues at home, illness or health concerns, conflicts with friends, academic failure, or problems in the classroom. For example, if six-year-old Franklin begins to display acting out behavior after his father is deployed to Afghanistan, the interventions required may involve counseling rather than specific teacher-directed interventions.

■ What are the events or actions that tend to trigger undesired behaviors? This is often called the antecedents for behavior (Scheuermann & Hall, 2008). Through this analysis, the teacher identifies the triggers that precede a behavior and influence the probability of misbehaviors. When teachers can control these triggers, they can minimize disruptive behaviors in the classroom. Because of the increased under-standing of the triggers for the behavior through the functional behaviorial assess-ment, teachers reduce the likelihood of inadvertently reinforcing behavior problems (Robinson & Ricord Griesemer, 2006). When such an assessment was conducted to determine why seventh-grader Audrey became sick at the beginning of fourth period, it was found that her teacher had announced that the students would have daily pop quizzes until their grades improved. The anxiety over the pop quizzes was the cause of Audrey's stomachaches. When the threat of the pop quiz was removed, Audrey's health improved.

■ How is the student being rewarded for the current behavior? Wheeler and Richey (2005) maintain that all behavior is purposeful, including challenging behavior, and the inappropriate behavior may be rewarded through tangible reinforcements, attention from teachers and peers, sensory reinforcement, and escape. Therefore, the reinforcements established for appropriate behavior must exceed the reward the student receives for continuing the inappropriate behavior.

■ Once the functional behavior assessment is complete, the stage is set for developing a hypothesis and an intervention plan (Colvin, 2009). Interventions can include chang-ing setting events, triggers, or rewards. In some cases, behavioral contracts are devel-oped that focus on increasing desirable behavior and decreasing problem behavior. The behavioral contract is an agreement between the student and teacher stating if the student exhibits compliant or cooperative behavior at a predetermined rate, then the student will be provided privileges or reinforcers. Contracts can also specify that the student will lose privileges when unacceptable behavior occurs. The case study of David at the end of this chapter is an example of how behavior was changed through a behavioral contract.

Scheuermann and Hall (2008) note that a functional behavior assessment is a process, not a single event. If the interventions do not produce the desired results, then the process will have to be repeated and new hypotheses and interventions developed.

## STRENGTHS AND WEAKNESSES OF THE BEHAVIORAL MODEL

Behavioral strategies are widely used in schools. In many cases, teachers are not aware that they are using researched methods, because the techniques seem a natural way of interact-ing with students, and advocates for behavior strategies would argue that this naturalness is precisely the strength of programs using a behavioral approach. Other strengths include the following:

■ Behavioral strategies work. A hundred years of research have shown that behaviors can be taught, changed, modified, or corrected. Doyle (1990) stresses that the techniques derived from laboratory studies of contingencies of reinforcement have been researched extensively and advocated widely in discipline strategies. Controlled studies, often in special settings, have indicated that behavior-analysis techniques are remarkably successful.

■ The use of behavioral strategies forces the teacher to be more aware of what is going on in the classroom. In many cases, the teacher becomes a more objective and precise observer of student behavior (Whitman & Whitman, 1971).

■ A behavioral program increases the likelihood that the teacher will be consistent in treatment of students. It gives teachers a systematic plan for dealing with discipline problems.

■ Behavior-management strategies provide all children a chance to be "good." For many students with behavioral disabilities, this may be their first opportunity to receive consistent reinforcement (Whitman & Whitman, 1971).

Critics of behavioral strategies cite philosophical and practical reasons for their objections to its use. Many find such programs to be manipulative and controlling and that the techniques used are more appropriate for use with animals than children (Landrum & Kauffman, 2006). Others think behavioral strategies teach children to work for rewards rather than for the intrinsic satisfaction that comes with doing a good job. Following are other weaknesses that have been cited:

■ The concept of ignoring undesirable behavior while praising desired behaviors is impractical for individual classroom teachers who lack the assistance of independent observers and support personnel and who work with large groups of students.

■ Teachers are less likely to examine their own teaching methods or other classroom factors as possible causes of students' unproductive behavior. Savage (1999) suggests that teachers using behavioral strategies are less likely to blame classroom problems on poor teaching methods, poor interpersonal skills, or inappropriate exercise of teacher authority. They may also not recognize that the student's behavior is an attempt to cope with boredom, anxiety, or anger.

■ Behavioral strategies can be harmful if used by insensitive and unethical teachers and administrators. The result may be a hatred of school.

■ Teaching children to avoid certain behaviors because they will be punished is not the same as teaching that the behaviors are wrong, immoral, or unethical. Kohn (1996) suggests that rewards only manipulate students; they do nothing to help children become kind or caring adults.

■ One student's reward may be another student's punishment. In a classroom of twenty to thirty students, it is difficult to find rewards that will appeal to every student.

## BEHAVIORAL MANAGEMENT IN THE CLASSROOM

### Scenario

Third-grade teacher Amy Collins is puzzled by David Brower's behavior. Every few minutes, David is out of his seat, going to the tissue box, the trash can, or to the pencil sharpener. Ms. Collins has told the students that they do not need to request permission to do these things, but only David abuses the privilege.

Sometimes, David will stand beside his desk, rummaging through his books and belongings, and at other times, he just stands at his desk, lost in thought. When Ms. Collins tells David to return to his seat, he quickly does so and never complains. David's constant roaming is becoming a problem for both Ms. Collins and the other students, who are distracted by his behavior and who feel that they, too, should be allowed to roam about the classroom constantly. During the past week, she punished David for his excessive out-of-seat behavior by giving him extra work and not allowing him to have recess; neither had any impact.

Ms. Collins talked to David's second-grade teacher about his behavior, but Ms. Smith couldn't remember David being a problem in her classroom. Ms. Smith suggested that Ms. Collins's expectations were too high. Concerned that she was making too much of David's misbehavior, Ms. Collins asked the school guidance counselor to observe her class and give her suggestions. The guidance counselor was amazed that during the two hours she observed the classroom, David was out of his seat twenty-seven times. The average number of times the other students left their seats during that same time period was three.

Working with the guidance counselor and David's mother, Ms. Collins developed a plan to shape David's behavior. Ms. Brower told Ms. Collins that David had been begging for a new pair of skates for several weeks. They decided that they would allow David to work for the skates by changing his out-of-seat behavior.

After school, David, his mother, the guidance counselor, and Ms. Collins met to talk about David's misbehavior. When Ms. Collins told David that he was out of his seat forty-three times the day before, David agreed that this seemed excessive. When asked why he thought he was out of his seat so often, David merely shrugged. Ms. Collins asked David if he was willing to work on staying in his seat more, and he quickly answered "yes."

Together, a plan was developed. With forty-three as a baseline, they agreed that for the next week, David would be out of his seat no more than thirty-five times a day. Each day Ms. Collins would send home a note telling how many times David had left his seat. Each day he met his goal, he would earn a point toward acquiring his skates. When he earned thirty points, he would receive the skates. They also agreed that they would reduce the times he could be out of his seat once David had earned five points. This reduction would continue until he was out of seat no more than ten times a day, the average number of times his classmates were out of their seats during a day.

The first day, David exceeded his goal and left his seat only thirty times. He was pleased with the note sent to his parents by Ms. Collins. Unfortunately, the second day, he forgot and did not meet his goal. After a few days, however, David's parents were receiving positive notes most days. It took seven weeks for David to meet his goal and to earn his skates. During that time, David became aware of his behavior and never returned to constant classroom roaming.

## Summary

Behavioral approaches to classroom management have their roots in the work of Pavlov (1849–1936), Watson (1878–1958), Thorndike (1874–1949), and Skinner (1904–1990). Based on the concept known as the Law of Effect, the premise is that rewarded behaviors will be repeated, and unrewarded behaviors will cease. Therefore, according to behaviorists, all behaviors—good and bad, appropriate and inappropriate—are learned and maintained by reinforcement. Therefore, the systematic application of reinforcement is the basis of behavioral techniques and is the foundation of many of the classroom models presented in this text.

## Key Terminology

Definitions for these terms appear in the glossary.

Activity reinforcer   31
Applied behavior analysis   32
Behavior modification   32
Behavioral techniques   21
Consequences   23
Continuous schedule of reinforcement   29
Exclusionary time-out   27
Extinction   28
Functional behavioral assessment   33
Intermittent schedule of reinforcement   29
Interval schedule of reinforcement   29
Law of Effect   21
Negative reinforcement   25
Nonseclusionary time-out   27

Positive reinforcement   24
Premack Principle   31
Presentation punishment   26
Primary reinforcements   30
Punishment   26
Ratio schedule of reinforcement   29
Reinforcement   24
Removal punishment   26
Seclusionary time-out   27
Secondary reinforcements   30
Shaping   32
Social reinforcers   31
Token reinforcer   31
Variable schedule of reinforcement   29

## Chapter Activities

### Reflecting on the Theory

1. Eleventh-grade history teacher Chris Bilyeu is having a problem with his fifth-period class. At the beginning of the semester, a few students were tardy for class. He thought it best to ignore the students and to continue with his lectures. Now, almost half the students in his fifth-period class are tardy, and many are five to ten minutes late for class.

   How would you handle this situation? How can the behavioral approaches presented in this chapter be used to resolve this problem?

2. In the scenario provided at the end of this chapter, Ms. Collins was successful in changing David's behavior. Consider the following:

   a. If the shaping activity had not worked with David, what might have been some of the reasons?
   b. Would you be comfortable using this method? Why or why not?
   c. What are the drawbacks to this method?

3. Give a classroom example of each of the following:

   | | |
   |---|---|
   | Positive reinforcement | Negative reinforcement |
   | Removal punishment | Ratio reinforcement |
   | Variable reinforcement | Interval reinforcement |
   | Extinction | Fixed reinforcement |

4. What is meant by a token economy? How is a token economy used in the classroom?

5. Are there types of students or students of certain grade levels who might not respond to behavior-management techniques? Explain why.

### Developing Artifacts for Your Portfolio

1. In the chapter-opening scenario, Ms. Johnson designed a reward plan for her class. Design your own plan for rewarding individual students and for rewarding the entire class. How will you reward *your* students for appropriate behavior?

### Developing Your Personal Philosophy of Classroom Management

1. One of the criticisms of behavioral strategies is the emphasis on extrinsic rewards. Do you think there is too much emphasis on extrinsic rewards in classrooms today?

2. Would you be comfortable using a behavioral approach to classroom management in your classroom? Why or why not? Are there some strategies that you will definitely incorporate into your classroom-management plan?

# Chapter References

Alberto, P. A., & Troutman, A. C. (2002). *Applied behavior analysis for teachers: Influencing student performance* (6th ed.). Upper Saddle River, NJ: Merrill/Prentice Hall.

Barrish, H. H., Saunders, M., & Wold, M. M. (1969). Good behavior game: Effects of individual contingencies for group consequences on disruptive behavior in a classroom. *Journal of Applied Behavior Analysis, 2,* 119–124.

Biehler, R. F., & Snowman, J. (1990). *Psychology applied to teaching* (6th ed.). Boston: Houghton Mifflin Co.

Brophy, J. (2006). History of research on classroom management. In C. Everston & C. Weinstein (Eds.), *Handbook of classroom management: Research, practice, and contemporary issues.* Mahwah, NJ: Lawrence Erlbaum Associates.

Colvin, G. (2009). *Managing noncompliance and defiance in the classroom.* Thousand Oaks, CA: Corwin.

Doyle, W. (1990). Classroom management techniques. In O. C. Moles (Ed.), *Student discipline strategies: Research and practice.* Albany: State University of New York Press.

Eggen, P., & Kauchak, D. (2001). *Educational psychology: Windows on classrooms* (5th ed.). Upper Saddle River, NJ: Merrill/Prentice Hall.

Kazdin, A. E. (1975). *Behavior modification in applied settings.* Homewood, IL: The Dorsey Press.

Kohn, A. (1996). *Beyond discipline: From compliance to community.* Alexandria, VA: Association for Supervision and Curriculum Development.

Landrum, T. J., & Kauffman, J. M. (2006). Behavioral approaches to classroom management. In C. Everston & C. Weinstein (Eds.), *Handbook of classroom management: Research, practice, and contemporary issues.* Mahwah, NJ: Lawrence Erlbaum Associates.

Morris, R. C. (1996). Contrasting disciplinary models in education. *Thresholds in Education, 22,* 7–13.

Premack, D. (1959). Toward empirical behavior laws: I. Positive reinforcement. *Psychological Review, 66,* 219–233.

Robinson, S., & Ricord Griesemer, S. (2006). Helping individual students with problem behavior. In C. Everston & C. Weinstein (Eds.), *Handbook of classroom management: Research, practice, and contemporary issues.* Mahwah, NJ: Lawrence Erlbaum Associates.

Savage, T. V. (1999). *Teaching self-control through management and discipline* (2nd ed.). Boston: Allyn & Bacon.

Scheuermann, B., & Hall, J. (2008). *Positive behavioral supports for the classroom.* Upper Saddle River, NJ: Merrill/Prentice Hall.

Skiba, R. J. (1983). *Classroom behavior management: A review of the literature.* Monograph No. 21. St. Paul: University of Minnesota Center for Research on Learning Disabilities.

Skinner, B. F. (1954). The science of learning and the art of teaching. *Harvard Educational Review, 24,* 86–97.

Skinner, B. F. (1968). *The technology of teaching.* New York: Appleton-Century-Crofts.

Smith, M. A., & Misra, A. (1992). A comprehensive management system for students in regular classroom. *The Elementary School Journal, 92,* 353–371.

Walker, J. E., & Shea, T. M. (1999). *Behavior Management: A practical approach for educators* (7th ed.). Upper Saddle River, NJ: Merrill/Prentice Hall.

Wheeler, J., & Richey, D. (2005). *Behavior management: Principles and practices of positive behavior supports.* Upper Saddle River, NJ: Merrill/Prentice Hall.

Whitman, M., & Whitman, J. (1971). Behavior modification in the classroom. *Psychology in the Schools, 8,* 176–186.

Zirpoli, T. J., & Melloy, K. J. (1997). *Behavior management: Applications for teachers and parents* (2nd ed.). Upper Saddle River, NJ: Merrill/Prentice Hall.

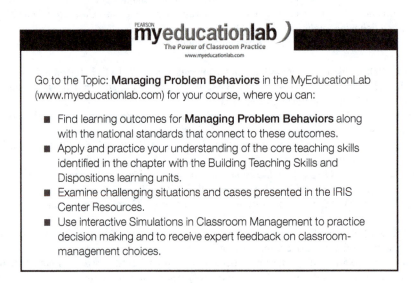

Go to the Topic: **Managing Problem Behaviors** in the MyEducationLab (www.myeducationlab.com) for your course, where you can:

- Find learning outcomes for **Managing Problem Behaviors** along with the national standards that connect to these outcomes.
- Apply and practice your understanding of the core teaching skills identified in the chapter with the Building Teaching Skills and Dispositions learning units.
- Examine challenging situations and cases presented in the IRIS Center Resources.
- Use interactive Simulations in Classroom Management to practice decision making and to receive expert feedback on classroom-management choices.

# Assertive Discipline

## Objectives

Chapter 3 prepares preservice teachers to meet
INTASC standards #5 (Motivation and Management),
#9 (Reflective Practitioner), and #10 (School and
Community) by helping them to

- understand the basic principles behind Assertive
Discipline.

- evaluate the rights of teachers and the rights of
students.

- determine the role of administrators and parents
in supporting rule enforcement.

- determine the appropriate consequences for
misbehavior.

- establish appropriate reward systems for individual
students and for classwide recognition.

- learn techniques for the effective use of Assertive
Discipline in the classroom.

- use the principles of Assertive Discipline to deal
with problem behavior.

## Scenario

Preservice teacher Helen Garcia has been assigned to observe fifth-grade teacher Marilyn Conner. During her first day of observation, Helen is intrigued by Ms. Conner's discipline plan and thinks it is one she would like to use. At the front of the classroom is a large poster outlining Ms. Conner's rules and consequences.

### The Rules for Ms. Conner's Class

- Come to class prepared.
- Stay on-task during instruction.
- No speaking out of turn.
- Keep hands, feet, and objects to yourself.
- No teasing or bullying.

### The Consequences for Misbehavior

| | |
|---|---|
| First Offense: | Receive a warning. |
| Second Offense: | Lose ten minutes of recess/playtime. |
| Third Offense: | Lose fifteen minutes of recess/playtime plus write in behavior journal. |
| Fourth Offense: | Teacher will call parents. |
| Fifth Offense: | Be referred to the principal. |

On a whiteboard beside the list of rules and consequences are twenty-four magnetic name tags with the name of each student in the class written on a plate. These name tags are lined up along one edge of the board. Across the top of the board are the words *First Offense, Second Offense, Third Offense, Fourth Offense,* and *Fifth Offense.* Unfortunately, before Helen can ask Ms. Conner how she uses the name tags, class begins.

During the first few minutes of class, Jonathan raises his hand and tells Ms. Conner that he has forgotten his pencil. Without stopping her instruction, Ms. Conner points to the whiteboard and the box of sharpened pencils on a table below the board. Without discussion, Jonathan places his magnetic name tag under the category First Offense and takes a pencil. Jonathan goes back to work, and Ms. Conner continues her instruction.

All goes well until midmorning when Ms. Conner notices two girls passing a note. As she takes the note from the girls, she points to the whiteboard, and both girls move their name tags to the First Offense category.

Later in the day, Ms. Conner notices Jonathan drawing rather than doing his assignment. Ms. Conner tells him to move his name tag to the Second Offense category. Later, when the class goes to the playground, Jonathan has to stay in the library and finish his assignment. When ten minutes has passed, he is allowed to join his classmates.

During the remainder of the day, two other students receive warnings, but no student goes beyond the Second Offense category. Helen also notices that the entire class is reinforced for good behavior. When the music teacher compliments the students on their good behavior during class, Ms. Conner tells the class they have earned a marble. All the students applaud as the marble drops into a jar among what appears to be hundreds of other marbles.

By the end of the day, Helen is eager to find out about the marble jar and the magnetic plates on the board. "Would you mind telling me about your classroom-management plan? I thought it really worked well."

"Well, it is certainly nothing new," Ms. Conner explains as she straightens the desks. "I first saw this procedure when I did my student teaching. My cooperating teacher said she had learned the method at a conference on classroom management. However, I've changed a few things about how I manage behavior. She had the students write their names on the board and then put a check behind their name for each infraction of the rules. I found the magnetic name tags at an office supply store, and they work well. Other teachers in this school are doing variations of this same concept. For example, Ms. Frazier, next door, still has students write their names on the board, and Mr. Rader keeps a clipboard for each day with the students' names and makes checks in it. I don't like that method as well, because he has to tell the student that they are getting a check."

"Will Jonathan start tomorrow with his name in the Second Offense category, or does he begin fresh?"

"No, I move the plates back after each day. Everyone starts with a clean slate each day. However, I do keep a daily record of what happened. Let me show you." Ms. Conner retrieves a notebook that contains record sheets for each student. "Each sheet contains a record for a month. I will record the problems that Jonathan had today. If I need to contact his parents, I can tell them about his behavior over a period of time. This notebook ensures that I have an accurate record of each student's behavior."

Helen looks at her watch and realizes that she is keeping Ms. Conner. "I didn't mean to keep you so long. This has been a great day for me; I really learned a lot. I hope you won't mind if I steal a few ideas."

"Not at all; that's what good teachers do. And you're welcome to come back anytime. You were a big help today."

# INTRODUCTION

Although Ms. Conner may not know the origin or name of her discipline plan, she is actually using the basic concepts of a classroom-management program, **Assertive Discipline,** developed by Lee and Marlene Canter in the early 1970s. Since that time, Assertive Discipline has become as common to classrooms as chalk and pencils. This model or variations of this model are used throughout the United States. Kizlik (2009) notes that Assertive Discipline is the most widely used discipline plan in schools.

Unlike the discipline models developed outside the classroom in the 1950s and 1960s, Assertive Discipline was developed to solve the problems of actual teachers. Lee and Marlene Canter realized that many of the problems found in classrooms were based on the failure of teachers to be assertive in having their needs met, resulting in many teachers feeling overwhelmed and powerless. Using theories and principles from assertiveness training and behavior modification, the Canters developed Assertive Discipline, which allows teachers to meet their needs by systematically applying behavioral strategies to classroom situations.

In 1989, Canter noted that he and his staff had trained 750,000 teachers. Since that time hundreds of thousands have read the numerous books published by Canter and Associates, attended workshops, and watched videos on the principles of Assertive Discipline. Through these means, teachers have been introduced to the following basic principles of Assertive Discipline:

- Teachers have the right to teach and to expect students to behave.

- Teachers must develop consistent and firm rules.

- Teachers must identify consequences to be used when students choose to misbehave.

- Teachers must provide positive consequences for appropriate student behavior.

- Teachers must create classroom plans to provide negative and positive consequences for behavior.

- Teachers must seek and expect support from parents and administrators.

**Step-by-Step Assertive Discipline**

To use Assertive Discipline in your classroom, you will need to do the following things:

1. Practice assertive responses to classroom conflict.

2. Establish classroom rules.

3. Establish a Hierarchy of Consequences for when rules are broken.

4. Determine a system for recording violations of the rules.

5. Establish a reward system for individual students and for the class as a whole.

6. Acquire support for your discipline plan from your school administrator.

7. Share plan with parents and secure support.

Unlike much of educational literature that focuses on the needs of students, Canter and Canter (1976, 1992) emphasize the wants, needs, and rights of the teacher. Canter and Canter stress that teachers have the right to

- establish classroom structure, rules, procedures, and routines that clearly define the limits of acceptable and unacceptable student behavior.

- determine and request appropriate behavior from students, so that the teacher's needs can be met while encouraging the positive social and educational development of the child.

- ask for assistance and support from parents and the school administration.

- teach students to consistently follow rules and directions throughout the school day and school year.

Although the Canters did not overlook the rights of children, the emphasis of such rights centered around supporting the teacher's ability to control the classroom. According to Canter and Canter (1976, 1992), students' rights include

- the right to know the behavior expected of them by the teacher.

- the right to have firm and consistent limits established, so that they can eliminate inappropriate self-disruptive behaviors.

- the right to have consistent encouragement, so that they will be motivated to interact appropriately.

- the right to know the consequences of inappropriate behavior.

- the right to be taught acceptable and responsible behavior.

## THE TEACHER VOICE

Canter (2010) notes that effective teachers have developed a strong teacher voice that demands students' attention and respect. The tenor, volume, and quality of the teacher's voice set the tone of the classroom and ultimately impact each student's self-esteem and

## Tips from the Field

Consistency and s ᵊᵐ item.
tools to use. On d
must be discusse
times multidaily ᵊᵈ
You'll find that
the year as w
need to have
the limit. Sta
remind ther

t choice and what they
ently in order to have

Kim Russell
Seventh-Grade Teacher
Vidor Junior High
Vidor, Texas

success. Can
students: no
in nature; t

**Nona**
to take ad
students ɯ
dents kn ᵊ
and less
Nonass
studen
filled

and,
scen
in f
ed.
ba

t

hen interacting with
tile styles are reactive

ʌn and allow students
washy, which confuses
ɪchers threaten, but stu-
students run the class,
are constantly violated.
nner hostility toward the
ofession or suffer a career

eds and feelings of students
students are negative, conde-
ial comments about a student
hen behavior must be correct-
ers describe the classroom as a
o so because students are afraid.
ds. They have positive expecta-
actions. Because they say what
nits in the classroom. When they
ent and fair. Because students are
because they consider the teacher
tions are met.

el Collins:

d his fourth-period class is a chal-
the class. After lunch, Mr. Collins
omentum. Today, when Mr. Collins
e sitting on the tops of their desks

engaged in an animated conversation about the events that took place at the ballgame the evening before. Vivian, a cheerleader, has the girls mesmerized with her account of postgame romance. Standing in the front of the class, Mr. Collins says, "Ladies, it is time to begin."

Vivian, giving Mr. Collins her most charming smile, says, "Can't you wait just a minute? I'm almost finished."

Mr. Collins, the *nonassertive teacher,* responds, "Well, how much longer will you be?"

Mr. Collins, the *hostile teacher,* responds, "Don't try your beauty-queen charm on me. I don't care how cute you are, it won't work on me. Now get your butt in your seat and your book on your desk."

Mr. Collins, the *assertive teacher,* responds, "You can finish after class. Now, I believe we were discussing the rise of Communism before we left for lunch."

## THE ASSERTIVE DISCIPLINE PLAN

Canter (2010) stresses that planning is essential to good teaching and to good discipline. Without a plan, teachers will have to choose an appropriate consequence at the moment of misbehavior. In the stress of the moment, the teacher may be unfair and inconsistent and may respond differently to students from different socioeconomic, ethnic, or racial backgrounds (Canter, 1989). Planning assures that students' rights are protected and that all students are treated fairly and consistently.

An effective plan must be in place the first day of class. To help guide a teacher in developing an individual classroom discipline plan, the following questions should be addressed:

- What behaviors does the teacher want students to eliminate or display?
- What negative consequences will be appropriate for the students?
- What positive consequences will be appropriate for the students?
- How can appropriate and inappropriate behaviors be tracked?

## STEPS IN DEVELOPING THE PLAN

The *first step* in development of the discipline plan is to seek approval from the administration and to plan for notification of parents. This is critical because the application of consequences will require the support of both the school's administration and the students' parents. Without their support, the plan will fail. Many teachers are hesitant to involve administrators and parents because, according to Canter (2010), there is a myth that a competent teacher will not need such assistance. He stresses, to the contrary, that *no* teacher is capable of working with each and every student *without* support.

The *second step* is the establishment of classroom rules. Canter and Canter (1992) give the following guidelines for rule development:

■ Rules must be observable. Whether a student has observed or violated a rule should not be debatable. Rules such as "Be nice" or "Always do your best" are too open for interpretation to be enforced.

■ Rules should be enforceable throughout the day. A rule such as "Students will not carry on conversations during work time" is inappropriate when the teacher divides the students into groups with instructions to work together. Rules that apply only during certain situations will confuse students and be ineffective.

■ Rules should be age appropriate. A rule such as "All cell phones are forbidden" would be as inappropriate for first-graders as "Only 12-inch voices in the hallways" is for twelfth-graders.

■ Rules should cover typical discipline situations. If the teacher plans to punish students for being tardy, "Come to class on time" must be one of the rules.

■ Rules must teach appropriate classroom behavior. A rule such as "Don't hit, kick, or touch anyone else with your hands, your feet, or any other object" is designed to teach younger children appropriate school behavior.

Assertive Discipline is often referred to by teachers as the "Marble in the Jar" plan. When the model was first introduced, Canter (1979) suggested that teachers drop a marble in a large jar whenever the class demonstrated good behavior. When the jar is full, the class could be rewarded by a party, extra free time, a movie, or a field trip. This focus on providing positive reinforcement is the *third step* in developing a discipline plan. Canter and Canter (1992) stress that such reinforcement is needed when one realizes that 90 percent of teachers' comments to students regarding their behavior are negative. Positive reinforcement is important because it creates a more productive classroom environment, reduces the frequency of problem behaviors, and maximizes the teacher's influence over students.

The discipline plan should include both individual and classwide recognition. Individual recognition can be done in a variety of ways. Praising students is the easiest and most fundamental way to positively recognize appropriate behavior. Positive notes or phone calls to parents should be a regular part of the reinforcement plan. Other reinforcements can include special privileges (computer time, being the classroom assistant, homework passes), awards, certificates, or tangible items.

Canter (2010) also recommends classwide recognition and states that such recognition (1) works well because of peer pressure, (2) is effective when working on a specific problem, and (3) should be implemented as needed rather than all year long. With classwide recognition, the class works together to earn points for a classwide reward. In addition to collecting marbles in a jar, classes can earn points on the board, collect letters to a special word, or bank play money as a way to earn the reward.

The *fourth step* in the discipline plan is to provide consequences for those students who choose to disobey the rules of the class. When this happens, Canter and Canter (1976, 1992) emphasize that the teacher must be prepared to deal with misbehavior

## Tips from the Field

As part of our character education program, we have been working with students to develop responsibility and citizenship. As we teach our students that they are part of our school community, we also teach them that they have a responsibility to their fellow citizens. We have developed a Golden Can (a small trash can painted gold) that is presented to a classroom, individual, or group to acknowledge their efforts in taking responsibility toward the care and cleaning of their classroom and area. Sometimes there might be a treat, like a small sucker or some stickers, in the can. Sometimes it is just the honor of being announced on the intercom that motivates the students. But whatever the motivation, it made a big difference in the appearance of our building. Our students are taking responsibility for the care of their building and learning valuable lessons about citizenship while doing it.

Doug McBride
Guidance Counselor
Stewart Elementary School
Washington, Iowa

calmly and quickly. If the teacher has planned ahead, there will be a clear course of action to follow. This will prevent a knee-jerk reaction to situations and allow the teacher to be consistent in the treatment of students. The effective use of consequences includes selecting appropriate consequences, developing a hierarchy of consequences based on the number of times rules are broken, and devising a tracking system for recording behaviors.

Canter and Canter give the following guidelines for selecting consequences:

- There should be no more than five consequences.
- Consequences must be something the students dislike, but they must never be physically or psychologically harmful. Canter and Canter never advocate corporal punishment.
- Consequences do not have to be severe to be effective. For 70 percent of students, a simple warning is sufficient. For another 20 percent who may need more than a warning, the consequences the teacher chooses do not have to be severe to be effective. Canter and Canter (1992) estimate that only 10 percent of students will cause real problems, and consequences should not be designed for this group. Instead, the Severity Clause (explained later) should be used with this population of students.
- Negative consequences should be applied *every* time a student chooses to behave inappropriately.

A consequence might be time-out, which is isolation from the other students. This isolation can occur in or out of the classroom. For secondary students, being required to stay after class and miss crucial time with their peers is an effective consequence. Having students write in a behavior journal is an often-used and especially effective consequence because it helps students focus on what they did and what they could have done differently. In a behavior journal, students write accounts of their misbehavior, the reasons they broke the rules, and what they should have done instead. Finally, the removal of a favored activity (recess, computer time) is an effective consequence. If the student's inappropriate behavior continues or escalates, parents or the principal must become involved. According to the Canters, the consequences need not be severe to be effective; their value lies in students knowing that they will occur each time a rule is broken.

Consequences should be applied through a **discipline hierarchy.** The hierarchy should begin with a warning, and with each infraction of a class or school rule, the consequences escalate. By the fourth infraction, parents should be contacted. If the misbehavior continues, the student should be sent to the principal.

For the hierarchy to work, teachers must have a system for keeping track of student misbehavior. In 1976, the Canters suggested that the first time a rule is broken, the student's name is written on the board. This constitutes a warning. When a rule is broken for a second time, or if a different rule is broken, a check is placed behind the student's name, and the consequence for a second offense is applied. If misbehavior continues, consequences are applied for each check mark earned. This continues until the student is required to go to the principal. The use of names and checks on the chalkboard was considered to be essential to Assertive Discipline. Canter and Canter originally used the check method to eliminate the need to stop the lesson and issue verbal reprimands. However, some parents and teachers considered this method humiliating to students. Canter (2010) now suggests using a clipboard, classroom-management log, or color-coded cards to track behavior. Regardless of the method used, Canter stresses that each day students should begin with a clean slate, and misbehaviors are not to be carried over from the day before.

## Tips from the Field

I have green, yellow, and red discipline cards on a chart for each student. At the beginning of the day each student has a green card showing on the chart. If a child is disruptive, he or she is told to pull their green card as a warning and their yellow card is exposed. After the yellow card is pulled, the child is given a five-minute time-out. After the red card is pulled, the child is given a ten-minute time-out. If the behavior continues, the child is sent to the school reflection room to talk to the educational assistant about how he or she can better handle a situation. Once a reflection sheet is satisfactorily completed, the child may return to class. Few students have to pull more than their green card before remembering to stay on-task.

Lolita Cox
Sixth-Grade Teacher
Museum Magnet Elementary School
St. Paul, Minnesota

**Table 3.1**   Sample Classroom Discipline Plan

### Ms. Jackson's Third-Grade Classroom-Management Plan

**Classroom Rules**

Do not talk while the teacher is talking, while other students are contributing, or during tests or quizzes.

Walk quietly and orderly in the hallways.

Don't hit, kick, or touch anyone else with your hands, feet, or other objects.

Bring all needed materials to class.

Don't bring food or drink in the classroom unless given special permission to do so.

**Consequences of Breaking Classroom Rules**

| | |
|---|---|
| First Time to Break a Rule: | Warning |
| Second Time to Break a Rule: | Five minutes in Quiet Corner writing in behavior journal |
| Third Time to Break a Rule: | Ten Minutes in Quiet Corner writing in behavior journal |
| Fourth Time to Break a Rule: | Fifteen Minutes in Quiet Corner and parents are called |
| Fifth Time to Break a Rule: | Sent to principal |

**Severity Clause:** Sent to principal

**Positive Recognitions**

| **Individual Rewards** | **Class Rewards** |
|---|---|
| Notes and phone calls to parents | Points toward party or special field trip |
| "No homework" passes | |
| Certificates of citizenship | |

Because classrooms will have a small percentage of students for which warnings and progression of consequences will not be effective, the *fifth step* in your discipline plan should be a **Severity Plan.** In cases of severe misbehavior that places students or the teacher in danger or prevents instruction from taking place, the student should not receive a warning or progress through the hierarchy. Instead, severe misbehavior requires immediate removal from the classroom and assistance from the school's administration. A sample discipline plan appears in Table 3.1.

## A MORE MODERN VERSION OF ASSERTIVE DISCIPLINE

Canter (1989) has expressed concern that both advocates and critics of Assertive Discipline have made its principles sound simplistic and overfocused on providing negative consequences. In *Assertive Discipline: Positive Behavior Management for Today's Classroom,* published in 2010, Canter maintains the basic elements of his original model but incorporates elements from recent research in redesigning his focus.

*The solution to many discipline problems begins with establishing a positive relationship with students.*

Realizing that children cannot obey rules they do not understand, Canter now encourages teachers to teach the rules and procedures at the beginning of the year. Canter suggests that teachers must focus on what he calls the "4th R"—responsible behavior. He asserts that responsible behavior can be taught in the same manner as any academic subject and that a curriculum to teach responsible behavior should begin the first day of class.

Canter's basic philosophy is that students are making a choice when they disobey or disrupt the class. In later versions of his theory, he acknowledges that for some students, misbehavior is not a choice. This change is acknowledgment of the inability of some children to follow rules because of emotional, mental, or behavioral disorders.

Whether the teacher is teaching history, math, literature, or personal responsibility, a critical part of any lesson plan engages the students. When students are engaged, off-task behavior is diminished and all students have the opportunity to learn. One way to engage students is through class discussion. However, questioning during class discussion can increase rather than prevent discipline problems unless the teacher understands the strategies for effcctive questioning. Table 3.2 provides Canter's strategies for engaging students in class discussions.

**Table 3.2** Effective Questioning Techniques

- **Direct Question to the Entire Class**—When specific students are called upon, all other students feel they no longer have to listen. Directing the question to the entire class keeps all students focused.
- **Use Wait Time**—Research shows that waiting a few seconds allows students to collect their thoughts and encourages more students to answer.
- **Don't Allow Students to Shout Out Responses**—Students must learn to wait until they are called upon. Aggressive students will dominate the class, and shy or quiet students will never have a turn to respond if students are allowed to shout out answers.
- **Have Students Check Each Other**—Once students have answered, ask by a show of hands if fellow students think the answer is correct. Ask those who vote in minority to explain why they think the answer is incorrect.
- **Randomly Call on Students**—One method is to pull names from a jar. This prevents the teacher from calling on only one gender, calling on only students from the center of the room, or calling on only students who are high achievers.
- **Provide an Opportunity for All Students to Answer**—One technique is to provide students with individual whiteboards on which they write their answers. The teacher can visually scan the room to see how many students understand the material. A more modern version of this method is through the use of electronic clickers.

*Source:* Cantor (2010).

## STRATEGIES FOR DEALING WITH DIFFICULT STUDENTS

Canter and Canter (1993) state that the disruptive behavior of just one student can prevent the teacher from teaching and the entire class from learning. Difficult students, as defined by Canter (2010) are those who engage in disruptive, off-task behavior with great intensity and frequency. These students refuse to comply after all steps in the classroom-management plan have been put in place. The solution to working with difficult students, according to Canter, begins with establishing a positive relationship with students. Canter (2010) notes that "when students test you, they are sending up a red flag that you need to immediately put some work into building a more positive relationship with them" (p. 78). Canter states that research clearly shows that establishing a positive relationship with students can reduce disruptive behavior by up to 50 percent. Canter provides the following suggestions for establishing trust:

- Know your students. Although teachers need to know about the academic ability of each student, they must also know about the things going on in the student's life outside the classroom. One way to learn this information is through a questionnaire given to students at the beginning of the year.

- Contact students and parents before school begins. This contact is twofold. One, it lets the students know they are welcome in your classroom. Two, it provides an introduction to parents so that if they need to be contacted later concerning a discipline issue, a positive relationship has been established.

- Attend extracurricular activities. It is important that students see teachers at concerts, plays, and sporting events. This opens the lines of communication by allowing teachers and students to discuss these events. Contact students after a difficult day. This goes a long way in reestablishing a relationship that is strained.

Students must understand that regardless of how the teacher feels about them personally, students will be held accountable for the choices they are making. Therefore, consequences for inappropriate behavior must be consistently applied. Canter and Canter (1993) stress that the goal of these consequences is to stop unacceptable behavior and to help the student make better choices.

Because consequences that have been established for the entire class have not worked, a separate plan should be put in place for difficult students. This individualized plan should be made during a one-on-one meeting between the teacher and student. The plan should identify specific behaviors that must be changed. A separate listing of rewards and consequences should be developed for these students. Once established, individual management plans should be shared with parents so they can support the teacher in carrying out the plan.

Canter and Canter (1993) note that when difficult students are being held to limits, confrontations will occur. Too often, they then become argumentative, critical, angry, and verbally abusive. Although it is tempting to respond to the student in the same manner, the teacher must remain calm and work to diffuse the situation.

Difficult students cannot be allowed to take over the classroom and prevent others from learning. When the behavior of the student becomes disruptive to the learning process, they must be given a choice—to comply with the instructions of the teacher or to leave the classroom. At this point the support of the administration is critical. Because some students will refuse to leave the classroom and go to the principal's office, a plan for how students will be removed from the classroom must be prepared with the school administration. The plan should follow all policies of the school and the school district.

Eventually, the disruptive student will return to the teacher's classroom. When this occurs, it is important that the student is treated as a valued member of the classroom and the process of establishing trust begin again.

## STRENGTHS AND WEAKNESSES OF ASSERTIVE DISCIPLINE

In the thirty years since the introduction of Assertive Discipline, the model has received both criticism and praise. The major strength of Assertive Discipline is its simplicity. This simplicity has been especially helpful for beginning teachers. Once the plan has been developed and approved by the administration, teachers are not required to make choices about how to react to student behaviors; they *know* how they will react to discipline situations. This prevents teachers from responding emotionally or being inconsistent in their responses. Fundamental to the model is the notion that teachers treat all students alike, applying the same standards and expectations for success to all students. Following are other strengths of Assertive Discipline:

- Research has shown its effectiveness. In 1989, Canter noted that the results of research on Assertive Discipline have consistently shown that teachers dramatically improve student behavior when they use Assertive Discipline. However, Emmer and Aussiker (1990) reviewed research on the effectiveness of Assertive Discipline and found that its use in the classroom had little or no influence on student behavior and attitudes.

- Assertive Discipline addresses student *behavior* rather than student *character*. When rules are broken, the teacher provides a consequence without making value judgments about the motivation or character of the student.

- The plan requires the support and involvement of administrators and parents. By presenting the discipline plan to parents and administrators before the first day of implementation, teachers are confident they will have their support.

- Assertive Discipline has evolved since it was first developed in 1976. Marzano (2003) states that these changes have been substantive. They have transformed Assertive Discipline into a program that employs a balance of negative and positive consequences as opposed to a focus on rule obedience and the application of consequences. Brophy (2006) agrees that Assertive Discipline has been revised to have less emphasis on reinforcement and more on clarifying the rationales for rules and supporting student self-regulation.

There is as much criticism of Assertive Discipline as there is praise. Weaknesses of the program include

- Some suggest that the principles of Assertive Discipline may be counterproductive. For example, McEwan (2000) quoted one student who suggested, "All students in class got to misbehave once, have their names written on the board, and then settle down, so no one faced consequences" (p. 155). Another concern is that students start with a clean slate each day. Some teachers complain that the names of the same students are written on the board day after day, with no real change in their behaviors from one day to the next. Some students may actually find the consequences for misbehavior rewarding, resulting in an increase in inappropriate behavior. These students see having their name on the board, check marks, or turned cards as a status symbol. One middle school teacher remarked that many of her students enjoyed the recognition of having their names on the board. As she put it, "For some of my students, having your name written on the board is a good thing. They like the chalk, but for them, spray paint would be even better."

■ Covaleskie (1992) expressed the opinion of many when he said, "A discipline program cannot be judged merely by asking whether it does a job of keeping children out of trouble in school; being a good person is more than that" (p. 174). He fears that programs such as Assertive Discipline fail to teach students to be truthful or teach them the reasons why they shouldn't lie. Instead, Covaleskie suggests that the lesson learned is to not get *caught* lying.

■ Assertive Discipline establishes an authoritarian environment in which students have virtually no rights and are mere recipients of the teacher's demands (Queen, Blackwelder, & Mallen, 1997). Kohn (1996) agrees and suggests that Assertive Discipline clearly places the blame for the discipline situation on the shoulders of the students: "The problem always rests with the child who doesn't do what he is asked, never with what he has been asked to do" (p. 13).

■ Assertive Discipline may only stop behavior for a short time and may not translate to other situations or areas. A rule such as "Don't talk when others are talking" may be viewed as a rule for the classroom, but not for the auditorium, gym, library, or other classes. Curwin and Mendler (1988) express concerns about such a focus on rules: "When rules are not developed from principles, students learn, for example, to be in their seats when the bell rings without understanding the importance of responsible work habits" (p. 68). Therefore, the effectiveness of Assertive Discipline would depend on the goals of the teacher. Assertive Discipline may meet the teacher's goal to change behavior for a moment in class but would not meet the goal of changing behavior for a lifetime.

■ There is no attempt to find the cause of misbehavior. Bromfield (2006) contends that Assertive Discipline treats the *symptoms,* but not the *causes* of behavior, because it makes no attempt to identify or treat the underlying causes of behavior. She stresses that child abuse, drug abuse, malnourishment, rejection, insecurity, loneliness, and emotional distress—all possible causes of misbehavior— do matter and in many instances can be treated by caring, competent teachers. According to Bromfield, if the cause of behavior is not discovered, the behavior will persist. The only question is where, when, and to what extent the behavior will be displayed.

■ There is limited opportunity for teacher discretion. It offers only one response when rules are violated and does not account for motivation or reason (Curwin & Mendler, 1988).

Assertive Discipline's success may be the cause of some of its failures. As Canter (1989) notes, Assertive Discipline has become a generic term. Many teachers and administrators have been trained by individuals who did not use or stress all the principles of Assertive Discipline. Unfortunately, according to Canter, not everyone follows the plan as originally intended.

## ASSERTIVE DISCIPLINE IN THE CLASSROOM

## Scenario

When June Wong was hired as principal of Henderson Elementary School, she pledged to have the best disciplined school in the system. After attending a workshop on Assertive Discipline, she spent the summer developing a discipline plan for her school. Before the school year began, she called a meeting of all the teachers in order to explain the plan. Her plan included

- schoolwide rules for nonclassroom situations.
- individual classroom rules to be established by each teacher.
- individual classroom consequences for a rule infraction.
- individual and classroom rewards.
- a schoolwide award system.
- notification of parents of the classroom teacher's rules and of the schoolwide discipline policies.

### The Schoolwide Rules Ms. Wong Established

- Walk in single file on the yellow line through the hallways.
- No talking in the hallways unless addressed by an adult.
- Use 12-inch voices in the cafeteria.
- Follow all directions from the teachers during drills and alarms.
- Don't tease or bully classmates.

### Consequences for Infractions of the Rules

| | |
|---|---|
| First Offense: | Warning. |
| Second Offense: | Ten minutes in detention and writing in behavior journal. |
| Third Offense: | Twenty minutes in detention and writing in behavior journal. |
| Fourth Offense: | Thirty minutes in detention and call to parents. |
| Fifth Offense: | Sent to principal. |

Any adult employee of the school could apply a consequence. The adult applying the consequence was to inform the classroom teacher of the schoolwide rule infraction. In addition to the schoolwide rules, each teacher was instructed to establish an individual class list of rules and consequences.

To reward students for good behavior, an afternoon of games and fun was planned for the last day of each six-week period. Throughout the six weeks, students could earn "Fun Bucks" for good behavior. Any adult employee could reward a student for good behavior with Fun Bucks. Students demonstrating excellent behavior could receive Fun Bucks from the cafeteria monitor, the custodian, or the school secretary. A student demonstrating good citizenship by helping a fellow student could be awarded with Fun Bucks by the classroom teacher, the custodian, the librarian, or the bus driver. Teachers could also reward students demonstrating good classroom behavior with Fun Bucks.

Students who were in detention during the six-week period were not allowed to participate in the reward afternoon. Instead, they were required to go to one classroom and continue with their schoolwork. Those allowed to participate could play games, buy prizes with their Fun Bucks, and win door prizes donated by local businesses.

On the day of the first reward afternoon, Ms. Wong realized she had a problem. First, there were more students who had to remain in the classrooms than were allowed to participate in the reward afternoon. In fact, in some classrooms, *no* students were allowed to participate. Second, one teacher had rewarded her students constantly, and her students had earned more Fun Bucks than all the other students combined.

The next day, Ms. Wong called the faculty together to discuss and refine the discipline plan. First, they agreed that students would have to be in detention twice during the six weeks to lose their chance to participate in the reward afternoon. They also discussed and agreed about what behavior was worthy of a reward.

By the end of the second six-week period, Ms. Wong is pleased with her discipline plan. The second reward afternoon is a huge success, with 80 percent of the students in the school participating. When students are in the hall, they quietly walk in a straight line. When she visits classrooms, she finds students on-task and well behaved. The cafeteria is a quiet place with few disturbances. After walking through the building, Ms. Wong returns to the office and tells the school secretary, "The building is so quiet, I almost forget there are children in the building. I'm very pleased by what we have accomplished."

## Summary

The most widely accepted classroom-management model throughout the 1970s and 1980s was clearly Lee and Marlene Canter's *Assertive Discipline*. This model, or variations of this model, are still used in schools throughout the United States. Using theories and principles from assertiveness training and behavior modification, Assertive Discipline has as its premise the right of the teacher to define and enforce standards for student behavior in the classroom. Assertive Discipline is a series of actions that are directed at clearly specifying expectations for student behavior.

## Key Terminology

Definitions for these terms appear in the glossary.

Assertive Discipline    43
Assertive teachers    45
Discipline hierarchy    49

Hostile teachers    45
Nonassertive teachers    45
Severity plan    50

## Chapter Activities

### Reflecting on the Theory

1. Eighth-grade teacher Natalie Cansler is having a problem with one of her students, Cary Kirby. Cary arrives each day without the required materials. Some days he forgets his pencil; other days it is his textbooks. Each day, he requests that he be allowed to return to his locker for some forgotten item. Ms. Cansler feels she is in a no-win situation. If she allows Cary to return to his locker, he loses valuable instructional time. If she refuses, he spends the hour unable to do his work. How could the principles of Assertive Discipline be used to change Cary's behavior?

2. In the scenario at the beginning of the chapter, Ms. Conner punished Jonathan for not having a pencil but then allowed him to select a pencil from a box of sharpened pencils. Did allowing Jonathan to take a pencil encourage Jonathan to forget his pencil in the future? Would you have given Jonathan a pencil or made him do without? Why?

3. Think of a teacher you consider "assertive." What are the behaviors that this teacher displays?

4. Are there types of students or students of certain grade levels who might not respond to Assertive Discipline techniques? Explain your reasoning.

5. The end of the chapter describes the discipline at Henderson Elementary School. Would you be comfortable working in a school that has adopted a plan such as Henderson Elementary School? Why or why not?

### Developing Artifacts for Your Portfolio

1. Canter and Canter suggest that teachers predetermine the consequences for rule violation. What consequences will you have for inappropriate behavior? Will you establish a discipline hierarchy? Why?

### Developing Your Personal Philosophy of Classroom Management

1. Would you be comfortable using Assertive Discipline as your classroom-management approach? Why or why not? Are there some strategies from Assertive Discipline that you will definitely incorporate into your classroom-management plan? Why?

2. Canter and Canter suggest that students "choose" to misbehave. Do you agree? Are students who misbehave choosing to violate the classroom rules, or are there other factors that might be impacting students' behavior? If so, what might they be?

## Resources for Further Study

Further information about Assertive Discipline and resources for its use in the classroom can be found by contacting

Solution Tree Press
Bloomington, IN
800-733-6786
812-336-7700

## Chapter References

Bromfield, C. (2006). PGCE secondary trainee teachers and effective behaviour management: An evaluation and commentary. *Support for Learning, 21*, 188–193.

Brophy, J. (2006). History of research on classroom management. In C. Evertson & C. Weinstein (Eds.), *Handbook of classroom management: Research, practice, and contemporary issues.* Mahwah, NJ: Lawrence Erlbaum Associates, Inc.

Canter, L. (1979). Taking charge of student behavior. *National Elementary Principal, 58*, 33–36.

Canter, L. (1989). Assertive discipline: More than names on the board and marbles in a jar. *Phi Delta Kappan, 71*, 57–61.

Canter, L. (2010). *Assertive Discipline: Positive behavior management for today's classroom* (4th ed.). Bloomington, IN: Solution Tree Press.

Canter, L., & Canter, M. (1976). *Assertive Discipline: A take charge approach for today's educator.* Santa Monica, CA: Canter and Associates.

Canter, L., & Canter, M. (1992). *Assertive Discipline: Positive behavior management for today's classroom.* Santa Monica, CA: Canter and Associates.

Canter, L., & Canter, M. (1993). *Succeeding with difficult students: New strategies for reaching your most challenging students.* Bloomington, IN: Solution Tree Press.

Covaleskie, J. F. (1992). Discipline and morality: Beyond rules and consequences. *Educational Forum, 56*, 173–183.

Curwin, R. L., & Mendler, A. N. (1988). Packaged discipline programs: Let the buyer beware. *Educational Leadership, 46*, 68–73.

Emmer, E. T., & Aussiker, A. (1990). School and classroom discipline programs: How well do they work? In O. C. Moles (Ed.), *Student discipline strategies.* Albany: State University of New York Press.

Kizlik, B. (2009). *Assertive discipline information.* ADPRIMA Education Information for New and Future Teachers. Retrieved May 11, 2010, from http://www.adprima.com.

Kohn, A. (1996). *Beyond discipline: From compliance to community.* Alexandria, VA: Association for Supervision and Curriculum Development.

Marzano, R. J. (2003). *Classroom management that works: Research-based strategies for every teacher.* Alexandria, VA: Association for Supervision and Curriculum Development.

McEwan, B. (2000). *The art of classroom management.* Upper Saddle River, NJ: Merrill/ Prentice Hall.

Queen, J. A., Blackwelder, B. B., & Mallen L. P. (1997). *Responsible classroom management for teachers and students.* Upper Saddle River, NJ: Merrill/Prentice Hall.

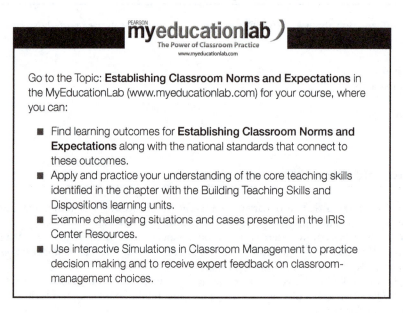

Go to the Topic: **Establishing Classroom Norms and Expectations** in the MyEducationLab (www.myeducationlab.com) for your course, where you can:

- Find learning outcomes for **Establishing Classroom Norms and Expectations** along with the national standards that connect to these outcomes.
- Apply and practice your understanding of the core teaching skills identified in the chapter with the Building Teaching Skills and Dispositions learning units.
- Examine challenging situations and cases presented in the IRIS Center Resources.
- Use interactive Simulations in Classroom Management to practice decision making and to receive expert feedback on classroom-management choices.

# Positive Classroom Discipline

## Objectives

Chapter 4 prepares preservice teachers to meet INTASC standards #5 (Motivation and Management), #6 (Communication), and #9 (Reflective Practitioner) by helping them to

- understand the basic principles behind Positive Classroom Discipline.

- understand the impact of nonverbal communication in setting limits in the classroom.

- learn techniques for the effective use of Positive Classroom Discipline in the classroom.

- evaluate classroom seating arrangements in maintaining appropriate classroom control.

- evaluate the relationship between instruction and classroom management.

- use the principles of Positive Classroom Discipline to deal with problem behavior.

## Scenario

Juan Morales is whispering to his friend Dion when he realizes the class has become unusually quiet. Turning toward the front of the class, he sees that Mr. McAdams has stopped talking and is giving him "The Look." "The Look" is famous throughout Miller High School, and Mr. McAdams has perfected the ability to stare so intently that students immediately stop whatever they are doing. Unable to maintain eye contact with Mr. McAdams, Juan picks up his pencil and turns his attention to the work on his desk. When Mr. McAdams is confident that Juan has turned in his seat and is now focused on the assigned work, he leans over to help another student.

As veteran sixth-grade teacher James Evans's class takes turns reading the chapter from their history text, two girls in the back of the room pass a note. As Doug reads the next paragraph, Mr. Evans moves to the back of the room and stands directly in front of the girls. He stands there until both girls turn to face him and begin to read silently from their book. When Doug reaches the end of the paragraph, he says, "Thank you, Doug." Then, putting his finger on the spot where she should begin reading, he motions for one of the note-passing girls to read the next paragraph. As she reads, he moves away from the girls and takes his position behind another student who needs a reminder to stay on-task.

Each week, the students in Marian Boyd's fifth-grade class can earn time for what Ms. Boyd calls the PAT (Preferred Activity Time). On Monday, Ms. Boyd announces that on Friday the class will have a PAT if they earn thirty minutes of free time during the week. After much discussion, the class decides they want to play their favorite review game as their PAT. Excited, they start to work, hoping to earn their PAT. During the afternoon, Ms. Boyd gives the students two minutes to put up their dictionaries, get out their math homework, and sharpen their pencils. When the two minutes is over, Ms. Boyd takes out a stopwatch and keeps track of the additional time it takes for everyone to get back in their seats and to be ready for math. She then subtracts the extra minutes it took to complete the task from the time allowed for Friday's PAT. The next day, Ms. Boyd gives the students five minutes to go to the bathroom as they return from lunch. When two girls take an additional two minutes, this time is subtracted for the PAT. Later in the week, Jamell is reading a comic book instead of finishing his seatwork. Without saying a word, Ms. Boyd takes out the stopwatch and starts tracking the time that Jamell is wasting. When several of the students notice what is happening, they tell Jamell to put the comic book away and to get back to work. At the end of the week, the class has twenty-five minutes left for their PAT and happily spends the time playing their favorite review game.

## INTRODUCTION

The three teachers described in the preceding paragraphs have two things in common. First, each is using negative reinforcement to manage their classroom. In each case, the teacher is using something the students find aversive (receiving the look, being in a student's space, losing time for preferred activities) until the students return to their work. In addition, these three teachers are using techniques that are the basis of Fredric Jones's **Positive Classroom Discipline** approach.

Fredric Jones (2007b) began investigating effective classroom-management techniques in the early 1970s. After spending thousands of hours observing both effective and ineffective classroom managers, Jones (1987) found that instruction can occur only in a well-controlled classroom and that teachers with poor classroom control can lose up to 50 percent of instructional time. In cases in which teachers must choose to discipline or to continue with instruction, Jones stresses that they must always choose to discipline.

Jones (1979) suggests that the major discipline problem in the classroom is not hostile defiance by a few students. According to Jones, the greatest discipline problem is the massive amount of time wasted by the majority of students. Jones found that in the average classroom, 80 percent of all disruptions are nothing more than students talking to their neighbors. Students wandering around the room cause another 15 percent of disruptions. Most of the remaining problems are minor disruptions, such as pencil tapping, note passing, or playing with an object. These disruptions are not severe and seem insignificant. However, it is hard enough to manage one child who is misbehaving, but when there are two misbehaving students, the drain on the teacher's skill and energy are squared. If there is a third child involved, this skill and energy drain is cubed. Simultaneously teaching and maintaining order in a class of twenty requires tremendous skill and energy. The lack of either skill or energy will result in a stressed teacher and a tremendous loss of instructional time.

By using proximity control, negative reinforcement, incentives, and good body language, Jones proposes that classroom control can be maintained and that learning can occur. Jones's theories are grounded in behavioral theory and classroom research at all grade levels. Jones (2007b) stresses that to control student behavior, an effective behavior-management program must systematically strengthen desired behavior while weakening inappropriate behavior. Strengthening desired behaviors must go hand in hand with eliminating undesired behavior. Too often, teachers focus on eliminating *undesired* behavior without having a plan to increase the *desired* behavior. Without a plan to increase desired behavior, however, whatever replaces inappropriate behavior is left to chance and may actually be another discipline problem. To obtain or strengthen desired behaviors, Jones advocates the use of positive and negative reinforcement. To stop inappropriate behavior, Jones uses a backup system that is punitive in nature.

In Jones's model, the enforcement of classroom standards and the development of cooperative behavior are combined, in order to maximize learning and minimize disruptions. Jones (2007b) stresses that an effective classroom-management system must be

- positive and affirm the student.

- economical. Jones uses the term *cheap* to describe systems that are practical and simple, require little paperwork, and are easy to use. Cheap systems are designed to reduce the teacher's workload.

- self-eliminating. An effective system will eventually become unneeded, because students will be trained to act appropriately. If the plan does not become self-eliminating, then it is either the wrong plan or is self-perpetuating. Self-perpetuating plans have built-in flaws; they actually reinforce unwanted behavior and feed the problem.

- low key, supportive, and almost invisible.

---

### Step-by-Step Positive Classroom Discipline

To use Positive Classroom Discipline in your classroom, you will need to do the following things:

1. Arrange your classroom for maximum proximity control.

2. Establish rules for your classroom.

3. Employ Limit Setting by using nonverbal methods to control behavior.

4. Provide backups for when Limit Setting is ineffective.

5. Train students to have responsibly for themselves and others through Responsibility Training.

6. Provide Preferred Activity Time (PAT) as reward for group behavior.

7. Use Omission Training for individual students who will not comply with classroom standards.

---

Positive Classroom Discipline focuses on the management of group behavior. The model consists of four main components:

1. Classroom structure

2. Limit Setting

3. Responsibility Training

4. Backup systems

## CLASSROOM STRUCTURE

Jones (2007b) considers classroom structure the centerpiece of classroom management. Preparing the structure of the classroom is a proactive step that prevents the majority of classroom disruptions. Issues to consider in providing structure include arranging the furniture and creating classroom rules and procedures. Consider the following example.

> At the end of the first six weeks, Heather Drapper asked her husband to meet in her classroom so they could rearrange the furniture. "I need to move my desk," she explained. "I want no more than eight feet between me and the student sitting farthest from the front of the room." Together they moved her desk and rearranged the students' desks. When they had finished, Heather walked to each desk. She stood in front of each desk and then moved around to stand behind the desk. Satisfied that she could be in any student's space in a matter of seconds, she rewarded her hardworking husband by taking him out to dinner.

In her short time in the classroom, Ms. Drapper had learned that one of the easiest ways to prevent discipline problems is location, location, and location. Most teachers recognize that the students who are closest to the teacher are the best behaved. To maintain appropriate control, teachers must constantly work the crowd by moving throughout the classroom and being at every desk. This method of classroom control is sometimes thought of as "management by walking around" or **proximity control.**

The classroom arrangement should allow for maximum teacher mobility, physical proximity to students, and the moment-to-moment accountability of students. There must be walkways so that teachers can reach each student quickly. The best possible room arrangement is one that puts the least distance and fewest barriers between the teacher and any student in the classroom. See Figure 4.1 for examples of effective and ineffective classroom arrangements.

### Figure 4.1

Effective and Ineffective Classroom Arrangements

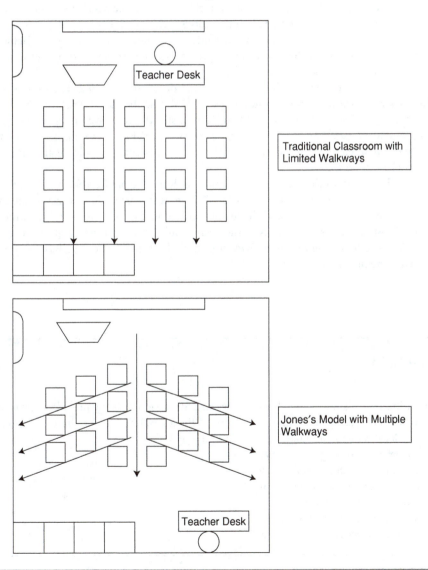

The main problem in most classrooms is the furniture arrangement. With the traditional arrangement of the desk in the front of the room, the distance from the chalkboard to the students in the front row can be anywhere from eight to thirteen feet. By moving the desk to a corner or to the back of the room, students are moved forward and closer to the area of instruction. Creating walkways between, in front of, and behind desks promotes easier access between students and teacher. Like Ms. Drapper, teachers should measure the time it takes to get to each student.

The location of overheads and teacher centers with computers and monitors creates additional problems. Because of the need for this equipment to be centrally located for maximum viewing by all students, they are typically placed at the front of the classroom. In some cases, teachers become trapped behind a table of electronic equipment. Jones (2007b) suggests that teachers move out and allow students to operate the equipment. Being the "overhead/computer operator" is rewarding to the student selected for the task, and it allows the teacher to work the crowd in the back of the room.

One of the most proactive things a teacher can do to structure the classroom is to establish classroom rules and procedures. Jones (2007b) describes general rules as those dealing with broad classes of behavior and that are best stated in positive rather than negative languages. He stresses that effective classroom rules are (a) limited in number, usually no more than five to eight; (b) enforceable quickly and consistently; (c) simple and clear; and (d) posted for all to see.

Procedures and routines are the techniques for doing the predictable things that occur normally throughout a school day. Jones (2007a) states that procedures must be taught as thoroughly as any other lesson and the lessons should include rehearsal and repetition to mastery. Most of the first two weeks of the term should be spent teaching procedures and routines. In the following example, Bridget Campbell's third-grade class has an effective routine for the beginning of each day.

## Tips from the Field

When I started using PowerPoint in my classroom, I quickly realized that using the computer trapped me in one location and eliminated my ability to control behavior through proximity control. I have eliminated this problem by assigning a "clicker" each day. The student selected sits by the computer and clicks the mouse when directed to do so. This allows me to move around the room as needed. The student is awarded for the job by being provided a printed copy of the notes. I never fail to have volunteers to be the clicker.

Michael Mosley
Seventh-Grade Social
Studies Teacher
Kenwood Middle School
Clarksville, Tennessee

As Bridget Campbell arranges the materials she will use throughout the day, her students begin to arrive. Taking a second to greet each student, Ms. Campbell answers individual questions and checks to make sure the pencil jar is full of sharpened pencils. As the students enter, they pull a card from an envelope on which their name is written. These envelopes are part of a large display on the bulletin board next to the door. They then place the card in one of two boxes, one marked "buying lunch" and the other marked "bringing lunch from home." The students know that they are then to put away their coats and backpacks and go immediately to their desks. Once seated, students are to place their homework on the right-hand corner and to begin working on the daily review. While the students work on the daily review, Ms. Campbell checks attendance by seeing whose card is still in its envelope. She then counts the cards in the "buying lunch" box and e-mails both the attendance and lunch reports to the office. When finished, she walks by each desk, checking to see whether homework has been completed. In just a few minutes, the class begins as Ms. Campbell discusses the daily review.

# LIMIT SETTING

"Rules define limits, but they do not establish limits" (Jones, 1987, p. 81). The establishment of rules is only the beginning of effective classroom management. To create limits in the classroom, Jones proposes a method, **Limit Setting,** through which teachers systematically teach students that they mean business. Through the teacher's interpersonal power, physical presence, and emotional tone, the message is sent to the students that the teacher's rules are for real. Limit Setting, according to Jones, goes beyond telling the class the rules: It is training them to follow the rules.

Limit Setting is rule enforcement. It is consistently disallowing infractions of the basic classroom rules. However, Jones (2007b) asserts that Limit Setting is done with the body, not the mouth. Jones (2007b) stresses that body language is the all-important medium through which teachers convey assertiveness and states that "body language allows the teacher to use finesse to protect students from embarrassment while dealing effectively with goofing off " (p. 35). In Limit Setting, the teacher is assertive but never aggressive, because the object of Limit Setting is to calm the students and to get them back on-task.

Jones's research (1979) shows that the training of students through Limit Setting techniques eliminates 70 to 95 percent of the disruptions in the regular classroom. Limit Setting begins with the following six steps.

**Step One: Eyes in the Back of Your Head**   Step one requires the "withitness" described by Kounin (1970). The teacher must be aware of everything that is going on in the classroom at all times. The teacher must catch disruptions as soon as they begin and respond immediately. Disruptions such as talking to one's neighbor are fun and self-rewarding. Ignoring the behavior will not make it go away, because the student may be rewarded for misbehaving by the student's peers.

**Step Two: Terminate Instruction**   The teacher must immediately terminate instruction to deal with the disruptive behavior. If the teacher does not, Jones stresses, students will have learned that the teacher places greater importance on instruction than on discipline. If the teacher does not take action, the amount of inappropriate behavior will continue until the teacher is forced to stop instruction.

**Step Three: Turn, Look, and Say the Student's Name**   The turn is the teacher's emotional response to inappropriate behavior. Before turning, the teacher should take a relaxing breath. Being calm, Jones stresses, is the key to effective Limit Setting. To appear calm and relaxed, hands should remain down by the side and the jaw should be slack. Waving hands show frustration, and the mouth will show distress if it is not slack. Face the student squarely, and say his or her name in a firm tone. Look the student in the eye and maintain unwavering eye contact.

Has the disruptive behavior stopped and has the student returned to work? The teacher should look at the student's knees and feet to determine compliance. According to Jones, the knees and feet tell the entire story. If they are facing the front of the room, the teacher can assume the inappropriate behavior has been stopped. If the feet and knees are not turned squarely in the chair, the teacher has only achieved pseudocompliance. Unless the student has turned squarely in the desk, the student plans to return to what he or she was doing as soon as the teacher's back is turned. Other pseudocompliance techniques include pretending to read or to write.

**Step Four: Walk to the Edge of the Student's Desk**   If the student does not turn around square in his or her seat, Jones advises the teacher to move toward the student at a deliberate pace until the teacher's leg is touching the edge of the desk. In a relaxed, calm manner, the teacher makes eye contact. Jones stresses that the teacher should remain at the edge of the desk until the student turns squarely in the desk. When the student returns to work, the teacher should watch for a few minutes, thank the student, and then move away.

## Tips from the Field

I believe in the power of "The Look." In my class, the students have an expression that goes, "When the eyebrows go up, it's going to get rough." Fortunately, each class tells the students in the next class this expression. Therefore, whenever students misbehave, all that is necessary for me to do is to arch my eyebrows and the students immediately stop whatever they are doing. "The Look" is a critical skill in classroom management.

Larry Bader
Fifth-Grade Teacher
Putman County Elementary School
Eatonton, Georgia

**Step Five: Prompt**   If the student did not return to work after the teacher stood at the student's desk for several minutes, the teacher should lean over at the waist until his or her weight is on one palm. Getting eyeball to eyeball with the student, the student should be given a prompt—a message that tells the student what to do next. The prompt might be moving work around in front of the student, pointing to the work to be done, or verbally telling the student to turn around and to begin to work. Once the student has complied, the teacher should thank the student and then move away.

**Step Six: Palms**   If the student does not comply during Step Five, the teacher should lean slowly across the desk and place both palms flat on the far side of the desk on either side of the student. The teacher should remain eyeball to eyeball with the student until the student complies. When the student complies, the teacher thanks the student and moves away.

If the student backtalks during Limit Setting or if two students are involved, the following steps are added to the process:

**Step Seven: Camping Out in Front**   If the student has been backtalking during this encounter, Jones stresses that Step Six should be continued and the teacher should "camp out" until the student complies. Jones (2007b) describes the golden rule of dealing with backtalk as "doing nothing"—"waiting out" the student. When the student stops talking, the teacher should give a prompt, wait until the student complies, and then move away. Jones stresses that the teacher should never move out until confident that the student has begun to work.

**Step Eight: Camping Out from Behind**   If backtalk involves more than one student, camping out in back may be more effective. The teacher should use the wide walkways and move around the desks to stand directly between the students. Leaning on the table of the first student, as described in Step Five, blocks the view of the second student. The teacher should totally ignore the second student and establish eye contact with the first student. Then the teacher should wait until the first student is back on target. Only when the first student is working is it time to focus on the second student.

Why does Limit Setting work? It works because students want the teacher out of their space. In order to have the teacher move away, almost all students stop the inappropriate behavior and return to their work. It works because Limit Setting uses behavioral research that shows that negative reinforcement increases desired behavior.

Jones (1987) stresses that Limit Setting shouldn't be necessary throughout the year. During what he calls the **acquisition phase** (when the students are first learning the classroom rules), the teacher may need to use Limit Setting several times a day. But Jones promises that once students realize that the teacher intends to enforce the rules and is consistent in this enforcement, Limit Setting will be needed less and less.

There are limitations to Limit Setting and Jones (1987, 2001) acknowledges that it will not work in all situations. Jones provides the following limitations of Limit Setting:

- If the teacher cannot be calm and shows anger and frustration, the effectiveness of Limit Setting is weakened. Calm is strength in Limit Setting.

- If the teacher has a poor relationship with the students, they may not return to work as a challenge to the teacher's authority. For Limit Setting to be effective, students have to trust that the teacher will move away when they return to work.

- If the teacher moves away too quickly, students may learn that only pseudocompliance is needed to get the teacher out of their space.

- If the teacher is trapped behind a desk or teacher center, the ability to move quickly to a student will be lessened. Students then know they have time to get back on-task before the teacher can reach them.

- If the lesson is boring or the students have been sitting too long, the interruption created by a Limit Setting episode may be rewarding. Students may then encourage each other to be off-task, just to break the monotony of the class.

- If the teacher is not aware of what is going on around the classroom, much behavior that could be solved by Limit Setting will be ignored. Inappropriate behavior will increase because students will realize that no one is watching.

- If the entire class is off-task, standing by one desk will do little to solve the situation.

- If the student is agitated or physically aggressive, moving into the student's space may be viewed as a threat. Teachers need to know their students well enough to read when Limit Setting will work and when it will not.

---

### Tips from the Field

I use PAT with all my classes, but it's important to adapt how you use it to each group of kids. How the classes spend their PAT time (and even how they gain time) is often not the same because of how different the dynamic of each period is. It takes me a month or more to figure out exactly what method fits each class, so if something doesn't work, I don't scrap PAT altogether; I simply try something else until I get it right. For instance, my regular and Pre-AP classes chose much different ways of spending their PAT this past year. My regular kids often chose "Heads-Up Seven-Up" or something similar. However, my advanced kids loved to play a game called "The Professor." I choose five students to come to the front of the class, and they become the one brain of the professor. A student in the audience asks the professor a question (it can be academic or plain silly), and the "professor" must answer by each saying one word. The sentence is complete when the last student gives an end punctuation. For example, if someone asked, "What's the capital of Texas?" the "professor" would answer like this: student #1—"The," student #2—"capital," student #3—"of," student #4—"Texas," student #5—"is," student #1—"Austin," student #2—"period." This becomes quite funny when the kids can't figure out what word should come next.

Stephanie Gilbert
Seventh-Grade Language Arts
McAdams Jr. High
Dickinson, Texas

## RESPONSIBILITY TRAINING

Classroom management is, as the name implies, management of the class. To be effective, rewards or incentives must be a group system rather than a collection of individual incentive systems (Jones, 2007b). To generate consistently good behavior from all class members, Jones proposes that teachers devise a complex, formal incentive system that utilizes (1) bonuses and (2) penalties. Essential are (1) group rewards and (2) group accountability. **Responsibility Training** is such a group incentive program, in which the philosophy is "One for all and all for one." The heart of Responsibility Training is the accountability students have for and to each other. Responsibility Training takes the teacher out of the enforcer, or nagging parent, role.

Basic to Responsibility Training are incentives. Incentives are used to increase productivity and to encourage students to follow classroom rules. In the first decade of the twenty-first century, however, there has been criticism of incentives and rewards because these teaching tools have been viewed as bribes. Jones (2007b) notes that a proactive incentive system (such as Responsibility Training) is an exchange that is established in advance and is, therefore, not a bribe. It is planned as a normal part of the day. However, a reactive system is established in the heat of the moment and should be considered a bribe.

*Jones stresses that a teacher's nonverbal behavior sends a clear message to students and prevents many misbehaviors from escalating.*

Incentive systems can be simple or complex. A simple incentive system provides a reinforcer in exchange for a specified behavior. Jones (1979) notes that incentive systems must have three parts: a task, a reward, and a system of accountability. One of Jones's (2007b) favorite incentive programs is what he calls **Grandmama's Rule.** Just as Grandmama told her grandchildren that they had to finish their dinner before they could have dessert, in Responsibility Training students are told that they must complete a required task in order to earn **Preferred Activity Time (PAT).** Grandmama's Rule is the juxtaposition of two activities: (a) the things students *have* to do and (b) the things the students *want* to do.

Preferred activities can be any educational activity students like to do. Jones (2001) suggests that these activities be readily available, easy to use, represent a reasonable amount of prep time for the teacher, and serve an educational purpose. PATs can be whatever activities students like and might include centers, games, and videos.

The success of PATs depends on students working together to earn the PAT. The group earns time for the PAT when *every* member of the class is productive, and the group loses time when *any* member of the class is off-task. Jones (2007b) suggests that in most classrooms, the peer group reinforces deviant behavior. With Responsibility Training, the teacher uses the power of the peer group to control class behavior.

For more than twenty years, Jones has trained teachers to successfully use Responsibility Training to change student behavior. In the majority of classrooms, the system works well. Nevertheless, he has found that in some classes a clique in the class will reinforce their own deviant behavior and are immune to peer pressure. Moreover, Jones stresses that the PATs must change often because reinforcement satiation is the eternal enemy of any incentive system.

## BACKUP SYSTEM

Although Jones (1987, 2001) proposes that most inappropriate behavior will be stopped through Limit Setting and Responsibility Training, a few students will force the use of negative sanctions. Jones's **Backup System** is a systematic, hierarchic organization of negative sanctions. He suggests the use of the Backup System when there is an obnoxious incident or a repeat disruptor who does not respond to Limit Setting or Responsibility Training.

The Backup System is composed of three levels: small backup responses, medium backup responses, and large backup responses. Table 4.1 provides examples of consequences at each level. As students work up the levels, the consequences become more severe and more professional assistance is involved.

Small backup responses are the first line of defense in the classroom. They are done privately, and in many cases the other students have no knowledge that they are being administered. Small backup responses are communications rather than sanctions. The objectives of the small backup system are (a) to inform students that they are entering the Backup System and (b) to invite students to return to their work.

Medium backup responses are more public. They can include being sent to time-out or having the student's name placed on the board. Medium responses are more punitive than corrective.

**Table 4.1**   Examples of Responses in Jones's Backup System

| Small Backup Responses | Medium Backup Responses | Large Backup Responses |
|---|---|---|
| Private—Between Student and Teacher | Public Within the Classroom | Public and Requires Two Professionals |
| Speaking privately to student<br>Catching the student's eye | Assigning time-out in classroom<br>Assigning time-out in colleague's room | Sending student to the office<br>Sending student to in-school suspension |
| Putting finger to lips | Warning student publicly | Requiring student to attend Saturday school |
| Pulling parent's address card | Sending student to the hall<br>Holding conference with parent<br>Requiring student to stay after school | Calling police<br>Giving detention<br>Expelling student |

Large backup responses require help from outside the classroom and the involvement of at least two professionals. Sending students to the office, assigning detention, and suspending a student are the most common examples.

Corporal punishment is never advocated by Jones. Jones (1987) states that of all the discipline techniques in existence, corporal punishment has the fewest assets and the greatest number of liabilities.

## SUMMARY OF THE FOUR-STEP MODEL

Jones (2007b) proposes a four-component model that includes Classroom Structure, Limit Setting, Responsibility Training, and Backup Systems. He suggests that teachers be proactive by establishing classroom limits through classroom rules and procedures. When these rules and procedures are challenged, Limit Setting is the first line of defense against typical disruptions in the classroom. Still, Limit Setting is mild social punishment and, as such, is incomplete. A reward system must be established to promote desired behavior. Responsibility Training provides balance by establishing such a reward system. In cases in which the first three components do not stop inappropriate behavior, Backup Systems must be in place. Jones (1987) cautions teachers, however, to extract as much management as possible from Classroom Structure, Limit Setting, and Responsibility Training before moving to punitive backup responses.

## STRATEGIES FOR DEALING WITH DIFFICULT STUDENTS

Jones (2007b) suggests that one of the oldest myths in education is that the solution to dealing with difficult students lies in the principal's office. Instead, he stresses, the solution lies in the classroom with the classroom teacher. According to Jones, the answer to dealing with difficult students is consistency. If the teacher has been consistent in following the steps outlined in Limit Setting, then small disruptions do not grow into big disruptions. When the teacher is consistent, smaller and smaller consequences are required to manage behavior. When the teacher is inconsistent, larger and larger consequences will be needed to govern misbehavior.

The types of disruptions caused by difficult students usually revolve around inappropriate interactions with fellow students or the teacher. In some situations, an individual student's behavior will cause the entire class to lose a reward, resulting in anger by fellow students. When that occurs, Jones (2007b) suggests that the teacher remove the student from Responsibility Training and use **Omission Training** to change the student's behavior. Omission Training is the name given to an incentive program system that rewards the omission, or avoidance, of unwanted behavior. In Omission Training, the teacher rewards the individual student for behaving appropriately for a certain period of time. To increase the likelihood of success, the class is also rewarded when the student is on-task. Therefore, the student has an opportunity to become a class hero and be accepted by the class, and the class helps the student learn new behavior.

The establishment of an Omission Training program requires that the teacher perform the following:

- Remove the defiant student from Responsibility Training so the class is no longer being punished for the student's inappropriate behavior.
- Talk to the student in a nonpublic place about the student's behavior.
- Establish an individual reward program for the student.
- Announce to the class that the student is now on an individual program. However, when the student earns time or a reward, the reward is shared with the entire class.
- Withdraw the student from Omission Training as the student learns appropriate behavior and is more accepted by the group.

The second type of unacceptable behavior comes from the student's interaction with the teacher. In many cases the student will respond to demands by the teacher in a negative way through inappropriate language or behavior. Jones (2007b) recommends that when confronted with a belligerent student, the teacher should do nothing. If the teacher responds with anger or harsh words, the student has succeeded. Therefore, when in doubt, do nothing.

Jones (2007b) stresses that the teacher's waiting and remaining silent does not mean that punitive action will not occur. Waiting simply gives the teacher time to think before acting and maintain professionalism. Depending upon the teacher's calmness and skill, a crisis can have a constructive end (Jones, 2008). Once the student has calmed, then the teacher should have a conversation with the student outside the presence of peers. Many times, all that is necessary for future disruptions to be avoided is what Jones calls a clinical conversation. After the conversation, however, the teacher may still feel it is necessary to use one of the large backups described in Table 4.1. These consequences occur outside the classroom in either the principal's office or in the juvenile justice system.

## FREDISMS

Since Jones wrote his first book in 1987, teachers have to come to appreciate what Jones has to say about classroom management as much as they appreciate his classroom-management system. His quotes have become famous and are called "Fredisms." Below are some of the favorite Fredisms.

It takes one fool to backtalk. It takes two fools to make a conversation out of it (Jones, 2007b, p. 224).

If the technology of discipline management could be likened to an animal, then corporal punishment would surely be its ass end (Jones, 1987, p. 344).

Almost every form of classroom disruption is its own reward. Being self-reinforcing, disruptions are self-perpetuating (Jones, 1987, p. 33).

Every student in your class has a Ph.D. in teacher management (Jones, 1987, p. 34).

Discipline management is an indoor sport. Basketball players know how to fake and poker players know how to bluff. Students know how to do both at the same time (Jones, 2001, p. 193).

Goofing off is its own reward. Goofing off is always the easy, pleasurable alternative to being on the ball (Jones, 1987, p. 241).

The most widespread management procedure in real classrooms is nag, nag, nag (Jones, 2007b, p. 7).

A roomful of students will always have more tricks up their sleeves than you will have in your bag of tricks. Bag of tricks represents to me the antithesis of a modern profession with an empirically based technology of professional practice (Jones, 1 987, p. 320).

## STRENGTHS AND WEAKNESSES OF POSITIVE CLASSROOM DISCIPLINE

Perhaps Jones's Positive Classroom Discipline's greatest strength lies in the fact that it is grounded in behavioral research. As stated in Chapter 2, behavioral theory is backed by a hundred years of research that shows that a student's behavior can be changed by reward and punishment.

An additional strength is that Jones specifies a set of steps or activities to follow when dealing with discipline problems. This provides a structure for the actions of teachers. Jones (1987) stresses that "knowing how to" in addition to "knowing about" is critical for teacher success in controlling a classroom.

Morris (1996) suggests that an additional strength is that Jones encourages teachers, administrators, and parents to work together to combat discipline problems.

There are, however, numerous weaknesses in the Jones discipline plan. Here are some of these weaknesses:

- Middle and high school students may become aggressive in response to the "in your face" approach. This approach may force a confrontation that neither the teacher nor the student wants.

- Student independence is not encouraged. Jones's model is one of absolute teacher control, with few student choices (Morris, 1996). Such absolute control can be seen in Jones's definition of Responsibility Training. "Responsibility training is an advanced type of time incentive that gets almost any student to do almost anything you want her or him to do when you want it done to your standards as a result of having asked only once" (Jones, 1987, p. 160).

- The use of students to keep fellow classmates in line can create problems rather than solve them. Resentment and revenge may be the result.

- Jones's insistence that instruction should be stopped when discipline problems arise may actually create problems in some classrooms. Some students may encourage each other to disrupt the class just so instruction will cease.

## POSITIVE CLASSROOM DISCIPLINE IN THE CLASSROOM

### Scenario

While part of the class works on math-review problems, fifth-grade teacher Janie Jandrokovic asks several students who are struggling with their vocabulary words to move to the computers so they can work on their words. As she helps a student load the software, she notices Zack passing a CD to Garrett. Stopping what she is doing, Ms. Jandrokovic turns to face the two boys. Caught, Garrett shoves the CD under his desk and pretends to work on his math. Upset that Garrett has kept his CD, Zack shoves him and says, "Give it back."

Garrett motions to let Zack know that Ms. Jandrokovic is watching, hoping that Zack will leave him alone and return to work. Unfortunately, Zack is more concerned about his CD than he is with his teacher. "I said give it back," he repeats.

Ms. Jandrokovic walks to the boys and moving behind Garrett and Zack, she stands between the boys. She leans down and sticks out her hand, indicating to Garrett that he is to place the CD in her hand. Seeing this, Zack exclaims, "Hey, you can't take that; it's mine. You give it back."

Ignoring Zack, Ms. Jandrokovic continues to lean down between the two boys, blocking Zack from view. Once she has been given the CD, she motions for Garrett to begin his math problems. The entire time she is dealing with Garrett, Zack keeps up a continuous stream of backtalk. "I want my CD back. Just because you can't afford

CDs for your own children doesn't mean you should take mine. You wait until I tell my dad. It's not right to take my things."

Ms. Jandrokovic ignores Zack until Garrett has been at work for a few minutes. Placing her hand on Garrett's shoulder, she says, "Thank you, Garrett." Then turning to Zack, she leans one arm on his desk and makes eye contact.

"You just wait until my folks hear that you stole my CD. Boy, are you going to be in trouble. You can't take my things," Zack continues. Realizing that Ms. Jandrokovic isn't going to argue back and plans to continue staring at him, he gives up and picks up his pencil.

Ms. Jandrokovic continues to stand by Zack's desk until he quits arguing and works three math problems. She then thanks Zack for getting back to work and returns to the computer station to finish loading the software.

When the class returns from gym a few hours later, Ms. Jandrokovic pulls Zack aside. When all the students have entered the classroom, Ms. Jandrokovic tells Zack, "I called your mother while you were in gym to tell her about the CD. She is coming to school this afternoon so the three of us can discuss your behavior. You are to stay in class this afternoon, and your mother will meet with us as soon as school is dismissed."

## Summary

Fredric Jones's discipline model, *Positive Classroom Management,* proposes that instruction can occur only in a well-controlled classroom. Therefore, he advocates that discipline must occur before instruction can begin. By using proximity control, negative reinforcement, incentives, and good body language, Jones proposes that classroom control can be maintained and learning can occur. Jones's theories are grounded in behavioral theory and classroom research at all grade levels. *Positive Classroom Discipline* consists of four main components: Classroom Structure, Limit Setting, Responsibility Training, and Backup Systems.

## Key Terminology

Definitions for these terms appear in the glossary.

## Chapter Activities

### Reflecting on the Theory

1. Fifth-grade teacher Angela Pruitt is dealing with one of the most common classroom problems: talkative students. Three girls constantly disrupt the class by talking. Ms. Pruitt has moved the girls so that they sit apart from each other, but they still manage to waste time talking, passing notes, and giggling over something one of them has said. How would Fredric Jones tell Ms. Pruitt to handle this situation?

2. Both Canter and Jones give suggestions for rule formation. How are the approaches similar? How do they differ?

3. What are the similarities and differences in Jones's approach to the techniques described in the chapter on behaviorism (Chapter 2)?

4. Do you agree with the way that Ms. Jandrokovic handled the situation with Zack and Garrett? What would you have done differently?

### Developing Artifacts for Your Portfolio

1. Jones believes that classroom arrangement is important to the success of classroom management. Analyze a classroom in which you have observed for the following:

   a. teacher mobility
   b. physical proximity to students
   c. moment-to-moment accountability of students
   d. walkways and aisles
   e. barriers between the teacher and any student in the classroom.

### Developing Your Personal Philosophy of Classroom Management

1. Jones's model has been called an "in your face" approach. Are there types of students or students of certain grade levels who might not respond to Jones's techniques? Would you be comfortable using this approach? Why?

2. Jones suggests that instruction should be terminated when discipline is needed, and if the teacher must choose between discipline and instruction, discipline should come first. Do you agree or disagree? Why?

3. With Jones's approach, the group earns time for the PAT when every member of the class is productive, and the group loses time when any member of the class is off-task. Do you agree with this philosophy? Why?

## Resources for Further Study

Further information about Positive Classroom Discipline and resources for its use in the classroom can be found by contacting

Fredric H. Jones & Associates, Inc.
103 Quarry Lane
Santa Cruz, CA 95060
(831) 425-8222
(831) 426-8222
http://www.fredjones.com

## Chapter References

Jones, F. (1979). The gentle art of classroom discipline. *National Elementary Principal, 58,* 26–32.
Jones, F. (1987). *Positive classroom discipline.* New York: McGraw-Hill.
Jones, F. (2001). *Tools for teaching.* Santa Cruz, CA: Fredric H. Jones & Associates, Inc.
Jones, F. (2007a). Teaching rules and routines. *Education World.* Retrieved June 16, 2010, from
    http://www.educationworld.com/acurr/columnists/jones/jones028.shtml.
Jones, F. (2007b). *Tools for teaching* (2nd ed.). Santa Cruz, CA: Fredric H. Jones & Associates, Inc.
Jones, F. (2008). Nasty backtalk. *Education World.* Retrieved May 15, 2010, from http://www.
    educationworld.com/acurr/columnists/jones/jones033.shtml.
Kounin, J. S. (1970). *Discipline and group management in the classroom.* New York: Holt,
    Rinehart and Winston.
Morris, R. C. (1996). Contrasting disciplinary models in education. *Thresholds in Education, 22,*
    7–13.

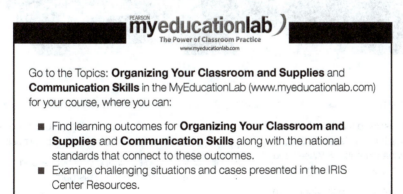

PEARSON
**myeducationlab**
The Power of Classroom Practice
www.myeducationlab.com

Go to the Topics: **Organizing Your Classroom and Supplies** and
**Communication Skills** in the MyEducationLab (www.myeducationlab.com)
for your course, where you can:

■ Find learning outcomes for **Organizing Your Classroom and
  Supplies** and **Communication Skills** along with the national
  standards that connect to these outcomes.
■ Examine challenging situations and cases presented in the IRIS
  Center Resources.

# Logical Consequences

## Objectives

Chapter 5 prepares preservice teachers to meet INTASC standards #2 (Student Development), #5 (Motivation and Management), #8 (Assessment), and #9 (Reflective Practitioner) by helping them to

- use knowledge about human behavior drawn from the research of Adler, Dreikurs, Albert, and Nelsen to develop strategies for classroom management.

- understand the motives for student behavior.

- evaluate research concerning the use of consequences as an alternative to traditional punishment.

- learn strategies for applying natural and logical consequences in the classroom.

- understand the basic principles of Logical Consequences.

- use the theory of Logical Consequences to deal with problem behavior.

## Scenario

At the end of her first year of teaching, third-grade teacher Sara Prabhu spent a few days reflecting on what she wanted to do differently the next year. Although she planned to change the physical setup of her classroom and revise several of her teaching strategies, the area she felt that needed the most improvement was her classroom-management plan.

When Sara began teaching, she adopted the discipline plan her cooperating teacher had used during Sara's student-teaching experience. This plan required the establishment of classroom rules and consequences. Throughout each day, students turned cards as they violated classroom rules. As more and more cards were turned, the consequences became more severe. After using this model for a year, however, Sara was frustrated and felt there were many flaws in her plan. The most critical flaw was that the consequences were not tied to the misbehavior or the motive for the misbehavior. Because Sara saw little connection between the behavior and the consequence, she was sure her students failed to see the connection as well.

During the summer, Sara was determined to find a classroom-management plan that better fit her teaching style and personal philosophy. She read numerous books and articles on classroom management and finally found an article written in the early 1970s on the use of logical consequences. Intrigued, she read the works of Rudolf Dreikurs. Dreikurs's model made sense to her, because the consequence for misbehavior was directly tied to the misbehavior. She felt certain that by using logical consequences, her students would see the relationship between their behavior and their punishment.

When school begins, Sara waits until she meets with the class before developing the classroom rules. After a discussion of what would make their classroom run smoothly, the class agrees upon a set of rules. They establish no consequences, because consequences are to be based on the behavior and on the motive for the misbehavior. A few days into the term, the lunchroom monitor tells Sara that a group of her students failed to clean their table and left it too messy for other students to use. Thinking of the appropriate logical consequence for such behavior, Sara sends the students to the cafeteria to clean the table and to apologize to the cafeteria staff. During the weeks that follow, Sara often has to struggle to find an appropriate logical consequence for each misbehavior but remains confident that students are learning from the consequences rather than simply feeling punished.

## INTRODUCTION

The last chapter in Part I on classroom management as discipline is based on the original work of Rudolf Dreikurs. Since the late 1960s and 1970s, many teachers, like Sara Prabhu, have adopted Dreikurs's model, **Logical Consequences.** When developed, Logical Consequences represented a shift from a behavioral focus on discipline to a more humanistic approach, using the concept that the motivation and goals of student behavior must be considered in the development of a discipline plan. But understanding the motivation behind behavior should not negate the need for appropriate consequences for misbehavior. Therefore, a major focus of Logical Consequences is to control student behavior while helping students recognize the consequences of their decisions.

Expanding Dreikurs's discipline concepts, Linda Albert and Jane Nelsen have provided a more current twist to Dreikurs's original theory. Albert (1996) and Nelsen (2006) stress that it is important to understand why students behave in a particular way. Through this understanding, teachers can develop strategies to handle particular problems. The premise behind Logical Consequences, however, is not just to control behavior but also to assist students in taking responsibility for their actions and behaviors.

Many of the concepts of Logical Consequences are based on the work of the Viennese psychiatrist Alfred Adler (1958), who proposed that all behavior has a purpose. According to Adler, each individual act by a student is goal driven. Unlike behavioral theorists, Adler did not see students as passively reacting to what is happening to them. Adler suggested that students are actively interacting with the environment and, even more important, that a student's behavior is a product of the student's appraisal and perception of the situation. Unfortunately, this appraisal is often subjective, biased, or inaccurate; yet to students, perceptions and assumptions are reality and are therefore not questioned. Consider the following example.

Because Cynthia's ninth-grade teacher asked students to work problems on the board, Cynthia always dreaded going to math class. Because she was overweight, Cynthia hated going to the board, knowing her classmates were staring at her. Today, she was assigned a problem that she hadn't been able to work the night before. Standing in front of the board, she felt her face redden as she struggled with the problem. She kept her face to the board, praying the answer would emerge. Then she heard laughter coming from the back of the room. Assuming the class was laughing at her, she turned and yelled, "I hate all of you. I hate this class." She ran from the room before she could learn that the class was actually laughing at a late-arriving student who was trying to sneak into the classroom without being seen by the teacher.

Adler's premise is that all people are social beings, and the need to belong or to be accepted is a basic human motivation. Every action of a student is an endeavor to find a place in the social structure of the classroom. Ideally, students discover that contributing to the welfare of the group is the best way to gain and maintain acceptance by others. Unfortunately, this is not always the case. All too frequently, students fail to understand what actions would help them to be accepted by the class. To help students find their place in the class and, ultimately, in society, Albert (1996) noted that teachers must understand the following:

- Students choose their behavior. Teachers have the power to influence, not control, student choices. She suggested that some students have a choosing disability rather than a physical or learning disability.

## Step-by-Step Logical Consequences

To use Logical Consequences in your classroom, you will need to do the following things:

1. Evaluate the goal of misbehavior to determine if it is
   - attention-seeking
   - power-seeking
   - revenge-seeking
   - failure-avoiding

2. Provide interventions based on the goal.

3. Impose a natural or logical consequence when rules are broken or misbehavior occurs.

4. Build community in the classroom by helping students connect to each other and to you.

- The ultimate goal of student behavior is to fulfill the psychological and emotional need to belong.
- Students misbehave to achieve one of four goals.

## GOALS OF MISBEHAVIOR

A student's behavior makes sense only when the teacher understands the reasons behind the behavior. Nelsen, Lott, and Glenn (2000) suggest that students are always making subconscious decisions based on their perceptions of their experiences in the classroom. The decisions they make become the basis of their behaviors. When students feel they do not belong, that they have no power, that they have been wronged, or that they cannot achieve, they act out in order to return balance to their lives. Perceptions and feelings become actions. In order to deal with the actions, Albert (1996) and Nelsen (2006) stress that teachers must understand the goals students are trying to achieve by their actions. Based on Adler's original theory, Albert and Nelsen identify four student goals:

1. To seek attention

2. To gain power

3. To seek revenge for some perceived injustice

4. To avoid failure

The most common goal for children is **attention seeking.** Students often have the mistaken idea that they have self-worth only when attention is paid to them. Although all children want and need attention, attention seeking becomes a problem when the goal is not to learn or to cooperate but to elevate the personal power of the student. For these children, being ignored is intolerable. In order to be noticed by the teacher or their peers, they are willing to accept punishment, pain, and humiliation.

Attention seeking plays out in numerous ways, some constructive and some destructive. In the passive form of attention seeking, the child may appear to be a model child and in some cases is the teacher's pet. Unfortunately, the demand for attention becomes stronger and stronger. When no longer satisfied with small amounts of attention, the student becomes a nuisance, a show-off, or the class clown. The attention-seeking student will constantly ask questions, not for information, but for attention. All of these behaviors are designed to keep the teacher and fellow students focused on the attention-seeking student.

Albert (1996) notes that there is a silver lining to attention-seeking behavior in that the student wants a relationship with the teacher. Therefore, the teacher can redirect inappropriate behavior so that the child gets attention in a more appropriate manner.

Albert (1996) states, "Young people don't lose their temper; they use it" (p. 41). This accurately describes the student who is **power seeking.** When the teacher tries to stop or redirect one of these students, a power struggle between the student and the teacher can ensue. In this situation, the student is trying to control the adult rather than get attention.

## Tips from the Field

As a means of maximizing one-on-one time with students, I make a point to stand outside my door during passing periods. As the students enter the room, I have the opportunity to greet them by name, congratulate them on their team's win the night before, ask them about their weekend, welcome them back if they have been absent . . . in short, acknowledge each of them so that they know they are an important part of my classroom. With a student load of 150 teenagers, it is a very efficient one-on-one connect *and* I am a presence in the hallway, which the administration appreciates!

> Kathy Koeneke Heavers
> Montrose High School
> Montrose, Colorado
> 2005 Colorado Teacher of the Year

The power-seeking student wants to be the boss and will contradict, lie, have a temper tantrum, or question the teacher's ability. Older students often have verbal tantrums and use what Albert (1996) calls the "lawyer syndrome" in which they drill the teacher as if the teacher were on the witness stand. Some power-seeking students are more passive. They are "sneaky," with their words representing one thing and their actions another.

Although the teacher may feel physically or professionally threatened, it is important that the teacher not engage in a power struggle with the student. Although power-seeking students can be extremely frustrating, Albert (1996) stresses that these students do have positive characteristics of leadership ability, assertiveness, and independent thinking, which can be redirected into more appropriate action.

**Revenge-seeking** behavior is the result of a long series of discouragements, in which the student has decided that there is no way to acquire the attention or power desired and that revenge will make up for the lack of belonging. Although the teacher and other students may be the target of a student's anger or pain, the cause of this anger and pain may actually be the result of personal circumstances, such as a broken home, parental unemployment, or racial prejudice (Albert, 1996).

Revenge-seeking students think everyone is against them. They believe teachers and fellow students are unfair to them, disregard their feelings, and hurt them. They are convinced that no one likes them, and because of this belief, they provoke others to a point at which relationships with the teacher and classmates are destroyed.

Students who feel beaten seek to retaliate. Revenge-seeking students are so deeply discouraged that they believe that only by hurting others can they find a place in the social atmosphere of the school. These students often threaten teachers and classmates. They can be the *victims* of a bully, or they can *become* the bully. Many harbor feelings that are manifested in violence toward themselves or others.

Revenge-seeking students know what the teacher holds dear and do what it takes to violate those values. Feeling personally attacked, the teacher feels hurt, disappointment, and dislike for the student. The behavior of these students often borders on the pathological and requires intervention from professionals. Therefore, it is important that teachers not retaliate or become emotionally upset. Only through an attitude of understanding and assistance can these students be helped.

**Failure-avoiding** students expect only failure and defeat, and after a while, these students simply give up. Feeling they cannot either achieve academically or find a place in the social structure of the class, they withdraw. Eventually, they sit alone and shrug off attempts by the teacher to help. Dreikurs, Grunwald, and Pepper (1982) describe these students as extremely discouraged and defeated. They may refuse to try, because they

- are overly ambitious and fear they cannot do as well as they want to.
- are competitive and fear they can't do as well as others do.
- feel pressured by parents and teachers and incapable of meeting their expectations.
- fear they will fail if they try.

Albert (1996) notes that a student who is avoiding failure rarely distracts or disrupts the classroom. Instead, the student sleeps or daydreams quietly throughout the class. The teacher may find it hard to determine whether the student *cannot* do the work or if the student *will not* do the work. Unfortunately, the student's discouragement is contagious, and soon the teacher feels helpless to reach the student. Often, the student is left alone to withdraw further from the teacher and other classmates.

Nelsen (2006) identified two clues to identifying mistaken goals. First, teachers should evaluate their reactions to students' misbehaviors. If the teacher feels irritated or annoyed, the student's goal is to get attention. If the teacher feels threatened, the student is displaying power-seeking behavior. If the teacher is hurt by the student's behavior, the student is probably seeking revenge. Finally, if the teacher feels inadequately prepared to help the student, the student is displaying failure avoidance.

The second clue is the child's response to the teacher's intervention. Attention-seeking students will stop their annoying behaviors for a short time if they receive attention from the teacher. The power-seeking student will continue to misbehave and may verbally defy the teacher. The revenge-seeking student's misbehavior will intensify when the teacher attempts to stop the behavior. Failure-avoiding students refuse to respond and withdraw further, hoping to be left alone. Consider the behavior of students in the following example:

> After Ms. Brentner gave the directions to the class, she allowed the class to start on their homework during the last fifteen minutes of class. Walking around the room to make sure everyone understood her directions, she noticed Garrett staring into space. Placing her hand on Garrett's shoulder, she said, "Garrett, you need to start to work."
>
> *Attention-seeking Garrett* looks up at Ms. Brentner, smiles, and begins his work.
>
> *Power-seeking Garrett* responds by loudly announcing, "This is stupid. It is the same stuff we did yesterday. Why do we have to do the same thing over and over again?"
>
> *Revenge-seeking Garrett* violently jerks away from Ms. Brentner's touch and shouts, "Get your stinky hands off me. I don't need your help."
>
> *Failure-avoiding Garrett* keeps his head down and looks at the paper on his desk. Speaking barely above a whisper, he says, "I can't. I don't understand how to do this."

## REACTING TO STUDENT BEHAVIOR

Dinkmeyer and Dinkmeyer (1976) stress that to effectively work with students, teachers need to understand the goals of the students' behaviors. To do this, the teacher must work to determine the real issues underlying behavior. Table 5.1 further explains how to determine these goals.

A teacher's reaction to misbehavior should be related to the goal for the behavior. For attention-seeking students, reinforcement should occur only when these students are acting appropriately. Often these students are not aware of how annoying their antics have become and will try to correct their behavior when the teacher talks to them about the

**Table 5.1** The Four Mistaken Goals of Students

| Mistaken Goal | Student's Belief | Example of Student's Behaviors | Teacher's Reaction to Behavior | Student's Reaction to Intervention by Teacher |
|---|---|---|---|---|
| Attention Seeking | The student feels part of class only when getting attention from the teacher or other students | Constantly demands attention / Desires to be teacher's pet / Shows off / Becomes the class clown | Annoyance/ Irritation | Stops momentarily but then resumes |
| Power Seeking | The student feels part of the class when controlling the teacher or other students | Contradicts / Lies / Has temper tantrum / Questions teacher's authority or knowledge | Professionally Threatened | Continues to verbally or physically defy the teacher |
| Revenge Seeking | The student feels left out of the social structure so strikes out at classmates or teacher | Is aggressive toward teacher or classmates / Becomes a bully / Threatens teachers or Classmates | Hurt | Intensifies behavior |
| Failure Avoiding | The student feels incapable of achieving socially or academically and no longer tries | Sleeps or daydreams through class / Attempts to be invisible | Inadequate to help student | Withdraws further from teacher or classmates |

*Source:* Dreikurs, Grunwald, and Pepper (1982); Nelsen (2006).

situation. In some cases, the teacher can provide a signal that indicates that the behavior needs to stop. Unfortunately, the teacher and the attention-seeking student are not alone in the class, and classmates may give the student the attention he or she seeks. When this occurs, the student may stop trying to get the attention of the teacher and act out even more.

When dealing with a power-seeking student, the first requirement is disinvolvement. Because there is no reinforcement for the student if power is not contested, it is critical that the teacher not engage the student in a power struggle. The teacher should avoid a direct confrontation. Because neither the student nor the teacher wants to lose face, discussion of the student's behavior should take place in private. Albert (1996) suggests that this allows both the teacher and the student to save face as everyone is allowed to escape a heated situation.

When the teacher's power is challenged, it is best for the teacher to allow a cooling-off period. After both the teacher and the student have had an opportunity to become calmer, they can discuss the student's misbehavior. It is important that students be allowed to have their say. Many times this will defuse the situation because for many students, having their *say* is as important as having their *way*.

Albert (1996) stresses that power seeking can be reduced when students are allowed a voice in the classroom. She advocates granting legitimate power by involving students in decision making. When students can have a choice, they feel they have power. When students have real responsibility, they are less likely to strive for power in destructive ways.

For dealing with revenge-seeking students, it is important that teachers try to build a caring relationship. This begins by talking with the student about the behavior. In some cases, students aren't aware that they are taking out their frustrations on the teacher. In other cases, the students know exactly what they are doing and must not be allowed to physically or psychologically hurt other students or the teacher. Regardless of the motive or reasons for the behavior, revenge-seeking students must be required to return, repair, or replace any damaged objects (Albert, 1995).

In dealing with students seeking to avoid failure, the teacher should try to determine the cause of the problem. Albert (1995) suggests that teachers modify the instructional methods, provide additional tutoring, encourage the student to use positive self-talk, and teach new strategies to use when the student wants to quit trying.

## CONSEQUENCES OF MISBEHAVIORS

Dreikurs rejected the use of punishment because he felt that students associate the punishment not with their own actions but with those of their punisher (Queen, Blackwelder, & Mallen, 1997). Nelsen (2006) agrees that too often punishment creates what she calls the four R's of punishment: resentment, revenge, rebellion, and retreat.

Rather than punishment, Nelsen (2006) advocates a method that advances the social order. The social order consists of a body of rules that must be learned and followed in order for a classroom to be a caring place where students can learn and grow. To learn responsibility, students must experience the consequences of behavior in order to preserve the "social order." The teacher is the representative of the social order, the person who imposes consequences for failing to respect the established rule.

Therefore, when a student breaks a class rule or behaves inappropriately, a consequence must follow. Every act has a consequence; some occur naturally, and some are teacher imposed. Natural and logical consequences are so called because their goal is to teach children to understand, anticipate, and make decisions based on the consequences of their actions in the real world (Nelsen, Lott, & Glenn, 2000).

**Natural consequences** are the results of ill-advised acts. They are the result of the evolution of events and take place without adult interference. Meyerhoff (1996) notes that there is no need for a teacher to provide natural consequences, because they will occur even without the teacher's intervention. It is the teacher's job, however, to make sure that the natural consequences of a student's behavior are not physically or psychologically harmful to the student.

Logical consequences are teacher arranged rather than being the obvious result of the student's own acts (Meyerhoff, 1996). Logical consequences are needed when the misbehavior substantially affects others or when the potential natural consequence is too severe.

Logical consequences are a subset of punishment, in the sense that they are imposed stimuli used to reduce a target behavior (Elias & Schwab, 2006). It is for this reason that students often perceive logical consequences as punishment. Therefore, it is critical that consequences be related to the student's actions and be discussed with the student. If the consequences are not understood and accepted by the student, the student may consider the consequences as punishment rather than as a logical result of the student's own behavior. To avoid consequences being viewed as a punishment, Dreikurs and Loren (1968) provided the following criteria distinguishing logical consequences from punishment.

- Logical consequences express the reality of what happens in society when one breaks a law or rule. They are tied to the social order because they represent the rules of living, which all human beings must learn in order to function in society. Punishment, on the other hand, only expresses the personal power of the teacher and the authority a teacher has over students.

- Logical consequences are tied directly to the misbehavior. Punishments rarely are.

- Logical consequences involve no element of moral judgment; punishment inevitably does. Logical consequences distinguish between the deed and the doer.

- Logical consequences are concerned only with what will happen now. Punishments are tied to the past.

- Logical consequences are applied in a nonthreatening manner. Often, there is anger in punishment.

- Logical consequences present choices for the student. Punishment demands compliance. When a teacher employs a logical-consequences approach, the student must be given the option of stopping inappropriate behavior or face the consequences of the misbehavior (Dinkmeyer & Dinkmeyer, 1976).

Only carefully and appropriately administered natural and logical consequences promote intrinsic motivation, self-control, and personal responsibility. Essential for these techniques to have their desired positive effect is that they are rooted in a caring relationship between teachers and students. Unfortunately, logical consequences are not always readily apparent or easily devised, but when used appropriately, they can have tremendous power

**Table 5.2**  The 5 R's of Logical Consequences

| | |
|---|---|
| **Related** | A consequence should be logically connected to the behavior. The more closely related to the consequence, the more valuable it is to the student. |
| **Reasonable** | A consequence should be equal in proportion and intensity to the misbehavior. The purpose is for students to see the connection between behavior and consequences, not to make them suffer. |
| **Respectful** | A consequence should be stated and carried out in a way that preserves a student's self-esteem. It addresses the behavior, not the character of the student. |
| **Reliably Enforced** | A consequence should follow misbehavior. Threats without action are ineffective. Consistency is the key. |
| **Revealed** | A consequence should be revealed (known) in advance for predictable behavior such as breaking class rules. When misbehavior occurs that was not predicted, logical consequences connected to the misbehavior should be established. |

*Source:* Albert (1996); Nelsen, Lott, & Glenn (2000).

in that they help students to learn accountability for their choices (Nelsen, Lott, & Glenn, 2000). In order to maximize the informational value of logical consequences while minimizing the control aspect, five elements are needed. To be effective, logical consequences must be related, reasonable, respectful, reliably enforced, and revealed. These five R's of logical consequences are explained in Table 5.2.

## HELPING STUDENTS CONNECT

One critical difference in the work of Dreikurs and Albert is that Albert's more current view of classroom management provides a more supportive, relational community in which students can take risks in thinking for themselves, take responsibility for their learning, seek teachers' help when necessary, and drive the cognitive benefits from peer interaction. Albert advocates a view of classroom management that focuses on creating classroom environments that are supportive of students' psychological needs and today's complex approaches to learning. Albert (1996) advises that providing consequences will not prevent students from misbehaving in the future if the consequences are not accompanied by encouragement techniques that build self-esteem and strengthen the student's motivation to cooperate and learn. It is important, according to Albert, that students be made to feel part of the classroom community by creating an environment where they feel capable, connected, and able to contribute.

Students can be made to feel capable by creating a classroom in which it is acceptable to make mistakes. The teacher needs to ensure that everyone can be successful by providing work appropriate for various learning styles and skill levels. The emphasis should be on completing work in a satisfactory manner and on continuous improvement.

Students need to believe they can develop positive relationships with teachers and fellow classmates. To help students connect, Albert (1995) suggests that teachers

- accept all students and encourage tolerance of diversity.
- give attention to students by listening and showing interest in their activities outside of class.
- show appreciation of students' kindnesses and good work through praise, phone calls, or written notes to parents.
- use affirmation statements that are specific about a student's positive qualities.
- build affectionate relationships with simple acts of kindness.

Teachers should also help students realize they need to contribute to the welfare of their classmates and to the positive atmosphere of the class. Allowing students to have leadership roles within the class can promote this awareness. Nelsen, Lott, and Glenn (2000) advocate the use of class meetings for that purpose. They suggest that class meetings can be the place where true dialogue and problem solving can begin. Class meetings should be held to discuss problems and issues of concern for the entire class.

Rather than using traditional classroom rules, Albert (1996) advocates the use of a classroom code of conduct. She suggests that students see classroom rules as adult driven. Codes of conduct provide a framework for how everyone in the class, *including the teacher,* will interact and treat each other. With a code of conduct, students are held accountable for their behavior at all times. A code of conduct allows students to feel they have a voice in how the class will act.

---

## Tips from the Field

To help my students feel a part of the class, we have classroom careers that rotate each week. Some of the careers include

*Courier:* Serves as the teacher's messenger to deliver items to the office.

*Game Show Host:* Assists teacher in drawing of names, prizes, and reading questions.

*Horticulturist:* Takes care of the classroom plants.

*Lunch Monitor:* Takes daily lunch count, hands out lunch tickets.

*Paper Passer:* Passes out new assignments.

*Technologist:* Responsible for keeping the computer area neat and shutting down computers at the end of the day.

Krisanda Venosdale
Fourth-Grade Teacher
Monroe School
St. Louis, Missouri

## STRATEGIES FOR DEALING WITH DIFFICULT STUDENTS

Nelson (2006) notes that the first step in dealing with difficult students is to understand the reasons behind the behavior. Most problem students at the elementary level are revenge-seeking students who think everyone is against them. They believe that teachers and fellow students are unfair to them, disregard their feelings, and hurt them. The results are students who lash out at administrators, faculty, and students.

Nelsen (2006) stresses that it is much harder to discover the goal for behavior after students enter their preteens. Although more teens display the mistaken goal of power or revenge than younger students, other factors are at play as well. Peer pressure is extremely important to teenagers, and Nelsen stresses that seeking peer approval is an additional goal for students. Teenagers also have the mistaken goal of excitement and often misbehave "just for the fun of it."

Students who are at risk for behavioral health concerns such as drugs, early pregnancy, delinquency, gangs, or chronic academic problems are weak in the following significant issues:

- the confidence that they can deal with life's challenges.
- the belief that they can make meaningful contributions to society.
- the belief that they are responsible for their personal choices.
- the ability to manage their emotions.
- the ability to effectively communicate, negotiate, and empathize with others.
- the ability to adapt with flexibility and integrity.
- the ability to make valid judgments and make decisions with integrity (Glenn and Nelsen, 2000).

### Tips from the Field

I believe a peaceful classroom begins with good **CONDUCT**. Students are instructed on the meaning of the following character traits:

*Cooperate*—work together, share, be kind

*Organize*—be prepared, turn in homework and assignments on time

*Negotiate*—admit your mistakes, learn to give and take

*Discipline Yourself*—exhibit self-control, follow directions

*Understand Your Feelings*—express your feelings, positive attitude

*Communicate*—listen, observe, speak softly

*Tolerate*—respect others' differences, abilities, feelings, and needs.

Andrea Galliano
Gifted Teacher K–3
Mulberry Elementary School
Houma, Louisiana

Difficult students feel they have little control over their own lives. When provided interventions that develop skills in the seven areas above, students can develop a strong personal base that gives them the strength and knowledge to face life's challenges.

## STRENGTHS AND WEAKNESSES OF LOGICAL CONSEQUENCES

Many see Dreikurs's Logical Consequences and the later variations of Dreikurs's theories by Albert and Nelsen as a positive way of promoting communication and respect between teacher and students. They suggest that the model promotes autonomy by allowing students to take responsibility for their actions and choices. However, the model is not without its critics.

One criticism is that first-year teachers may have a difficult time identifying and understanding students' motives for misbehavior, because children often send false or mixed signals (Morris, 1996). Queen, Blackwelder, and Mallen (1997) contend that within the context of a classroom, it is impossible for even a veteran teacher to determine the goal of each child's behavior.

Kohn (1996) also questions Dreikurs's idea that student behavior is a choice. He states, "Adults who blithely insist that children choose to misbehave are rather like politicians who declare that people have only themselves to blame for being poor" (p. 17). He further suggests that such a concept removes the need for teachers to consider their own decisions and classroom demands in creating problem students.

Even after teachers have established the motives for misbehavior, it may still be difficult to know how to respond to inappropriate behavior. Unfortunately, there is not always a natural or a logical consequence to fit the misbehavior.

Kohn (1996) calls logical consequences "punishment lite." He states that it is difficult to differentiate between punishment and logical consequences and questions whether there is a real difference between Dreikurs's model and other models that promote punishment for misbehavior.

Nelsen (2006) was once an advocate of logical consequences but no longer supports the practice because the basic concepts of logical consequences are misunderstood. Too often, she suggests, humiliation is added to logical consequences in the belief that students should suffer. When this occurs, punishment becomes disguised as logical consequences, and results are ineffective.

## LOGICAL CONSEQUENCES IN THE CLASSROOM

### Scenario

When Erica McCaslin began her first year of teaching sixth grade at Bracey Middle School, she decided to use Cooperative Discipline as her classroom-management model. Rather than establishing a set of classroom rules, she allowed the students to spend the first few days of school establishing a classroom code. Dividing the class into groups, each group wrote what they thought the code should be. After putting all the codes on the board, parts from several were incorporated and the class agreed on the following class code:

> We, Ms. McCaslin's sixth-grade class, believe that all students should be treated with dignity and courtesy. We believe that we have the responsibility of helping everyone learn, and we will do nothing that prevents Ms. McCaslin from teaching or anyone from learning. We will show respect for each other, our teacher, our classroom, and the school.

Each student in the class signed the code of conduct and a copy was posted above the whiteboard.

The class agreed that if a problem developed between a student and Ms. McCaslin, Ms. McCaslin would handle the situation and provide the consequence for mis-behavior. If a problem developed between two students, the students would be sent to a classroom tribunal who would decide the consequences. So that all students would have a chance to serve on the tribunal, three students were picked each month to serve as the tribunal, and no student could serve twice until all students had an opportunity to serve.

During the first month, Ms. McCaslin has several opportunities to see how well her plan is working. When Bethany fails to finish her assignment, Ms. McCaslin decides

*Assigning students as classroom helpers increases the sense of community.*

that Bethany would miss the opportunity to attend the assembly and would remain in the classroom to finish her work. When Jamal broke the aquarium when he leaned back in his chair, the tribunal decides he would have to pay to replace the aquarium. Jamal's parents agreed that Jamal would have to contribute three dollars a week from his spending money to the replacement of the aquarium. When Nick pulled the chair from under Kristin, causing her to fall to the floor, the tribunal decides that Nick would have to spend one hour in time-out writing a letter of apology to Kristin.

Although Ms. McCaslin sometimes finds it difficult to find an appropriate consequence for each misbehavior, she feels the plan helps students make the connection between their behavior and the consequence of their behavior.

## Summary

Rudolf Dreikurs's Logical Consequences and Linda Albert's Cooperative Discipline are the last models presented with a focus on control. When developed, Logical Consequences represented a shift from a behavioral focus on discipline to a more humanistic approach based on the concept that the motivation and goals of student behavior must be considered in the development of a discipline plan. Expanding Dreikurs's discipline concepts, Linda Albert proposes a cooperative approach to help students connect, contribute, and feel capable. Based on Adler's original theory, Dreikurs and Albert identified four student goals: (1) to seek attention, (2) to gain power, (3) to seek revenge for some perceived injustice, and (4) to avoid failure. The idea that the consequence must fit the crime is the key to their theories, in that every act has a consequence; some occur naturally, and some are teacher imposed.

## Key Terminology

Definitions for these terms appear in the glossary.

Attention-seeking students   83
Failure-avoiding students   85
Logical consequences   81

Natural consequences   88
Power-seeking students   84
Revenge-seeking students   84

## Chapter Activities

### Reflecting on the Theory

1.  As Mr. Hoernschemeyer prepared to leave his seventh-grade class, he noticed that someone had carved the letters "JK" into a desk. Since Jack Kelly occupied the desk each sixth period, it was not difficult for Mr. Hoernschemeyer to guess who had damaged the desk.

What should Mr. Hoernschemeyer do now? How can he apply the principles of Logical Consequences to resolving this situation?

2. In the opening scenario, Ms. Prabhu designed consequences based on the misbehaviors and the students' motives for them. Do you agree with this method for determining the appropriate consequence for misbehavior? What problems might this method create in a classroom?

3. Kohn suggests that logical consequences are just "punishment lite" and that they are just punishments with a less offensive name. Do you agree, or are logical consequences different from punishment?

### Developing Artifacts for Your Portfolio

1. Describe five typical classroom misbehaviors. Describe a natural consequence, a logical consequence, and a typical punishment that might be used for each.

2. Observe the behaviors of three students. Describe the behaviors of these students. How does the teacher react to their behaviors? How do the students react to the teacher's intervention? Based on your observations, classify the students' behaviors as attention seeking, power seeking, revenge seeking, or failure avoiding.

### Developing Your Personal Philosophy of Classroom Management

1. Would you be comfortable using Logical Consequences as your classroom-management approach? Why or why not? Are there some strategies that you will definitely incorporate into your classroom-management plan?

2. Many consider a strength of Assertive Discipline to be the consistency with which punishment is administered. Logical Consequences provides for a more individual approach to discipline. Which do you consider to be more critical—to be consistent or to deal with students as individuals?

## Resources for Further Study

Further information about Logical Consequences and resources for its use in the classroom can be found by contacting

Dr. Linda Albert
8503 N. 29th Street
Tampa, FL 33604
813-931-4183 (Phone)
813-935-4571 (Fax)

Dr. Jane Nelsen
Empowering People, Inc.
P.O. Box 1926
Orem, UT 84059-1926
1-800-456-7770 (Phone)

## Chapter References

Adler, A. (1958). *What life should mean to you.* New York: Capricorn.

Albert, L. (1995). Discipline: Is it a dirty word? *Learning, 24,* 43–46.

Albert, L. (1996). *Cooperative discipline.* Circle Pines, MN: American Guidance Service.

Dinkmeyer, D., & Dinkmeyer, D., Jr. (1976). Logical consequences: A key to the reduction of disciplinary problems. *Phi Delta Kappan, 57,* 664–666.

Dreikurs, R., Grunwald, B. B., & Pepper, F. C. (1982). *Maintaining sanity in the classroom.* New York: HarperCollins.

Dreikurs, R., & Loren, G. (1968). *A new approach to discipline: Logical consequences.* New York: Hawthorn Books.

Elias, M. J., & Schwab, Y. (2006). From compliance to responsibility: Social and emotional learning and classroom management. In C. Evertson & C. Weinstein (Eds.), *Handbook of classroom management: Research, practice, and contemporary issues.* Mahwah, NJ: Lawrence Erlbaum Associates, Inc.

Glenn, H. S. & Nelsen, J. (2000). *Raising self-reliant children in a self-indulgent world.* Roseville, CA: Prima Publishing.

Kohn, A. (1996). *Beyond discipline: From compliance to community.* Alexandria, VA: Association for Supervision and Curriculum Development.

Meyerhoff, M. K. (1996). Natural and logical consequences. *Pediatrics for Parents, 16,* 8–10.

Morris, R. C. (1996). Contrasting disciplinary models in education. *Thresholds in Education, 22,* 7–13.

Nelsen, J. (2006). *Positive discipline.* New York: Ballantine Books.

Nelsen, J., Lott, L., & Glenn, S. (2000). *Positive discipline in the classroom* (3rd ed.). Rocklin, CA: Prima Publishing.

Queen, J. A., Blackwelder, B. B., & Mallen, L. P. (1997). *Responsible classroom management for teachers and students.* Upper Saddle River, NJ: Merrill/Prentice Hall.

PEARSON
**myeducationlab**
The Power of Classroom Practice
www.myeducationlab.com

Go to the Topic: **Maintaining Appropriate Student Behavior** in the MyEducationLab (www.myeducationlab.com) for your course, where you can:

- Find learning outcomes for **Maintaining Appropriate Student Behavior** along with the national standards that connect to these outcomes.
- Apply and practice your understanding of the core teaching skills identified in the chapter with the Building Teaching Skills and Dispositions learning units.
- Examine challenging situations and cases presented in the IRIS Center Resources.

# PART II
# Classroom Management as a System

Four models that emphasize a systems approach to classroom management are presented in Part II, "Classroom Management as a System." Chapter 6 presents Richard Curwin and Allen Mendler's model, Discipline with Dignity. The research of Carolyn Evertson is the foundation of her model, Classroom Organization and Management Program (COMP). Her model is presented in Chapter 7. Chapter 8 focuses on building communities and provides the philosophy of Alfie Kohn. Marvin Marshall's Discipline without Stress® Punishments or Rewards is the focus of Chapter 9. The models presented in Part II share the following characteristics:

- Classroom management is systematic.
- Classroom management and instruction are interwoven.
- Teachers and students share the responsibility for managing classroom behaviors.
- Rule development is a joint effort between students and teachers.
- A range of consequences should be provided to meet the diverse needs of students.
- Students must be taught appropriate behavior.
- The focus is on *prevention* of misbehavior rather than *reacting* to discipline problems.
- Planning is essential to effective classroom management.
- Teachers should teach the rules and procedures of the classroom rather than assuming students understand their meaning.
- Classroom communities provide a safe, caring learning environment.

# Discipline with Dignity

## Objectives

Chapter 6 prepares preservice teachers to meet INTASC standards #4 (Instructional Strategies), #5 (Motivation and Management), and #9 (Reflective Practitioner) by helping them to

■ understand the basic principles behind Discipline with Dignity.

■ maintain student dignity while dealing with discipline situations.

■ learn a systematic approach to classroom management.

■ evaluate the needs of teachers and students.

■ evaluate the impact of teaching style and strategies on discipline.

■ determine the appropriate consequences for misbehavior.

- prevent situations requiring discipline from occurring.

- learn strategies for dealing with students with the potential for violence and aggression.

- use the principles of Discipline with Dignity to deal with problem behavior.

## Scenario

A heated debate is going on at West Creek Elementary School. For over a week, a committee charged with establishing a schoolwide discipline plan has been meeting, and each day, the meeting has ended with more disagreement than agreement. The principal of West Creek directed the group to establish a list of rules and consequences that will be used consistently by each teacher in the school. Unfortunately, the discipline committee has discovered that few teachers agree as to what the rules should be and what the consequences should be if the rules are broken.

"All right," says Heather Jarman, chair of the committee, "I think we have finally agreed on our first rule, 'All homework will be due the day after it is assigned.'"

Leaning back in his chair, Drew Austin asks, "Then are we also going to have a rule that all teachers have to return the graded homework the day after it is turned in?"

Frustrated after a week of chairing a committee that appears to be accomplishing nothing, Heather snaps back, "No, Drew. Our job is not to make rules for the teachers. Our job is to make rules for our students, and I could use your help in getting this accomplished. Now, what should be the consequence for not having homework?"

Adopting a more serious tone, Drew suggests, "Homework not turned in on time will receive a grade of zero."

Veteran teacher Shelby Gibson sighs. "I have students who *never* do their homework. They are already getting a zero and could care less. I don't think giving zeros will motivate these students. We need to take away something they want—like recess."

"Okay, I will revise my suggestion. The consequence for missing homework should be that students not having homework will miss recess to complete the work."

First-year teacher Emily Caldarelli speaks up. "So if I understand what we are saying, all students should have the same consequence. If I have two children who come without their homework, they should both miss recess. What if one is a child who *never* does his homework and the other is a child who didn't do his homework for the first time because of some emergency? Should they be punished in the same way?"

"Why, yes, of course they should both miss recess. They broke a rule. Didn't you understand our charge? Mr. Evans wants consistent rules and consequences for all classes and all students. You can't treat children differently."

Shaking her head in disbelief, Emily counters, "But I treat children differently every day. I have children for whom I adapt instruction because they have a learning disability. I try to adapt to different learning styles. In fact, I'm evaluated on how well I individualize instruction! Yet when it comes to discipline, I'm told I should treat children as if they are made by cookie cutters. What we are doing doesn't seem right."

## INTRODUCTION

Emily Caldarelli is not alone in her concern that when it comes to discipline, children are treated as if they are cookie-cutter cutouts. For over twenty years, Allen Mendler and Richard Curwin have stressed that a "one size fits all" policy for classroom management is ineffective and inherently unfair. After writing their first book *The Discipline Book,* in 1980, Curwin and Mendler gained national recognition with the publication of *Discipline with*

*Dignity* in 1988. While staying current by constantly updating their research and adapting their books to meet the changing needs of students and teachers, Curwin and Mendler have remained true to their belief that effective discipline comes from the heart and soul of an individual teacher and should not be a generic "one size fits all" program.

Several principles are central to the theory behind **Discipline with Dignity** (Curwin & Mendler, 1988a). The most fundamental of these principles is the idea that everyone in the school setting is to be treated with dignity. This means that students are treated with the same dignity that is granted teachers, administrators, and staff. Curwin and Mendler propose that effective discipline can occur only when decisions for managing student behavior are based on a schoolwide core value system that maintains the dignity of each student in all situations.

Central to treating individuals with dignity is the creation of a school environment in which the needs of both students and teachers are met. Curwin and Mendler (1980) state that the needs of students and teachers fall into one of four sets of needs:

1. *Personal identity,* which can be met through a positive self-image.

2. *Connectedness,* which can be met through a sense of positive affiliation with others.

3. *Power,* which can be met by having a sense of control over one's own life.

4. *Achievement,* which can be met by being enabled to achieve academically.

Discipline problems develop within the classroom when the needs of an individual student, a group of students, or the teacher are not fulfilled. Curwin and Mendler (1980) stress that discipline problems do not occur in a vacuum; they are part of a total classroom environment and can be prevented when the classroom is an environment in which both individual and group needs can be met with minimum conflict.

In many cases, Curwin and Mendler (1988a) argue that a discipline problem is a means of conveying to the teacher that something is wrong in the classroom. They suggest that when discipline problems occur, teachers should look at their own role in creating the problem. It may be that the problem is the result of how the teacher interacts with students or the way in which the teacher conducts the class. Many teachers create minor discipline irritations, such as out-of-seat behavior, foot stomping, pencil tapping, and talking, by ignoring the attention span of students or by failing to vary the way information is presented. In *Discipline with Dignity,* teachers are encouraged to look at their own actions as critically as they look at those of their students.

Curwin and Mendler (1980) view classroom management as a process that evolves in an individual classroom, based on the needs of a specific teacher and his or her students. They do not support one system of classroom management or advocate a particular approach but rather provide a framework within which teachers can develop their own style of classroom management by helping them to recognize and accept feelings, to develop their awareness of themselves and their students, and to establish a classroom structure for dealing with discipline problems when they do occur.

Finally, Curwin and Mendler (1988b) suggest that the job of a teacher includes dealing with student behavior as well as teaching their subject matter. The teacher's goal should not be to eliminate all forms of misbehavior, because students need opportunities to test limits, but rather to help students make appropriate choices and decisions.

## Step-by-Step Discipline with Dignity

To use Discipline with Dignity in your classroom, you will need to do the following things:

1. Work with students to create a classroom principle that reflects the type of classroom you desire.

2. Determine the "flag rules" that you require in your class.

3. Establish classroom rules with the students. These should include the flag rules you identified.

4. Establish a range of consequences to be used when rules are broken.

5. Evaluate your contribution to misbehavior when it occurs.

6. Provide a consequence from the list of choices based on the individual needs of the student.

7. Create personal contracts for those students who cannot benefit from traditional consequences.

In fact, they suggest that discipline is not the critical issue that many believe it is because of what they call the **70-20-10 Principle.** In each classroom, Curwin, Mendler, and Mendler (2008) propose that there are three groups of students. In the first group, 70 percent of the students rarely break rules or violate principles. The second group is made up of the 20 percent of students who break rules on a somewhat regular basis. The final 10 percent are chronic rule breakers and are generally out of control most of the time. The trick of a good discipline plan, according to Curwin and Mendler, is to control the 10 percent of students who regularly break rules without alienating or overly regulating the 20 percent who rarely do so, and without backing the 10 percent of chronic rule breakers into a corner.

## THREE-DIMENSIONAL PLAN

In order to meet the needs of all students, Curwin et al. (2008) recommend the creation of a three-dimensional discipline plan that focuses on preventing discipline problems from occurring. However, the plan provides actions for when problems do occur and resolves the more serious discipline issues of the 10 percent of students who are chronic discipline problems. The three-dimensional plan is an integration of many discipline approaches and includes elements from Skinner, Jones, Dreikurs, Canter, and Glasser. However, Curwin and Mendler's focus is on maintaining student dignity and teaching responsible behavior.

Unlike models that focus on teaching obedience, the cornerstone of Curwin and Mendler's model is the teaching of personal responsibility. The goal is to teach students to make wise decisions by allowing them to make choices and mistakes in a safe environment. "Teaching responsibility requires motivating students to want to change, teaching them decision-making skills, and providing them with new skills for better behavior" (Curwin & Mendler, 2000, p. 17). In Curwin and Mendler's three-dimensional plan, teachers and students work together to develop the discipline plan.

---

## Tips from the Field

The most difficult classroom management situation is when the entire class is unruly and it is hard to pinpoint who is creating the problem. In these situations, I think it is important to consider the following:

1. Look at yourself: Do you fully understand the material that you are teaching and have anticipated the problems that students may have? Are you presenting material that is too hard? Too easy? Are you connecting with your students? Do you have enough structure? Are you presenting yourself as a firm, but caring teacher? Are you engaging in mannerisms that give away that you are insecure?

2. Are you allowing time to explain the new material? Or are you constantly going over homework for most of the period, barely having time to present the new lesson, assigning new homework at the last minute, thus creating a cycle where students are truly frustrated? Your timing may be off. Allow time to clearly present a lesson. Allow for practice in class.

Terri Husted
Boynton Middle School
Ithaca, New York

---

## Prevention

The prevention component of Curwin and Mendler's three-dimensional plan is designed to minimize or prevent classroom problems from occurring by providing structure and direction in the classroom while accommodating the daily issues that arise. The heart of the prevention dimension is the establishment and implementation of social contracts. The **social contract** is a system for managing the classroom and is designed to enhance human interaction in the classroom. Social contracts give students a sense of ownership by involving them in the creation of classroom rules and regulations. Curwin and Mendler (1988a) stress that teachers who exclude students from classroom policy making run the risk of widespread dissatisfaction with rules that students perceive as arbitrary and unfair. When students have a part in the creation of the guidelines they will live by, they feel empowered.

The successful contract begins with the establishment of **classroom principles** that represent the value system of the classroom. Principles, unlike rules, cannot be enforced. Principles define attitudes and expectations for long-term behavioral growth (Curwin & Mendler, 1988b). Although students must be involved in the creation of classroom principles, the process begins with teachers carefully considering their own values in order to determine how they want to manage their classrooms, how they want to treat their students, and how they want students to treat each other. This self-analysis is essential. Curwin and Mendler (1988b) found little difference in the effectiveness of teachers who were permissive, authoritarian, or moderate. The difference lies in how aware teachers are about their own beliefs concerning how a classroom should be managed. Each individual teacher has a different tolerance for noise, movement, humor, and classroom activity. Trying to conduct the class in a way that is not congruent with the teacher's personality and preferred methods will result in increased agitation and anxiety for both students and the teacher.

Once the classroom principles have been established, specific rules, driven by those principles, must be developed. The teacher begins by providing **flag rules,** which are non-negotiable (Mendler, 2007). These rules represent the value system of the teacher. Once the flag rules are presented, the students develop rules for each other and for the teacher. Mendler and Curwin (1983) state that rules are critical to successful classroom management because unclear limits lead to discipline situations.

Consider how the personalities and teaching styles of the teachers on South Hamilton Middle School's sixth-grade team differ.

> The teachers on the Bronco team at South Hamilton Middle School are a very diverse group. Second-year social studies teacher Jody Brundage enjoys a lively active classroom. Primarily utilizing cooperative learning groups, she considers herself a facilitator rather than a teacher. Science teacher Catherine Dobrowolski is very structured in her classroom. Always wearing a white lab coat, she encourages her students to use what she calls quiet professionalism as they conduct experiments. Math teacher Garry Guier uses a traditional approach to teaching. In his class, students have assigned seats and spend much of each hour listening to Mr. Guier present material using the overhead projector. Finally, language arts teacher Gabriel Quintero considers his classroom a stage and his students his audience. Each day he fascinates his students by dressing as the characters they are studying, reciting long pieces from plays, and doing anything necessary to maintain their attention. Although each teacher is different in personality and teaching style, the hundred students who make up the Bronco team easily adjust as they move from teacher to teacher, because the teachers on the Bronco team all agreed that there would be clear rules and regulations for each classroom. The rules might be different for each classroom, but students are aware of the limits and the consequences for misbehavior.

Once the students have developed a list of rules, the class votes on the rules. The rules should have at least 75 percent agreement before a suggested rule becomes a classroom rule. This process is important because it gives ownership of the rules by all the class.

It is important to establish consequences for each rule established by the class. Although the enforcement of these consequences falls in the second dimension of the three-dimension plan, *action,* the creation of the consequences occurs during the *prevention* phase (Curwin & Mendler, 1980). Mendler and Curwin (1983) note that too often teachers wait until a rule is broken before thinking of a consequence. Students need to know the consequences for breaking each rule so they can make suitable choices and become effective decision makers.

Curwin and Mendler (1988a) suggest that a **range of consequences** be established for each rule. Unlike theorists who suggest that the consequences be sequential in their application, Curwin and Mendler recommend that a consequence be selected from the established list based on the needs of individual students. A student who purposely disobeys a rule may have a harsher consequence than a student who accidentally breaks the rule. Curwin and Mendler (1984) emphasize that in all cases, consequences should be instructional rather than punitive and should be regarded as natural and logical extensions of the rules.

The purpose of consequences is not to punish but to help the student learn responsibility and how to make better choices (Curwin et al., 2008). Ultimately, teachers want students to understand that misbehavior produces effects. Therefore, to be effective, consequences must be clear and specific, provide alternatives based on motivation, be natural and logical, preserve the student's dignity, and be tied to classroom rules (Curwin & Mendler, 1988b). Consider how Jody Brundage from the Bronco team helped her class establish consequences:

"Now that we have established our rules, we need to establish a list of consequences for breaking the rules. We need a range of consequences. For example, the consequence might be less severe if someone does something the first time than it would be if a student repeatedly breaks a rule. All right, let's think of our first rule, 'We will not touch each other without permission.' What consequences do you think we should have for this rule?"

Lauren's hand goes up. "If it were an accident, like they just bumped into someone, I think the student should just apologize."

"Yes, but what if they meant to do it," Demari stresses. "I think something else should happen. They need to be punished."

"Maybe they should go to the office," another student adds.

After several suggestions were given, the class voted on the consequences they thought best for the first rule. Ms. Brundage then says, "So, our list of consequences for breaking our first rule will be

Student apologizes to classmate.

Student is sent to office.

Student's parents are called.

Student is given in-school suspension.

Are we all in agreement?"

Once the students have created the list of rules and consequences and 75 percent of the students have agreed to them, the class reviews all the rules and consequences to ensure that there are no misunderstandings. This can be done in many ways, but Curwin and Mendler suggest that one effective way is to actually test for understanding. Once established, parents and administrators are notified of the classroom rules. Curwin and Mendler (1988a) stress that the established list of rules and consequences needs to be revised throughout the year to determine whether they are working effectively and whether they need to be changed to meet the changing needs of the classroom.

## Action

The action dimension of Curwin and Mendler's three-dimensional plan serves two purposes:

1. When a discipline problem occurs, something must be done to stop the problem.

2. Dealing with the problem quickly and effectively prevents minor problems from escalating.

The first step in the action dimension is to implement the consequences associated with rule violation. However, Curwin and Mendler (1988a) stress that *how* a consequence is implemented is at least as important as the consequence. Tone of voice, proximity to the student, body posture, use of contact, and other nonverbal gestures determine the effectiveness of a consequence as much, or more, than the actual content of the consequence. Curwin and Mendler provide nine principles to guide in the implementation of consequences:

1. *Be consistent.* A consequence from the approved list must be implemented each time a rule is broken. The consequence may be a simple reminder of the rule, but students must realize that the teacher is aware that a rule has been broken. Consistency creates order and predictability in the classroom and shows that the teacher honors the social contract and expects the students to do so as well.

2. *Remind the student which rule has been broken.* Lecturing, scolding, and making the student feel guilty are unnecessary. These tactics only escalate the problem by generating anger and hostile feelings.

3. *Use the power of proximity control.* The teacher should move toward the student. Typically, this is enough to gain the student's attention and stop inappropriate behavior. This will assure all students that the teacher is aware of everything that happens in the classroom. A word of caution: The age and personality of the student should be considered with proximity control. For some students, an invasion of personal space is considered a threat and will escalate rather than de-escalate the situation.

4. *Make direct eye contact when delivering the consequence.* Much can be delivered by this unspoken message. But the teacher must be aware of cultural differences. In some cultures, a lowering of the eyes is a sign of respect. A student should not be forced to behave in a manner that is uncomfortable or counter to cultural norms.

5. *Use a soft voice.* Shouting and yelling are signs of a lack of control. The softer the tone, the more impact it will have on students.

6. *Acknowledge appropriate behavior.* Too often, the only students who get attention from the teacher are those acting out. Mendler (1997) cited research showing that teachers fail to recognize 95 percent of appropriate behavior. Therefore, finding ways to acknowledge desired behavior should not be hard if teachers pay attention.

7. *Do not embarrass students in front of their peers.* Part of treating students with dignity is allowing them to save face in front of their peers. Speaking quietly to a student or asking a student to step outside the classroom may prevent the escalation of the situation by not forcing a public confrontation.

8. *Do not give a consequence when angry.* It is important to be calm and to model the appropriate way to handle emotionally charged situations. An overly aggressive delivery will create hostility, resentment, and fear. Teachers who lose self-control fail to model the very behavior they desire in their students.

9. *Do not accept excuses, bargaining, or whining.* Implement the consequence as directly and expeditiously as possible.

## Tips from the Field

During student teaching I had a group of fourth-grade girls who loved to talk and pass notes. Nothing seemed to work with these girls. I tried the traditional rewards and punishments. Because these were very social little girls, I decided to use dance as a reward. I promised the students that each Friday I would teach the class a new dance step. At the end of six weeks, we would have a dance party where all the new dance steps could be used. Each day I evaluated individual and group behavior. If students had had no major discipline issues during the week, they were allowed to learn a new dance step on Friday. If they had had more than one discipline issue during the week, they were excluded from the dance class and had to move to another location to continue with their work. Not being a dancer, I had to research dance moves for our Friday dance lesson. Therefore, each Friday was full of giggles as I attempted to teach the students new moves. Because I allowed students to laugh at my mistakes, it gave approval for students to laugh at themselves. Everyone loved the time we spent together, and as the weeks went on, behavior for all students drastically improved.

Rachel Ann Meeks
First-Grade Teacher
Montgomery Central Elementary School
Clarksville, Tennessee

Although the manner in which consequences are delivered influences their effectiveness, Curwin and Mendler (1988a) noted other reasons teachers fail to provide appropriate consequences. One of the most common reasons is that the consequence has not been established by the teacher or the students, but instead by a schoolwide committee. The teacher may find the consequences too harsh or incongruent with the teacher's belief system. A rule or consequences not valued by the teacher will not be implemented.

The second reason is that rule violations often occur at inconvenient times or places. Students know when the teacher is busy or distracted and will test the teacher during these times. If the teacher fails to deal with inappropriate behavior, incidents will occur more and more often during these times.

Teachers often resent the need to play police officers. Teachers would like to walk to the lounge to enjoy their lunch without having to monitor the halls. They would like to watch a pep rally or assembly without having to be on alert for misbehaving students. Unfortunately, students expect and depend on the adults in a school to react and stop inappropriate behavior. They want teachers to be vigilant. This vigilance makes the school a safer place for all to be.

## Resolution

Teachers need a method of managing the 10 percent of students who won't obey the rules, who do not respond to the established consequences, and who are a danger to themselves and others. The resolution dimension of Curwin and Mendler's three-dimensional plan provides the teacher with techniques for working with these students.

---

**Sample Behavioral Contract**

I, _____, will change my behavior by:

_____

_____

_____

If I meet my goals and do not display unacceptable behavior, I will be rewarded with the following on Friday of each week until this contact ends:

_____

_____

_____

If I do not meet my goals and have unacceptable behavior, I will have the following consequences:

_____

_____

_____

This contract will be reevaluated on _____.

_____                    _____
Student's Signature                                      Teacher's Signature

---

**Figure 6.1**

Sample Behavioral Contract

The resolution aspect of the three-dimensional plan involves the establishment of **individual contracts** when the social contract in the classroom fails to work. Figure 6.1 provides an example of such a contract. Such contracts are negotiated with the student to determine the cause of the behavior, the means of preventing misbehavior from occurring in the future, and the needs of the students that can be met by the teacher. In many cases, other school professionals (social workers, guidance counselors, administrators) and the student's parents must be involved in the resolution phase (Curwin & Mendler, 1988a).

---

**Tips from the Field**

Use humor to diffuse difficult situations. Children are less defensive and become willing to go along with virtually any teacher expectation when their teacher approaches a situation with a smile instead of a growl. (This works well when dealing with administrators, too!)

Tracy Callard
Intermediate Teacher
Horace Mann Elementary School
Wichita, Kansas
2002 Kansas Teacher of the Year

---

The purpose of the individual contracts is to help students identify what they need or want from the class and ways of having their needs met without resorting to disruptive actions that violate the classroom social contract. The establishment of an individual contract requires that the teacher carry out the following:

- Identify those students who are having trouble following the social contract.
- Get in touch with personal feelings about the student. An effort should be made to eliminate any perceptions or biases held toward the student.
- Arrange a time for a private conversation with the student.
- Develop a plan based on the student's needs, maturity, and ability to follow through with the required action.
- Put the plan in writing so that the student will understand what has been determined.
- Meet with the student to revise the plan if he or she cannot carry it out.
- Provide assistance to make the plan work. Determine what went wrong. Determine what interventions are needed.
- Seek outside help from counselors, parents, administrators, and others if additional assistance is needed.

Curwin and Mendler (2000) state that students cannot learn "the three R's" until they learn the most important "R"—responsibility. The three-dimensional plan teaches responsibility by allowing students to make choices within limits and to face the consequences of their choices.

## STRATEGIES FOR DEALING WITH DIFFICULT STUDENTS

Since writing their first book in 1980, Mendler and Curwin (2007) acknowledge that more students than ever are displaying problem behaviors. They estimate that the number of students who present challenging behaviors have increased from 5 percent to 10 percent of the student population. Teachers would stress that not only have the number of students displaying problem behavior increased but the seriousness of the offenses have changed. In the twenty-first century, teachers have to worry about fights, weapons, bullying, insulting language, severe disrespect toward adults, and total disregard for rules. These types of misbehavior begin at a younger age, and for many, rewards and punishments have only temporary results.

Many schools have responded to the increase in difficult students by implementing zero tolerance policies in their schools. Curwin and Mendler (1999) dismiss the effectiveness of such policies and state that they have zero tolerance for zero tolerance. They stress that teachers, administrators, and parents should have zero tolerance for the idea of doing anything that treats all students the same way. In 1997, they wrote *As Tough as Necessary* to provide an alternative to zero tolerance by providing a balance between being strong and

**Table 6.1**    Strategies for Difficult Students

| Strategy | Crisis Management | Short-Term Strategies | Long-Term Strategies |
|---|---|---|---|
| **Purpose of Strategy** | Restoring order to classroom during acting-out behavior by student | Stop misbehavior and preserve the dignity of student and teacher | Prevent acting-out behavior |
| **Goal of Strategy** | Ensure safety and survival of all class | Redirect the energy of the class back to instruction | Understand why student behaves in the manner he/she does |
| **Techniques** | ■ Have a plan for receiving assistance from administration<br>■ Have a plan for where students will go and what they will do during crisis<br>■ Evaluate effectiveness of how crisis was handled and make adjustment in anticipation of next event | ■ Respond with dignity to offensive student behavior<br>■ Preserve your own dignity<br>■ Keep offending student in class if possible<br>■ Model alternatives to aggression<br>■ Use "I" messages when talking to student<br>■ Use PEP (Privacy, Eye Contact, and Proximity)<br>■ Defer interaction until a later time | ■ Acknowledge positive behavior of problem student<br>■ Structure cooperative learning activities that involve problem student<br>■ Determine out-of-school issues that need interventions<br>■ Create a network of support for student |

*Source:* Mendler and Curwin (2007).

being fair. The message in *As Tough as Necessary* is that violence will not be tolerated, but that students should not be dealt with in a cookie-cutter fashion. In some cases, however, Curwin and Mendler (1999) agree that the zero-tolerance approach is necessary and that students may have to be removed from the school in order to provide a safe environment for everyone.

In most cases, zero tolerance is not the answer, and Mendler and Curwin (2007) stress that "we may be able to remove difficult students from our class, but we cannot remove them from our lives" (p. xx). They stress that we will deal with these students whether that interaction occurs in schools, the community, or in the courts. Therefore, they propose that strategies must be put in place to deal with difficult students in the school setting.

When choosing a discipline strategy to use with difficult students, teachers must consider three types of strategies: crisis, short-term, and long-term. Crisis strategies are concerned with restoring order when chaos occurs, ensuring the safety of all students. Short-term strategies are designed to defuse classroom escalation and end power struggle between the difficult student and the teacher. Long-term strategies have a more preventive focus when the teacher or faculty teams work with individual students to change the behavior on a more permanent level. Table 6.1 provides specific techniques for each strategy.

## STRENGTHS AND WEAKNESSES OF DISCIPLINE WITH DIGNITY

Perhaps the greatest strength of Discipline with Dignity is that it requires teachers to consider their values, their interactions with students, their contributions to discipline situations, and their teaching methods. Another strength is that Curwin and Mendler have used the feedback they have received from classroom teachers to keep the model current as students and classrooms change.

The Discipline with Dignity approach does have its critics though. Blumefeld-Jones (1996) was surprised that Curwin and Mendler would criticize Lee Canter's Assertive Discipline program, because Blumefeld-Jones finds little difference between the two models. He emphasizes that "teacher control is no less central to Curwin and Mendler but is also more subtle since they explicitly argue against such obedience" (p. 14). Kohn (1996) agrees and suggests that Discipline with Dignity places too much emphasis on getting students to do what they are *supposed* to do rather than thinking about what they *should* be doing.

Another criticism of Discipline with Dignity has been its emphasis on rule development by students. Many teachers view rule development as the role of the teacher and question the idea of students developing rules for the teacher. Others question whether young children are developmentally able to develop rules. Many high school teachers consider the process of rule and consequence development too elementary to use with older students.

*Curwin and Mendler advocate the use of individual contracts with students who continually violate the classroom's social contract.*

## DISCIPLINE WITH DIGNITY IN THE CLASSROOM

### Scenario

After greeting her students on the first day of school, Ms. McBryant asks, "I wonder how many of you noticed that I don't have any rules posted in our classroom? That is because I want you to help me write our classroom rules and procedures. Over the next few days, we are going to establish the rules that you will follow, and you are going to create some rules that I will follow, as well. Now, to begin, we need to think bigger than specific rules; we need to think of some general principles that we want to guide our class."

Noting the confusion on the faces of her students, Ms. McBryant explains, "For example, one of the principles I want for this class is that every student will reach his or her potential. I can't write a rule about that, but I want that principle to guide what I do in the classroom. Now this is what I want you to do. I want you to move your desks so that you are in groups of four. Then, as a group, I want you to think of two or three principles that you think should guide our class. Any questions?"

Later, each group presents the list of principles they have developed. Suggestions include the following:

Every student is to be respected.

All opinions are respected.

No one is ridiculed in this class.

Every student will be safe.

Every student is appreciated.

After reviewing all the suggestions, the class agrees to the following statements that summarize their classroom principles:

In Ms. McBryant's class, everyone is treated with respect. This means that all opinions are honored, we help each other learn, and we respect each other's property.

The next day, Ms. McBryant prepares the class to establish the rules that would reinforce the class principles. "Class, now that we have written our classroom principles, we need to develop rules that will determine how our principles are enforced. Now, in a few minutes, I will allow you to develop a list of rules for our class and a list of rules that you think I should follow. However, I have the right to veto any rule that I think will prevent me from doing my job as a teacher. I am also going to give you two rules that are nonnegotiable. These two rules are necessary for our classroom principles to work. My first rule is 'We will not touch each other without permission.' The second rule is 'We will speak in appropriate voices.' Now, let's gather into groups and establish a list of rules."

After each group has developed a list of rules and the class has voted on the rules they would adopt, Ms. McBryant says, "All right, class, I think we have agreed on our classroom rules, and I have combined your list and mine. For you, the rules will be

We will not touch each other without permission.

We will speak in appropriate voices.

We will not call each other names.

We will not take something that does not belong to us without permission.

For me, you have decided that the rules will be

Ms. McBryant will not give homework over the weekend or during school breaks.

Ms. McBryant will not yell at students.

I am very proud of you, I think you have developed a list of rules that will make our class run smoothly."

## Summary

In *Discipline with Dignity,* Richard Curwin and Allen Mendler contend that a "one size fits all" policy for classroom management is ineffective and inherently unfair. They stress that the school environment must meet the needs of each student and teacher by assuring that everyone in the school is treated with dignity. Discipline with Dignity is a three-dimensional discipline plan that focuses on preventing discipline problems from occurring. The three elements of this model are prevention, action, and resolution. In the twenty plus years since Curwin and Mendler wrote *Discipline with Dignity,* their theories have evolved to meet the changing needs of teachers and classrooms. In 1997, Curwin and Mendler wrote *As Tough as Necessary* in response to the need of teachers to deal with more violent students.

## Key Terminology

Definitions for these terms appear in the glossary.

70-20-10 Principle    102            Individual contracts    108
Classroom principles    103          Range of consequences    104
Discipline with Dignity    101       Social contract    103
Flag rules    104

## Chapter Activities

### Reflecting on the Theory

1. In Chapter 3, the following scenario was presented:

   Eighth-grade teacher Natalie Cansler is having a problem with one of her students. Cary Kirby arrives each day without the required materials. Some days he forgets his pencil; other days it is his textbooks. Each day, he asks to return to his locker for some forgotten item. Ms. Cansler feels she is in a no-win situation. If she allows Cary to return to his locker, he loses valuable instructional time. If she refuses, he spends the hour unable to do his work.

   How would Curwin and Mendler suggest that Ms. Cansler deal with Cary's behavior? How does their strategy differ from that of Lee and Marlene Canter?

2. Curwin and Mendler suggest that discipline situations are a fundamental part of the job of a classroom teacher and state, "The teacher's goal should not be to eliminate all forms of misbehavior, because students need opportunities to test limits, but to help students make appropriate choices and decisions." Do you agree or disagree? Why?

3. Curwin and Mendler encourage teachers to avoid a "cookie-cutter" approach to discipline. Is there a way to be consistent while meeting the needs of individual students? Explain your reasoning.

4. Curwin and Mendler identify needs of both students and teachers. How will you meet your needs of identity, connectedness, power, and achievement in your role as a classroom teacher?

## Developing Artifacts for Your Portfolio

1. Describe your teaching style. What instructional strategies will be common in your classroom? What discipline problems might occur as a result of your style or strategies? How can you eliminate these problems while maintaining your preferred style of teaching?

2. At the end of Chapter 1, you were encouraged to develop a list of the rules you will establish for your classroom. Review the list and change as needed. Develop a "range of consequences" for each of these rules.

## Developing Your Personal Philosophy of Classroom Management

1. In the last scenario, Ms. McBryant stated that one of the principles she wanted for her class was for every student to reach his or her potential. What principles will guide your instruction, your interaction with students, and your classroom-management plan?

2. What will be your "flag rules"? Why do you consider these rules nonnegotiable?

3. What strategies from the Discipline with Dignity model will you incorporate into your classroom-management plan?

## Resources for Further Study

Further information about Discipline with Dignity and resources for its use in the classroom can be found by contacting

Solution Tree Press
Bloomington, IN
800-733-6786
812-336-7700

## Chapter References

Blumefeld-Jones, D. S. (1996). Conventional systems of classroom discipline. *Journal of Education Thought, 30,* 5–21.

Curwin, R. L., & Mendler, A. N. (1980). *The discipline book.* Reston, VA: Reston Publishing.

Curwin, R. L., & Mendler, A. N. (1984). High standards for effective discipline. *Educational Leadership, 41,* 75–76.

Curwin, R. L., & Mendler, A. N. (1988a). *Discipline with dignity.* Alexandria, VA: Association for Supervision and Curriculum Development.

Curwin, R. L., & Mendler, A. N. (1988b). Packaged discipline programs: Let the buyer beware. *Educational Leadership, 46,* 68–71.

Curwin, R. L., & Mendler, A. N. (1997). *As tough as necessary: Countering violence, aggression, and hostility in our schools.* Alexandria, VA: Association for Supervision and Curriculum Development.

Curwin, R. L., & Mendler, A. N. (1999). Zero tolerance for zero tolerance. *Phi Delta Kappan, 81,* 119–120.

Curwin, R. L., & Mendler, A. N. (2000). Six strategies for helping youth move from rage to responsibility. *Reaching Today's Youth, 4,* 17–20.

Curwin, R. L., Mendler, A. N., & Mendler, B. D. (2008). *Discipline with dignity* (3rd ed.). Alexandria, VA: Association for Supervision and Curriculum Development.

Kohn, A. (1996). *Beyond discipline: From compliance to community.* Alexandria, VA: Association for Supervision and Curriculum Development.

Mendler, A. N. (1997). Beyond discipline survival: Reclaiming children and youth. *Journal of Emotional and Behavioral Problems, 6,* 41–44.

Mendler, A. N. (2007). *What do I do when . . . ?* Bloomington, IN: Solution Tree.

Mendler, A. N., & Curwin, R. L. (1983). *Taking charge in the classroom.* Reston, VA: Reston Publishing.

Mendler, A. N., & Curwin, R. L. (2007). *Discipline with dignity for challenging youth.* Bloomington, IN: Solution Tree.

PEARSON
**myeducationlab**
The Power of Classroom Practice
www.myeducationlab.com

Go to the Topic: **Creating Positive Student–Teacher Relationships** in the MyEducationLab (www.myeducationlab.com) for your course, where you can:

- Find learning outcomes for **Creating Positive Student–Teacher Relationships** along with the national standards that connect to these outcomes.
- Apply and practice your understanding of the core teaching skills identified in the chapter with the Building Teaching Skills and Dispositions learning units.
- Use interactive Simulations in Classroom Management to practice decision making and to receive expert feedback on classroom-management choices.

# Classroom Organization and Management Program (COMP)

## Objectives

Chapter 7 prepares preservice teachers to meet INTASC standards #1 (Content Pedagogy), #3 (Diverse Learners), #4 (Instructional Strategies), #5 (Motivation and Management), #7 (Planning), #9 (Reflective Practitioner), and #10 (School and Community) by helping them to

■ understand the basic principles behind Classroom Organization and Management Program (COMP).

■ recognize the importance of collaboration in supporting changes in teaching practices.

■ determine appropriate instructional strategies to be used in teaching classroom rules and procedures.

■ use the techniques presented in the six components of COMP.

■ evaluate the research based on effective classroom management, which is the foundation for COMP.

- determine the characteristics and actions of effective classroom managers.

- recognize that management and instruction are integrally related.

- take into account the student differences in attention spans, learning modalities, and

- intelligences as they develop a personal classroom-management plan.

- evaluate how subject-area content impacts classroom-management strategies.

- use research by Carolyn Evertson to deal with problem behavior.

## Scenario

First-year teachers Nick Napolitano and Monique Mathis have spent the weeks before school began preparing their lessons and their classrooms. After a long morning of work, Nick enters Monique's room with thoughts of lunch on his mind. "Do you want to get a pizza? Remember," he reminds Monique, "it won't be long before we can't go out for lunch."

"Sure, just give me five minutes to put this away," Monique says as she moved large poster boards to her desk.

Looking at one of the poster boards, Nick notices that it is divided into four columns: Teacher Tasks, Student Tasks, Rules, and Procedures. Confused, he asks, "What is all this? What are you doing?"

"Well, I started to develop my classroom rules, and it occurred to me that I needed a set of different rules and procedures for each of the activities we will do. For example, the rules and procedures the

students need when working on the computers are different from those they need when working independently. So, I've been thinking through each activity. See," she says as she shows him a completed poster board, "these are the rules and procedures I've been working on for my computer center. I've thought through what I will have to do to make the center work well. I've listed the tasks the students will perform at the computer. Then I've developed rules for computer use, and I've developed the procedures I think we will need."

"This is way too much work. I think I'll wait and see what problems develop and deal with them then."

Grabbing her purse, Monique says, "Well, I keep remembering what I was told in my teacher-education program. My professor said that the returns of careful planning are one thousand percent. I'm hoping she was right. Now, let's get that pizza. I'm starving."

## INTRODUCTION

Even though she is just beginning her first teaching assignment, Monique is already demonstrating the characteristics of an effective classroom manager. Monique is being proactive by planning ways to prevent student confusion and misbehavior, and she understands that management and instruction are interwoven. These same two elements are part of a classroom-management plan, **Classroom Organization and Management Program (COMP),** created by Carolyn Evertson. COMP is the result of 30 years of research by Evertson and her colleagues that included over 5,000 hours of classroom observation. COMP was originally developed through a series of related studies funded by the National Institute of Education and conducted through the Research and Development Center for Teacher Education at the University of Texas in Austin and the Arkansas Department of General Education in Little Rock (Evertson & Harris, 1995). Since 1989, COMP has been implemented in thousands of schools in the United States and the American territories.

*The creation of classroom procedures is a fundamental element of an effective classroom plan.*

COMP was developed from descriptive, correlational, and experimental research studies designed to discover successful key management practices and strategies. For over 30 years, Evertson and nationally recognized researchers such as Edmund T. Emmer, Julie P. Sanford, Barbara S. Clements, Linda M. Anderson, Catherine H. Randolph, Alene H. Harris, and Jere Brophy have examined successful classroom-management practices. Their research identified the following characteristics of successful classroom managers:

- Teachers whose students consistently gained in achievement organized classrooms in such a way that they ran smoothly, with a minimum of disruptions (Brophy & Evertson, 1976).

- Teachers whose classrooms were well managed analyzed classroom tasks in precise detail to determine the procedures and expectations required for students to be successful (Emmer, Evertson, & Anderson, 1980; Evertson & Anderson, 1979).

- Teachers in well-managed classrooms saw the classroom through the students' eyes. They were, therefore, able to analyze the students' needs for information (Emmer et al., 1980; Evertson & Anderson, 1979).

- Teachers who were effective classroom managers monitored student behavior in order to quickly deal with disruptive behavior and potential threats to their system (Emmer et al., 1980; Evertson & Anderson, 1979; Evertson & Emmer, 1982).

## Step-by-Step Classroom Organization and Management Program (COMP)

To use COMP in your classroom, you will need to do the following things:

1. Organize your classroom to maximize learning opportunities and to prevent misbehavior.

2. Establish classroom rules. Involve students in the process.

3. Establish classroom procedures to promote learning and good behavior.

4. Plan lessons on classroom rules and procedures. Teach students how to follow rules and procedures.

5. Manage student work and provide for student accountability.

6. Maintain good behavior by providing both positive and negative consequences for behavior. Implement corrective consequences when students need to be guided toward other avenues for behavior.

7. Plan and organize instruction with a focus on the procedures needed to enhance learning.

8. Maintain momentum during instruction.

- Junior- and senior-high-level teachers who were effective classroom managers clearly communicated needed information, reduced complex tasks to essential steps, and had a good understanding of student skill levels (Evertson & Emmer, 1982).

- Teachers who were more effective classroom managers kept students engaged in academic work by organizing instruction (Evertson & Emmer, 1982).

- Teachers who were effective classroom managers not only created workable management systems but also taught the systems to their students from the first day of the school year (Emmer et al., 1980). The importance of this was verified by later research by Evertson, Emmer, Sanford, and Clements (1983) that found that after the beginning of the year, classroom patterns become established and midyear changes require stronger, more intensive interventions.

- Teachers who were successful at blending academic and social skills had students who tended to stay on-task, engage in appropriate behavior, and demonstrate higher achievement. These teachers recognized that they were teaching both academic and social skills, and that both academic and social behaviors are developmental (Evertson & Harris, 1996).

All the variables identified as being significant in producing student achievement and reducing inappropriate and disruptive students are incorporated into COMP. Since Evertson began her research in the 1970s, classrooms have become more diverse, and a greater variety of academic activities are needed to meet students' needs. This increase in complexity demands even greater expertise in classroom management, and strategies for meeting the changing needs of classrooms are incorporated into COMP (Evertson & Harris, 1995).

The changing complexity of the classroom has also brought about a need for a definition of classroom management that more closely reflects the changing dynamics of modern classrooms. In an interview with Marchant and Newman (1996), Evertson said, "For a long time, classroom management has been and still is associated with control and discipline, and with questions about the best ways to get students to comply. We are simply saying that these notions of management are not compatible with building the kinds of learning communities we are trying to build where students have a stake in their own learning and their own community" (p. 31).

As teachers move from traditional teaching methods to methods for building community, they also must move from traditional methods for managing the classroom. Often, teachers find that managing learning-centered classrooms provides additional challenges as teachers struggle to manage cooperative groups, learning centers, and collaborative learning activities (Evertson and Neal, 2006). In the most effective classroom environment, teaching and classroom management blend seamlessly to support these types of activities.

Evertson and Harris (1999) suggest that a broader definition of classroom management is needed and that classroom management must be viewed as a holistic descriptor of teachers' actions in orchestrating all that teachers do to encourage learning in their classrooms. This includes creating predictable, orderly classrooms, establishing rules, gaining student cooperation in tasks, and coping with the procedural demands of the classroom. A holistic definition of classroom management is one that emphasizes a teacher's ongoing choices and actions rather than narrowly considering responses to misbehavior. Today's view of classroom management must be "all that teachers must do to encourage learning in their classrooms, including proactively setting up an environment that encourages learning and discourages wasting time, and orchestrating instruction in ways that promote and maintain student engagement" (p. 251).

When classroom management is viewed as orchestrating all that goes on in a classroom, a system of classroom management is needed. COMP was developed to provide such a system to teachers (Evertson & Harris, 1995). The central goal of COMP is to help teachers improve overall instructional and management skills through planning, implementing, and maintaining effective classroom practices. Additional goals are the improvement of student task engagement, the reduction of inappropriate and disruptive behaviors, the promotion of student responsibility for academic work and behavior, and the improvement of student academic achievement. Evertson and Harris (1996, 1999) note the following key principles of COMP:

- Effective classroom management prevents problems rather than handling them after they occur.
- Management and instruction are integrally related.
- Students are active participants in the learning environment, and classroom management must take into account student differences in attention span, learning modalities, and intelligence.
- Professional collaboration supports changes in teaching practice.

COMP provides for the uniqueness of each classroom setting and seeks to promote thinking about classroom-management decisions, rather than simply presenting teachers

## Tips from the Field

I teach my students simple forms of sign language to use in the classroom setting. Bathroom/water/pencil sharpening/and other requests never interrupt instruction as students use the appropriate sign symbol. I, in return, acknowledge their request with the appropriate sign language symbol. I don't miss a beat in the instructional lesson as the Beat Goes On!

Samuel Bennett
Fifth-Grade Teacher
Garner Elementary
Winter Haven, Florida
2006 Florida Teacher of the Year

with a "recipe" for effective management. COMP comprises of six major components: Organizing the Classroom, Planning and Teaching Rules and Procedures, Managing Student Work and Improving Student Accountability, Maintaining Good Student Behavior, Planning and Organizing Instruction, and Conducting Instruction and Maintaining the Momentum (Evertson & Harris, 1997). Few of these components are new to teachers. As Evertson (1985) states, however, the ordering of these components and the rationales for their use provide a conceptual framework from which teachers can make the critical decisions about their teaching on an everyday basis.

## KEY ELEMENTS OF COMP

Just as the rationale for COMP developed from the research on effective classroom management, the six components of COMP are products of years of research into the characteristics of effective classroom managers. The rationales and key elements for each of the six components follow.

### Organizing the Classroom

In many cases, the first impression about a teacher comes not from an interaction between the teacher and a student or a teacher and a parent but from the way the teacher has prepared the classroom. Everything in a classroom—the way the furniture is arranged, the types of materials displayed, the colors selected for the wall and bulletin boards, and the presence of or lack of clutter—sends unspoken messages about the teacher to students and their parents.

Teachers must be aware of the messages their classrooms convey and be sure that the messages are consistent with their values and goals. For example, Evertson and Harris (1997, 1999) state that classroom design sends a signal to students about how they are to interact and learn in the classroom. If desks touch or students sit together in groups at tables and chairs, the arrangement signals that collaboration and cooperation will be expected. If desks are arranged in traditional rows or are standing alone, the message is that their work will be done independently. Easily accessible learning centers and computer stations signal that they are there to be used by students. Comfortable chairs or pillows in a reading nook suggest that students will be expected to linger over a favorite book.

Problems develop when the message sent by the classroom arrangement does not match the teacher's style of instruction. If students are grouped together, they will talk to one another. If that is not the teacher's desire, traditional desks may be more appropriate. If materials are not to be used by students, teachers only invite problems when these materials are accessible to inquisitive hands. Teachers must analyze different arrangements for consistency with their instructional goals (Evertson & Harris, 1997).

Unfortunately, there are few ideal classrooms (Evertson, 1987). Few teachers have been fortunate enough to be able to design the space they will use as a classroom. Most teachers, especially new teachers, take the space assigned to them and strive to make it functional. However, regardless of the limitations of the space provided, teachers must consider three elements for effective organization of the classroom: visibility, accessibility, and distractibility.

**Visibility.**  Every student must be able to see teacher-led instruction, demonstrations, and presentations. Any instructional material that is presented via overhead, whiteboard, or monitor must be visible to every student without requiring them to move their chairs, turn their desk, or crane their necks (Evertson & Harris, 1997). Before the first day of class, teachers should sit in each student's desk to determine whether the student will be able to see and hear all teacher-led instruction.

It is equally important for the teacher to see all students, the student work areas, and learning centers. As Emmer and Evertson (2009) note, if students cannot be seen, it is difficult to determine whether they need assistance or are participating in off-task behavior.

**Accessibility.**  In order to provide the assistance needed and to maintain on-task behavior by proximity control, the teacher should be able to reach every student in the classroom quickly and without disturbing other students. High-traffic areas should be clear and separate.

---

### Tips from the Field

My classroom is in the computer lab. Instead of having students raise their hands for help while they are working on the computer, I use colored plastic cups as a help signal. The students set the cup on top of their monitor. This allows students to keep working until I assist them, and many times, they are able to answer their own questions. It also keeps my younger students in their seats. I change the color of the cups with different seasons to add a little fun and color to my room.

LeAnn Morris
Empire Elementary School
K-5 Technology
Carson City, NV
2008 Nevada Teacher of the Year

Careful attention must be paid to traffic patterns around pencil sharpeners, waste cans, and in-room water fountains. If areas for storing materials are poorly placed, distractions may occur when students get or return supplies. Easy access to and efficient storage of instructional materials maintain lesson momentum and minimizes wasted time. However, only teaching materials that students are allowed to touch should be left in places where students gather.

**Distractibility.**   Before the first student arrives, the teacher should scan the room for distractions that might compete for the teacher's attention or encourage off-task behavior. Although teachers want classrooms that are attractive and inviting, they sometimes forget that excessive decoration can visually overstimulate some students. Other distractions include displays, toys, animal cages, and a myriad of other things that students may find more interesting than the material being presented. Remember that what might not be a distraction for the teacher or some students may distract others. Such distractions must be moved to another part of the classroom and away from the view of an individual student. Distractions that disrupt the entire classroom should be removed from the classroom.

Evertson and Randolph (1999) stress that the way classroom space is used will have important implications for how students participate in class activities and how they interact with the teacher and each other. It is important to remember that how the classroom looks and feels will either hinder or support class activities. Consider how Nick, from the opening scenario, discovered that he had created a problem with the placement of his computer center.

> After his lunch with Monique, Nick decided that he needed specific rules and procedures for his computer center. He was pleased with the result and thought his center was creative and very usable. However, he was disappointed the first day students used the center. Until students were working at the computers, he had not realized that students sharpening their pencils would have to lean over the students sitting at the computers to do so. After a day of quarreling and complaining by students either sharpening their pencils or working at the computers, Nick realized that he had to move the pencil sharpener or the computer center in order to resolve the problem.

## Planning and Teaching Rules and Procedures

Evertson and Randolph (1999) stress that rules and procedures are necessary to maintain lesson flow, continuity, and students' engagement in academic work. A carefully planned and systematically taught system of rules and procedures is necessary to communicate behavioral expectations to students and to ensure that the teacher's goals are met (Evertson & Harris, 1997). Efficient procedures and workable rules allow a variety of activities, or even several activities at a given time, to take place during a class with minimum confusion and wasted time.

Evertson and Harris (1997) state that rules are expected norms of general behavior. They make up the "constitution of the classroom" (p. 2.05e). They function to prevent or encourage certain behaviors. Unlike procedures, which change to meet classroom demands, rules do not change.

---

**Table 7.1** Points to Consider in Rule Development

- The rules should be stated so expectations are clear.
- Rationales for each rule should be provided.
- Rules that encourage a positive class climate should be selected.
- The list of rules should be kept as short as possible.
- Classroom rules should be consistent with school rules and policies.
- The students should be involved in rule development.
- Examples should be given to illustrate the rules.
- Rules should be taught in the same manner as other content.

---

*Source:* Evertson, C. M. (1987). Managing classrooms—A framework for teachers. In D. Berliner & B. Rosenshine (Eds.), *Talk to teachers.* New York: Random House.

Evertson and Harris (1997) consider rule and procedure development the teacher's responsibility, and the teacher must make certain that the set of classroom rules and procedures is adequate and appropriate. On the other hand, many teachers do include their students in the process of developing rules and procedures in order to promote ownership of rules and to encourage students to take responsibility for their behavior. The decision to involve students in rule making will depend on the maturity level of the students and the teacher's level of comfort in sharing responsibility with students.

Although it is important to keep the number of classroom rules short and manageable, the actual number of rules is not as critical as how rules are developed. Specific guidelines for rule development appear in Table 7.1.

Whereas rules lay out basic behavioral expectations, **procedures** are often the specific "how to's" that show students step by step how to successfully follow the rules (Evertson, 1987). Procedures function to make tasks routine, to communicate expectations for student behavior during a specific activity, and to aid in the transition from one activity to another. Unlike rules, they change according to needs that arise, and they have no prescribed number (Evertson & Harris, 1997).

Evertson and Harris (1999) note that both rules and procedures should be taught to students and that the teaching of rules and procedures is no different from teaching other content. Rules and procedures must be taught with an emphasis on developing rationale for the rules and procedures and on providing students with cues for self-monitoring. Teachers must remember that skills must be practiced, and a single presentation of a procedure is not adequate for student comprehension or continued use of the procedure. Consider how Monique teaches her classroom rules and procedures to her students:

> "Class, yesterday we looked at our second rule: 'We ask permission to use someone else's things.' Today we are going to discuss our third rule: 'We will use appropriate voices.' Who wants to tell me what this means?"
>
> Several hands went up and Monique called on Murray. "I think it means that we should be quiet and not disturb others."

"Well, yes, there are times when we should be quiet, but does this mean we have to be quiet all the time? Are there times we can make lots of noise? Dana, when is it all right to make lots of noise?"

Hesitating, Dana said, "I guess it is all right to make lots of noise on the playground or in the gym."

"Dana, that is a great answer. Of course, you can make lots of noise on the playground. In fact," she says, as she moves to the tape recorder, "I made a tape of you when you were at recess yesterday. Let's hear how you sounded." As Monique played the tape of the children on the playground, several students laughed when they heard their own voices shouting or calling out to someone.

"Wow, you were making a lot of noise, but you weren't breaking a rule. That is how I *expect* you to sound when you are on the playground. Does everyone understand what I mean?" Monique looked around the room and noticed that all students appeared to understand. "Now, I want us to develop a procedure so you will know when you are and when you aren't making the correct amount of noise. I thought we might develop a number system. Let's create a system that goes from one to five. One will be the quietest you should be, and five will be the loudest you can be. So, when you can be really noisy, like on the playground, we would be at our highest level of noise. So, if I hold up five fingers, you know you can be as loud as you want. Let me write this on the board." Monique wrote a 5 on the board and then wrote beside it, "Loud shouting, yelling, laughing—appropriate for the playground or the gym."

"Now, let's think of the opposite of our number five. Can you demonstrate how you would sound if I held up one finger?" Monique watched as every student got still and became very quiet. "Wow, that is really quiet. When would we need to be that quiet?"

For the next hour, the students and Monique talked about the appropriate noise levels for their class. "Okay, let's practice our procedure." Monique held up one finger and everyone got very quiet. When she held up two fingers, the students whispered to the person next to them. "Great job, now I think we will have to wait to practice level five until we are on the playground. Does everyone understand our procedure? Any questions?"

Table 7.2 provides specific instructions for how to teach a procedure.

## Managing Student Work and Improving Student Accountability

Evertson and Harris (1997, 1999) suggest that the ultimate goal of an effective classroom-management system is to teach student responsibility. Unfortunately, many students do not understand the connection between their effort and the results of their effort. Therefore, effective teachers not only hold students accountable for their academic work and their behavior but also teach them how to be accountable (Evertson & Randolph, 1999).

Accountability is encouraged by establishing a system of clearly communicated expectations for students and providing as much responsibility to students as possible. Evertson and Harris (1997) note that effective student-accountability systems consist of two essential

**Table 7.2** Steps for Teaching Classroom Rules and Procedures

**Step One:** **Explain**

- Define a procedure or rule in *concrete* terms. This is especially important when the rule contains words that might not be understood or open for interpretation, such as the term *respect*.
- Describe the acceptable behaviors with words and actions.
- Provide a rationale for why the rule or procedure is needed. This begins the process of helping students look beyond their own needs and desires.
- Model how the rule or procedure would look in action. Have several students demonstrate how the rule or procedure should be followed.
- Present step-by-step directions for carrying out procedures. These steps should be written as well as verbalized.

**Step Two:** **Rehearse**

- Have students practice the procedure, step by step, until all students can do the procedure correctly.
- When students break a rule or do not follow a procedure, review the steps again and have students model the appropriate behavior.

**Step Three:** **Test Knowledge of Rule or Procedure**

- Allow students to demonstrate their knowledge of rules and procedures by testing in written form or having students demonstrate.
- Provide feedback on the accuracy of their knowledge and skill.
- Have students observe students as they move about the school or on the playground and record when rules or procedures are not followed. Discuss the consequences of not following rules and procedures.

**Step Four:** **Reinforce**

- Acknowledge when rules and procedures are followed.
- Provide praise and rewards for following rules and procedures.

**Step Five:** **Reteach When Necessary**

- Plan to review rules and procedures after breaks in the school term or after long absences from the classroom.
- When procedures or rules aren't followed, take the time to remind students of the rules.
- Reteach and rehearse when necessary.

*Source:* Adapted from Wong and Wong (1998) and Evertson and Harris (1997).

elements that must be designed and managed. One element establishes student responsibility by providing clear explanations about what students must do to be successful. The second element requires teachers to model responsible behavior by being consistent in their grading and feedback to students. For these two elements to be successful in developing independent learners, teachers must

- *Provide clear and specific instructions for overall work requirements.* Evertson and Harris (1997) recommend that assignments and important instructions be put on a whiteboard, overhead projector, or flip chart and that assignments requiring detailed instructions should be provided both orally and in writing.

- *Communicate assignments and instructions so that every child understands.* Teachers should go over instructions orally with the class, questioning students about their understanding of the directions and providing examples of the work expected. For large projects and assignments, substages should be developed with clear deadlines and goals for each of the substages.

- *Monitor students' work; keep track of what students are doing.* Evertson and Randolph (1999) stress that effective classroom managers monitor their classes and students for signs of student confusion. Monitoring indicates the importance and appropriateness of the assignment. Monitoring student progress helps identify students who are having difficulty and allows the teacher to encourage other students to keep working.

- *Establish routines for turning in work.* To enable teachers to keep accurate records about who completed their work, students should be told when and where assignments are to be placed.

- *Provide regular academic feedback to students; check their work.* Students' work should be checked in order to provide feedback and correctives and rechecked to make certain students are learning concepts correctly (Evertson, 1987). Evertson and Harris (1997) suggest that teachers plan specifically and in advance how they will handle student work, how they will check the work, and what portion of students' grades will be based on tests, daily assignments, homework, and special projects.

- *Establish routines for handling makeup work.* Student accountability often fails when students are absent. Absent students miss instructions and directions for assignments. Establishing routines for handling makeup work is critical for effective teaching. Consider how Nick solved his makeup-work problem.

One morning Nick was waiting for Monique when she arrived at school. "Hey, Monique, come to my room. I want to show what I did over the weekend. You are going to be very impressed."

Laughing, Monique followed Nick into his room and to the computer on his desk. "All right. I'm waiting. Impress me."

"Look," Nick said as he pulled up the new Web site he had developed for his class.

"Nick, I *am* impressed. How did you know how to do this?"

"Well, I knew some basics and just figured out the rest. But I want you to see the best part. When you click on homework, you not only see each day's homework, you can also actually print out the assignment. Now, if a student is absent, the student or the student's parents can just go to the Web site and see what was missed. If students don't have a computer at home, they can go to the computer center and print out their assignments. I don't have to remember to tell the students what they missed, and students have no excuse for not keeping up with the homework. Now, let me show you what else you can do."

## Maintaining Good Student Behavior

Unfortunately, even the most effective teachers will have students who challenge the classroom rules and procedures. In some cases, these challenges disrupt the classroom and interfere with other students or class activities (Evertson, 1989). In other cases, the challenge is not disruptive to others but results in off-task behavior. In either case, the teacher must intervene and redirect the student's behavior. But as Evertson and Harris (1997) note, teaching, not punishment, is the goal.

Maintaining good student behavior requires a combination of consequences, intervention strategies, and communication. Having a reasonable set of positive, negative, and corrective consequences for rules and procedures, and consistently using them when appropriate, makes classroom expectations predictable to students and encourages them to be self-governing. It is important to have a range of consequences for two reasons. First, a range of consequences allows the teacher to deal appropriately with the level of misbehavior. Second, what might be punishment to one student might be rewarding to another. Having a preplanned set of consequences and intervention strategies will increase the teacher's ability to manage the classroom (Evertson & Harris, 1999).

**Positive consequences,** in the form of extrinsic incentives or rewards, follow behavior and serve to increase or maintain behavior. Incentives and rewards can be emotional, psychological, or academic. The incentive and reward selected will depend on the student's age, interest, and maturity level.

**Corrective consequences** are specific strategies for helping students manage their own behavior. In using a correcting consequence, the teacher has the student practice the desired behavior or procedure. In some cases, it is necessary to reteach the procedure to ensure that students understand what they are to do. The goal of corrective consequences is to help students consciously think about their actions. Evertson and Harris (1997) provide suggestions for two corrective consequences: self-recording and self-instruction. In self-recording, the students take responsibility by recording each time they exhibit a desired behavior. In self-instruction, students verbalize what they are to do.

**Negative consequences** are undesired consequences that follow a behavior and are used to decrease the unwanted behavior. However, Evertson and Harris (1992) note that punishment or negative consequences neither teach desirable behavior nor instill a desire to behave. They recommend that negative consequences and punishments be used only when it is necessary to respond to repeated misbehavior. Evertson and Harris (1997) remind teachers that "Your ultimate goal is to teach students appropriate behavior and to have them increase and/or maintain that behavior, not just stop behaviors that are disruptive or inappropriate" (p. 4.25e).

**Intervention strategies** redirect budding student misbehavior. Intervention strategies stop misbehavior, reinvolve students in the lesson, keep the climate of the classroom positive, and do not disrupt teaching. Selecting the best time to use intervention strategies depends on the teacher's belief about the cause of the problem. Possible intervention strategies include making eye contact, using proximity control, reminding students of the rule or procedure, and questioning students about their behavior.

When dealing with student misbehavior, it is always important to choose battles carefully. It is impossible to respond to each and every situation of off-task or inappropriate behavior. Some behaviors can be ignored, and others should never be ignored. In addition, the battles are different for different teachers. What one teacher considers important to control may not be important to another. For example, Monique and Nick found they disagree as to which behaviors to battle.

> When Monique joined Nick in the faculty lounge at lunch, she noticed that he was unusually quiet. "Hey, what's wrong? Have you had a rough morning?"
>
> "No, I guess not. Mr. Silkowski evaluated me this morning. He ranked me high on everything but classroom management. He said that often my students are too loud. I don't think they are too loud, do you?"
>
> Avoiding eye contact, Monique said, "Well . . ."
>
> "Monique, do you agree with him? I realize I don't keep my students as quiet as your students, but the noise doesn't bother me. Why should it bother Mr. Silkowski?"
>
> "Nick, I realize that the noise doesn't bother you, but it might bother other teachers. I have to admit that sometimes my class can hear your students when they are playing a game or having a discussion. Then my students wonder why they have to be so quiet. And there is another problem."
>
> "What? What other problem?"
>
> "Well, have you considered what happens to your students when they leave you? I doubt that most teachers will be as tolerant as you are. Won't your students be confused about how much noise they are allowed to make?"
>
> Nick thought about what Monique had said. "Maybe. I will have to think about what you said. But, Monique, I don't want to have to use some one-to-five system like you do. That is just not me. I don't want to punish them for being excited about learning."
>
> "Then don't punish them. Reward them instead. Determine some reward you can give when students are talking at an appropriate level. Classroom management isn't only about punishing, you know."

## Planning and Organizing Instruction

Too often, traditional classroom models overlook the critical relationship between instruction and management. Evertson and Randolph (1999) suggest that effective classroom management has typically been regarded as a precondition for instruction. In reality, however, the concept that management is isolated from content is faulty because management carries messages about the value of content. How the classroom is being managed during particular learning activities must be considered with content as plans and activities are developed. Evertson and Randolph (1999) see good classroom-management practices as inseparable from good instructional practices. A critical element of COMP is planning for the interplay between management and instruction.

How teachers teach has changed as classrooms have moved from a teacher-centered focus to a student-centered focus. As Evertson and Randolph (1999) note, "Silent children seated in straight rows portray the history of American education, not its future" (p. 249). Teachers now present content using a full range of instructional strategies that include whole-group instruction, teacher-led groups, cooperative groups, student pairs, centers and stations, computerized and online instruction, and individualized instruction. Management demands in these classrooms are significantly different from those in teacher-centered classrooms (Randolph & Evertson, 1994).

For every classroom task, there are both academic and social dimensions (Evertson & Harris, 1997; Randolph & Evertson, 1994). In each situation, students not only have to determine what they are to learn but also how they are to participate in the learning process. Teacher-centered activities make different demands on both students and teachers than activities that are student centered. The more complex the instruction, the more important it is that teachers plan for both instruction and management. Regardless of the instructional method, it is the teacher's job to think through the learning process with a focus on the tasks of both the teacher and the students. Consider how Monique manages her class as she prepares her classwork using learning centers.

> After Monique's students completed their morning review, she asked them to gather around her on the reading rug. "Who noticed that the classroom looks different this morning?" Monique waited as every hand went up. "Well, today we are beginning a study of the Southeast. Now, around the room, I have created six learning centers. Each center focuses on one of the states we will be studying. Each center has activities you and your team members are to do at the center. You will spend two days at each center, and then you will move to the next center. You have worked in cooperative groups before, and our procedures for working in groups apply when you work in the centers. Katlin, will you tell us the procedures for working in groups?"
>
> When Katlin finished telling the procedures, Monique says, "Great job! Now, today I want to go over the rules and procedures for working in centers, and I want to go over what you will be expected to do at each center. Tomorrow, you will actually work in your centers. All right, our first center focuses on the state of Florida. Ginny, please read the written directions for this center."

## Conducting Instruction and Maintaining the Momentum

The first five elements of COMP are designed to establish a well-managed classroom from the beginning of the school year. The final element, Conducting Instruction and Maintaining the Momentum, provides consistency in maintaining the management system. Evertson and Harris (1997, 1999) state that in order to reduce potential behavior problems and maintain student involvement in the instructional activities, teachers must

- *Provide clear instructions.* Communicating information and directions in a clear, comprehensible way is an important teaching skill. This begins with the teacher establishing appropriate objectives and helping students understand the relevance of what they are learning. Clarity includes providing clear procedural directions that enable students to know what to do and how to perform the task.

■ *Check for students' understanding of what they are to do.* Instructions for assignments must be given precisely, and the teacher must be able to respond to students' questions with understandable explanations. It also involves checking student understanding in other ways, such as questioning them, having students demonstrate the steps, or using other means of detecting potential problems with academic material.

■ *Monitor students' behavior.* Monitoring involves regularly surveying the class or groups to watch for signs of confusion. Teachers should make a practice of routinely checking students and attending to nonverbal cues in order to catch problems before errors are practiced and reinforced.

■ *Provide for smooth transitions.* It is during transitions that students most often waste time, wander off-task, or engage in inappropriate behavior. Teachers must plan for transitions as carefully as they plan for instruction.

At the end of a long day, Monique stopped by Nick's classroom to find him working on his lesson plans. "Trying to get ready for tomorrow?"

"No, I'm just making notes. Today was a disaster. The students were to start their social studies project today. I thought I was clear in my instructions, but no one seemed to understand what I wanted them to do. Then I tried to explain again, and things just got worse. So, I'm making notes. You know, if I teach this again next year, I don't want to make the same mistakes. Sometimes I find I spend more time thinking about what didn't work than I do making new plans."

"Well, don't stay too late. Hopefully things will go better tomorrow."

Returning to his plans, Nick said, "I'm working out all the details tonight, so that I make sure that tomorrow goes better than today did. Good night."

---

## Tips from the Field

As a thirty-two-year teaching veteran at the secondary level, I have seen a strong shift from a classroom full of presumably well-behaved, somewhat motivated, parentally supported adolescents to a classroom of many behaviorally challenged, unengaged, often-on-their-own students who need direction. As a result, the initial strategy of modeling, practicing, and teaching desired behaviors has a real place in my classroom. From the simple (trash can usage, asking permission to speak or leave the room) to the complex (managing makeup work and daily classroom protocol),

I find that most students want direction and structure. Although they might not verbalize a fascination with direction and structure, my students want a place within where they can work effectively, the playing field is equal, and their ideas are valued. I firmly believe that students learn and perform as one teaches them.

Bridget Kay Call
Matewan High School
Matewan, West Virginia
2006 West Virginia Teacher of the Year

## STRATEGIES FOR DEALING WITH DIFFICULT STUDENTS

Evertson and Harris (1999) suggest that at times all students will display inappropriate behavior. How a teacher handles these situations will depend on the following factors:

- the teacher's level of tolerance
- the severity of the behavior
- the impact on other students
- the cost of intervening in terms of lost instructional time
- the probability of success if the teacher intervenes

One criticism of COMP is that it provides little information on how to deal with difficult students. COMP does not specifically address how to handle difficult students, because the program is designed to provide methods of preventing discipline problems rather than strategies for reacting to behavior problems. However, Carolyn Evertson does address this issue in two of her classroom-management books.

Evertson and Emmer (2009) stress that the interventions to be used with problem students will depend on the goal of the teacher. One goal is to immediately stop the behavior and return the classroom to order. The second goal is to prevent the behavior from happening in the future. The ideal intervention meets both of these goals. Evertson and Emmer (2009) have classified interventions that put these two goals into three categories: minor, moderate, and extensive.

Evertson and Emmer (2009) note that many minor interventions are effective because they make students aware of their behavior. Therefore, useful minor interventions include the following:

- using nonverbal cues such as eye contact or signaling
- making a smooth and efficient transition from one activity to another
- using proximity control
- redirecting the behavior
- providing additional instruction if the students appear confused about directions
- giving a desist in a firm voice
- giving the student a choice
- using "I" messages that describe the behavior and its effects on the classroom

Moderate interventions like the following take more time and effort on the part of the teacher:

- withholding a privilege or desired activity
- isolating or removing the student from an activity
- using a fine or penalty

- assigning detention
- referring the student to the office

When students do not respond to minor or moderate intervention and their behavior continues, a more extensive intervention is needed. These interventions are much more individualized and consist of creating individual behavior plans for the students. This is often done in conjunction with the functional behavior analysis process described in Chapter 2.

## STRENGTHS AND WEAKNESSES OF COMP

Perhaps the greatest strength of COMP comes from its research base. COMP was created from the research designed to identify the characteristics and actions of effective classroom managers. Since its creation, the success of the program has been extensively researched, and this research is what provides credibility to the program.

Program results have been measured with observational field studies, teacher's self-evaluation reports, and administration reports of observed classroom, teacher, and student change (Evertson & Harris, 1995, 1999). Following are the three main findings from this research:

1. Students of teachers who had participated in COMP obtain greater gains in academic achievement, as measured by standardized tests, than do students of teachers who had not participated in the program.

2. Teachers who participated in COMP instituted classroom practices that resulted in classroom environments more conducive to students' learning.

3. Students of teachers trained to use COMP showed a significant decrease in inappropriate and disruptive behavior and a significant increase in academic achievement.

Weinstein (1999) suggests that an additional strength of COMP is its emphasis on preventing inappropriate behavior rather than simply reacting to inappropriate behavior. COMP provides a body of knowledge and a set of practices that require thoughtful decision making by the teacher.

## COMP IN THE CLASSROOM

### Scenario

By the end of their first year of teaching, Nick and Monique are proud of their accomplishments. They realize that part of their success has resulted from their friendship and collaboration. Throughout the year, they shared teaching ideas, discipline problems, and successes. Nick has become a better classroom manager because of Monique's influence. Nick helped Monique create a class Web site and taught her strategies for incorporating computer activities into her instruction. When Nick agreed to direct the Founder's Day pageant, Monique helped by designing and making the costumes. Recognizing what Nick and Monique had accomplished through their collaboration, Mr. Silkowski established a mentor program for all first-year teachers.

## Summary

*Classroom Organization and Management Program (COMP),* created by Carolyn Evertson, is the result of thirty years of research. COMP was developed from descriptive, correlational, and experimental research studies designed to discover successful key management practices and strategies. A proactive approach, COMP is designed to help teachers improve overall instructional and management skills through planning, implementing, and maintaining effective practices. COMP provides a system of classroom management through proactive planning at the beginning of the school year and thoughtful decision making throughout the year. The system emphasizes the integration of management and instruction as a means of creating a positive learning environment.

## Key Terminology

Definitions for these terms appear in the glossary.

Accessibility   123

Classroom Organization and Management
       Program (COMP)   118

Corrective consequences   129

Distractibility   124

Intervention strategies   130

Negative consequences   129

Positive consequences   129

Procedures   125

Visibility   123

## Chapter Activities

### Reflecting on the Theory

1. Ms. Booker is reconsidering her teaching strategies. She had hoped to use collaborative learning as her primary teaching strategy. However, she is finding that she is uncomfortable with the noise level in the classroom. She finds she is constantly telling the students to lower their voices, and everyone is miserable, especially Ms. Booker.

   How can Ms. Booker use the strategies presented in COMP to resolve her classroom problems?

2. One of the fundamental principles of COMP is that classroom management and instruction are integrally related. Do you agree? Why or why not?

3. Throughout the chapter, Nick and Monique worked together to improve their teaching and classroom management. What lessons did they learn from each other? Have you found that such cooperative collaboration occurs in most school settings? Explain your answer.

4. Evertson's research clearly shows a correlation between management and academic achievement. What might be some of the reasons for such a correlation?

### Developing Artifacts for Your Portfolio

1. Consider one classroom procedure you will need in your classroom. Analyze this procedure and provide a listing of the behaviors expected of your students.

2. Evertson contends that the way a classroom looks and is designed sends messages to parents and students. Analyze a classroom where you have observed to determine what message the classroom is sending about

- the teacher's instructional style
- the teacher's personal values
- the teacher's organizational skills
- the teacher's classroom management

3. Analyze the classroom in question 2 for accessibility, distractibility, and visibility.

4. Evertson contends that for every classroom task, there are both academic and social dimensions, because students must not only determine what they are to learn but also how they are to participate in the learning process. Consider the subject-area content you will teach. What are the social dimensions of learning your content? How must students participate in the learning process to learn your content? How will your subject-area content influence how you manage your classroom?

### Developing Your Personal Philosophy of Classroom Management

1. Evertson and Randolph state, "Silent children seated in straight rows portray the history of American education, not its future." What is your reaction to this quote?

2. Would you be comfortable using COMP as your classroom-management plan in your classroom? Why or why not? Are there some strategies that you will definitely incorporate into your classroom-management plan?

## Resources for Further Study

Further information about Classroom Organization and Management Program and resources for its use in the classroom can be found by contacting:

Dr. Carolyn Evertson
Dr. Alene H. Harris
Classroom Organization and Management Program
Vanderbilt University
Box 541
Peabody College
Nashville, TN 37203
615-322-8050

# Chapter References

Brophy, J. E., & Evertson, C. M. (1976). *Learning from teaching: A developmental perspective.* Boston: Allyn & Bacon.

Emmer, E. T., & Evertson, C. M. (2009). *Classroom management for secondary teachers* (8th ed.). Upper Saddle River, NJ: Pearson Education.

Emmer, E., Evertson, C. M., & Anderson, L. (1980). Effective management at the beginning of the school year. *Elementary School Journal, 80,* 219–231.

Evertson, C. M. (1985). Training teachers in classroom management: An experimental study in secondary school classrooms. *Journal of Educational Research, 79,* 51–58.

Evertson, C. M. (1987). Managing classrooms: A framework for teachers. In D. Berliner & B. Rosenshine (Eds.), *Talk to teachers.* New York: Random House.

Evertson, C. M. (1989). Improving elementary classroom management: A school-based training program for beginning the year. *Journal of Educational Research, 93,* 82–90.

Evertson, C., & Anderson, L. (1979). Beginning school. *Educational Horizons, 57,* 164–168.

Evertson, C. M., & Emmer, E. (1982). Effective management at the beginning of the school year in junior high classes. *Journal of Educational Psychology, 74,* 485–498.

Evertson, C. M., & Emmer, E. T. (2009). *Classroom management for elementary teachers* (8th ed.). Upper Saddle River, NJ: Pearson Education.

Evertson, C. M., Emmer, E. T., Sanford, J. P., & Clements, B. S. (1983). Improving classroom management: An experiment in elementary school classrooms. *The Elementary School Journal, 84,* 173–188.

Evertson, C. M., & Harris, A. H. (1992). What we know about managing classrooms. *Educational Leadership, 49,* 74–78.

Evertson, C. M., & Harris, A. H. (1995). *Classroom organization and management program: Revalidation submission to the program effectiveness panel, U. S. Department of Education.* Nashville, TN: Vanderbilt University. (ERIC Document Reproduction Service No. ED403247.)

Evertson, C. M., & Harris, A. H. (1996). *COMP: Classroom organization and management program: An inservice program for effective proactive classroom management.* Washington, DC: National Diffusion Network.

Evertson, C. M., & Harris, A. H. (1997). *COMP—A workbook manual for elementary teachers* (5th ed.). Nashville, TN: Vanderbilt University.

Evertson, C. M., & Harris, A. H. (1999). Support for managing learning-center classrooms. In H. Jerome Freiberg (Ed.), *Beyond behaviorism: Changing the classroom management paradigm.* Boston: Allyn & Bacon.

Evertson, C. M., & Neal, K.W. (2006). *Looking into learning-centered classrooms— Implementations for classroom management.* Washington, DC: National Educational Association.

Evertson, C. M., & Randolph, C. H. (1999). Perspectives on classroom management in learning-centered classrooms. In Hersholt C. Waxman & Herbert J. Walberg (Eds.), *New Directions for teaching practice and research.* Berkeley, CA: McCutchan.

Marchant, G. J., & Newman, I. (1996). Mentoring education: An interview with Carolyn M. Evertson. *Mid-Western Educational Researcher, 9,* 26–28.

Randolph, C. H., & Evertson, C. M. (1994). Images of management for learning-centered classrooms. *Action in Teacher Education, 16,* 55–63.

Weinstein, C. S. (1999). Reflections on best practices and promising programs: Beyond assertive classroom discipline. In H. Jerome Freiberg (Ed.), *Beyond behaviorism: Changing the classroom management paradigm*. Boston: Allyn & Bacon.

Wong, H. K., & Wong, R. T. (1998). *How to be an effective teacher: The first days of school*. Mountain View, CA: Harry K. Wong Publications.

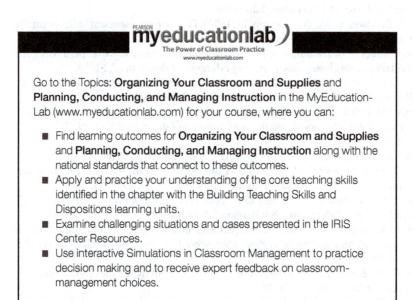

PEARSON
**myeducationlab** )
The Power of Classroom Practice
www.myeducationlab.com

Go to the Topics: **Organizing Your Classroom and Supplies** and **Planning, Conducting, and Managing Instruction** in the MyEducation-Lab (www.myeducationlab.com) for your course, where you can:

- Find learning outcomes for **Organizing Your Classroom and Supplies** and **Planning, Conducting, and Managing Instruction** along with the national standards that connect to these outcomes.
- Apply and practice your understanding of the core teaching skills identified in the chapter with the Building Teaching Skills and Dispositions learning units.
- Examine challenging situations and cases presented in the IRIS Center Resources.
- Use interactive Simulations in Classroom Management to practice decision making and to receive expert feedback on classroom-management choices.

# Building Community

## Objectives

Chapter 8 prepares preservice teachers to meet INTASC standards #4 (Instructional Strategies), #5 (Motivation and Management), #6 (Communication), and #9 (Reflective Practitioner) by helping them to

■ evaluate the use of external rewards as a way to control student behavior.

■ learn to distinguish between productive praise and evaluative praise.

■ evaluate the impact of teacher/student interactions on discipline.

■ evaluate the impact of teaching style and strategies on discipline.

- learn to develop a sense of community within the classroom.

- involve students in resolving classroom problems.

- involve students in discussions of curriculum, procedures, and class problems.

- use suggestions by Alfie Kohn to deal with problem behavior.

## Scenario

Preservice teacher Kelly Gaines has been hired to substitute-teach for Daniel Herrera while he is on sick leave. She had spent some time with Mr. Herrera and had thought she was familiar with his classroom-management plan. She is surprised, however, when upon returning from lunch, a student asks if the class has earned a marble for the quiet way in which they have returned to class.

"I don't understand. What do you mean that you earned a marble?"

A student explains, "Mr. Herrera puts a marble in the jar if we walk back from the cafeteria quietly and

in line. When the jar is full, we are given an afternoon with no work."

Confused, Ms. Gaines asks, "But aren't you *supposed* to walk quietly in the hall so that you don't disturb the other classes? Why should you earn a marble for doing what is right?"

The students look to each other, confused by the question. Finally, Kevin tries to explain. "Well, we *always* get a reward for following the rules. *Why else* should we follow the rules?"

# INTRODUCTION

Kelly Gaines is not the first person to question the use of classroom rewards and punishments. In 1996, Alfie Kohn questioned such behavioral approaches to classroom management in a groundbreaking book, *Beyond Discipline: From Compliance to Community.* In this book, Kohn challenges teachers to give up current practices of handling behavioral problems through coercion and reward and to solve problems by providing an engaging curriculum and caring community. Kohn stresses that the ultimate goal of classroom management should not be on simple obedience, but on having students behave appropriately because they know it's the right thing to do and because they can understand how their actions affect other people.

Kohn proposes that the purpose of education is to produce not just good *learners,* but also good *people.* Such a goal, he stresses, cannot be achieved through behavioral techniques. Praise, privileges, and punishments can change student behavior, but they cannot change the student. Kohn contends that behavioral manipulation does not develop a commitment to being a caring and responsible person. Rewarding good behavior does not provide the motivation for continuing to behave appropriately when there is no longer any reward to be gained for doing so. In fact, Kohn maintains that the more teachers control their students through reward systems, the more difficult it is for students to become moral people who think for themselves and care about others (Kohn, 1991, 2006).

Therefore, Kohn stresses that the focus in classrooms must change from an emphasis on curbing negative behaviors to an emphasis on promoting positive ones. Haim Ginott held a similar view and, as early as 1972, noted that ethical concepts such as responsibility, respect, loyalty, honesty, charity, and mercy cannot be taught directly but are taught

---

### Step-by-Step Building Community

To use Building Community in your classroom, you will need to do the following:

1. Evaluate your interactions with students. Is your interaction positive or negative? Determine if you are the source of conflict within the classroom.

2. Evaluate the curriculum. Are you meeting the needs of the students? When students are off-task, ask "What's the task?" Is it appropriate and stimulating?

3. Change from a punisher to a problem solver. Work with students to find solutions to classroom disturbances rather than focusing on means of punishment.

4. Reduce or eliminate you and your students' dependence on extrinsic rewards to achieve desired behavior.

5. Create a classroom community where students value each other and work together cooperatively.

---

through concrete life situations from people one respects. According to Kohn and Ginott, the only way to help students become ethical people, as opposed to people who merely do what they are told, is to have them construct moral meaning. Kohn (1991) suggests that if the goal is to have children take responsibility for their behaviors, teachers must allow students to make decisions about what is right and wrong.

Because Kohn suggests that classroom management involves all classroom activities, his concepts are included as a system of classroom management. He stresses that effective classroom management requires the building of communities, and that to do so, teachers must evaluate the manner in which they communicate with students, find alternatives to traditional punishments, and eliminate the focus on rewards and praise.

## LOOKING AT STUDENT–TEACHER INTERACTIONS

Kohn (2006) proposes that central to effective classroom management are self-evaluations by teachers of what they consider important in the classroom, how they interact with students, and what they ask students to do. Too often, when problems develop, teachers automatically look at the students as the cause without evaluating their own roles in the problem. Kohn notes that teachers must always look first to their responsibility for creating situations.

Kohn (2006) proposes that what is needed is not another discipline plan but a whole new curriculum, because a huge proportion of unwelcome behaviors can be traced to a problem with what students are being asked to learn. In the past, teachers focused only on students who did not do as they were asked, rather than on what it was they were asked to do. When students are asked to spend their days completing endless worksheets, problems are going to develop and students will misbehave to make the time pass faster and to eliminate boredom.

## Tips from the Field

I teach in a rural school, so students are in my classroom for all their high school math classes. Their seventh-grade year begins with me talking about communication and the important role it plays in having a productive class atmosphere. I tell my students that I intend to communicate with every student every day; and if I fail to interact with any one of them, he or she should let me know (this in itself encourages them to communicate with me). The interaction that takes place between my students and me in seventh-grade math sets the tone for the rest of the high school math classes they may take from me.

> Fred P. Strand
> Hatton High School
> Mathematics Instructor
> Hatton, North Dakota
> 2006 North Dakota Teacher of the Year

## ELIMINATING THE USE OF REWARDS AND PRAISE

In 1972, Ginott cautioned teachers and parents about the overuse of classroom praise and suggested that some children might actually get hooked on praise. Kohn (1993a, 1993b) also warned teachers about the overreliance on rewards and praise. In an interview with Brandt (1995), Kohn noted that at least seventy studies showed that extrinsic motivators such as grades, praise, and tangible rewards are not merely ineffective but are also actually counterproductive to producing ethical, responsible individuals. Still, the use of praise and rewards has come to seem so natural to many teachers that even questioning the practice is surprising to them. After all, rewards and praise work. Countless teachers can attest that students will do tasks they dislike and find boring just to earn a sticker, piece of candy, or verbal praise.

Kohn (1991, 1995) objected to the use of praise for several reasons. First, rewards and praise work only for a short while and eventually lose their effectiveness. Unfortunately, the more rewards are used, the more they seem to be needed. Second, many students work for the reward but may never see the value of what they are learning. Learning becomes what one does to get a reward. Kohn identified two dozen studies that show that people expecting to receive a reward from completing a task simply do not perform as well as those who expect nothing. Third, and perhaps most important, Kohn (Brandt, 1995) suggested that much of the praise used by teachers is fundamentally fraudulent, in that the teacher is pretending to talk to the student but is actually using the student to make a point or to criticize the behavior of other students. For example, most teachers would be embarrassed and humiliated if the principal said, "I like the way you come to faculty meetings on time and are always prepared." Yet, such interactions happen in the classroom each day.

**Table 8.1**  Characteristics of Effective Praise

Don't praise students, only what students do.
Make praise as specific as possible.
Avoid phony praise.
Avoid praise that sets up competition.
Give praise in private.
Avoid praising a student's character.
Avoid praise that compares or condescends.

*Sources:* Ginott, H. G. (1972). *Teacher and child: A book for parents and teachers.* New York: Collier Books; Kohn, A. (1993a). *Punished by rewards.* New York: Houghton Mifflin Company.

Unlike Kohn, Ginott (1972) did find some value in praise if the praise is appreciative rather than evaluative. When our statements describe a student's work, action, or accomplishments, the student's self-evaluation is positive and productive. **Appreciative praise does not evaluate personality or judge character.**

Students also make conclusions about themselves when they receive **evaluative praise.** Unfortunately, these conclusions are typically negative and destructive. Evaluative praise is often viewed as a threat and brings discomfort and fear. Ginott (1972) cautioned teachers to avoid praise that attaches adjectives to a student's character. Only praise that places no judgments on a student's character or personality makes the classroom a safe place where students are free to try and to make mistakes. Table 8.1 outlines Ginott and Kohn's suggestions for using praise.

## ALTERNATIVES TO PUNISHMENT

Kohn (2006) encourages teachers to find alternatives to punishment and to treat inappropriate behavior as a problem to be solved together in a supportive classroom community. In such an environment, disciplinary problems become opportunities for conveying values, providing insights, and strengthening self-esteem.

Therefore, Kohn (2006) is critical of traditional discipline programs that focus on punishment. He argues that such programs may temporarily change behavior but cannot help students become ethical adults. He further suggests that the goal of traditional discipline programs is to make children behave a certain way and to comply with adult demands rather than to support or facilitate children's social and moral growth (Brandt, 1995). Too often, in traditional programs, the lesson that is learned is that the price for displeasing adults is pain or embarrassment. Kohn suggests that corporal punishment is the worst example of the impact of traditional discipline, because it teaches children that aggression is acceptable.

More current discipline programs emphasize consequences and choices rather than merely focusing on punishment. In his interview with Brandt (1995), however, Kohn stated that the use of terms like *consequences* and *choices* is misleading. Kohn maintains that in most situations consequences are just **punishment lite,** because the focus is still on controlling students. The creators of these discipline plans suggest that students choose their behavior, but Kohn fears that students actually have no choice, because they must decide between the lesser of two evils: choose to do what the teacher wants or choose to be punished. New disciplines, Kohn argues, are old disciplines with a new twist, designed to appeal to educators who are uncomfortable with the use of bribes and threats.

Kohn's primary problem with both traditional and more current discipline programs is that they fail to achieve what teachers desire and may actually interfere with what teachers are trying to accomplish in the classroom. Central to his argument is that punishment usually works only as long as the punisher is around. Kohn fears that traditional discipline warps the relationship between the punisher and the punished, with the result that the caring relationship between teacher and student is significantly compromised. Perhaps most disturbing is that when students are told to think of the consequences of their behavior, they focus only on the consequences to themselves, never to others. Kohn contends that traditional discipline fails to teach students to be compassionate or caring individuals. Consider the following examples of how traditional discipline fails to achieve what educators desire for their students.

> Nathan has had a hard time concentrating during class. He had accidentally pushed a fellow student as they got on the bus and had been warned that he "would get it" when he got on the bus that afternoon. After observing that Nathan was distracted and had spent most of the morning staring out the window, Ms. Gamez warns, "Nathan, if you don't get back to work, I'm calling your mother and having you stay after school until you complete your work." Having suddenly found a way to avoid the trip home on the bus, Nathan continues to stare out the window.

> As Justin and Kason return to the classroom, they noticed that the door to the storeroom has been left open. Peeking inside, they find boxes of candy that will be sold by the school baseball team for a fund-raiser.
>
> "Wow, look what's here. Grab some," Justin tells Kason as he stuffs a bar of candy in his coat pocket.
>
> "We can't take this. We'll get in trouble."
>
> "Not if we aren't caught. We'll just take one bar from each of the boxes. That way, no one will realize any is missing. It won't matter if no one catches us."

> Laura O'Malley takes a deep breath and flops onto the couch in the faculty lounge. "You won't believe the morning I've had. I have got to find a new discipline plan."
>
> Krystal Mathis turns from the soft-drink machine. "Why? What happened?"
>
> "I have a list of consequences listed beside my rules, and the first time students break a rule, they are given a warning. Then if they break the rule again, they have to write in their behavior journals. Every day, Carman breaks one of the rules.

Today, I had had it and asked him why he continues to do the same thing day after day. You know what he said? He said, 'Well, I always get a warning before it counts, right?'"

As noted, discipline that only produces compliance when the punisher is present is worthless. Therefore, Kohn feels discipline must be much more than punishment. Effective classroom discipline, he suggests, should be a means of helping students become caring, ethical individuals.

## BUILDING A CLASSROOM COMMUNITY

Many teachers fear that if traditional approaches to classroom management are removed as options for dealing with classroom problems, they will be powerless. Kohn (2006) stresses, however, that there isn't just one alternative to traditional discipline strategies, but an unlimited number of options that are available to classroom teachers. These alternative approaches require more than a change in teacher behaviors. They require that teachers and students build a community of learners where it is safe to try new ideas and even to fail. Therefore, according to Kohn (2006), the goal should not be finding another discipline plan but transforming our current educational structures by creating classroom communities where students care about each other, their teachers, and the school.

When students come together on the first day of school, they are a group, not a community. It takes time and the intervention of a caring teacher to create a community within the classroom.

Building a **classroom community** begins with students having a positive relationship with an adult who respects and cares about them. Kohn (2006) stresses that communities are built upon a foundation of cooperating throughout the day, with students continually being allowed to work together. Classrooms should have classwide activities in which students are provided an opportunity to work together toward a common goal. Students acquire a sense of significance from doing significant things, from being active participants in their own education. Finally, academic instruction can be used to build community.

---

### Tips from the Field

When doing group work, I appoint a "job foreman." This person is the leader of the group and has the job of answering questions that may arise, keeping students on-task, praising good work, and reporting to me. Through-out the year, leaders rotate so everyone has a turn.

Mary Schlieder
Norris High School
Firth, Nebraska
2008 Nebraska Teacher of the Year

*Cooperative learning is the key to building a classroom community.*

Community building should not be separate from what students are learning. Students should be provided explicit opportunities to practice **perspective taking,** through which they can imagine how the world looks from someone else's point of view (Kohn, 1997). Activities that promote an understanding of how others think and feel foster intellectual growth while helping students become more ethical and compassionate.

Most of the discussion of how to resolve classroom problems and how to build a community can take place in class meetings. Kohn (2006) states, "Apart from the invaluable social and ethical benefits of class meetings, they foster intellectual development as well, as students learn to reason their way through problems, analyzing possibilities and negotiating solutions" (p. 90). When students meet in a class meeting, they get the positive message that their voices count, they experience a feeling of community, they learn to problem-solve and make decisions, and they develop the ability to reason and analyze (Kohn, 1994).

Kohn (2006) is not an advocate of rule development, for several reasons. First, he finds that rules turn children into little lawyers who look for loopholes and ways around the wording. Second, rules turn teachers into police officers who emphasize enforcement rather than learning. Finally, when rules are broken, the typical reaction is to provide a consequence. Therefore, the emphasis is on punishing students rather than helping them grow into self-disciplined individuals.

Rather than creating rules, Kohn suggests that students engage in conversation about the type of community they wish their classroom to be. He argues that even very young

### Tips from the Field

One of my favorite classroom-management ideas is to put every student's name from a class on a Popsicle stick and place the sticks in a cup. I use these sticks to pick pairs, arrange random small groups, and to call on students randomly when we are discussing concepts in class. (I put the stick back in the cup, so no one is ever "off the hook" after they answer a question). In the beginning of the year, I talk a lot about working with others and the importance of getting along with others. I coach my students not to make any signs (positive or negative) when they are placed in teams so no one's feelings are hurt. I promise them they will work with every other student in the class throughout the year.

Anne Keith
Eighth-Grade Teacher
Chief Joseph Middle School
Bozeman, Montana
2010 Montana Teacher of the Year

children can begin with specific ideas of how they should treat one another. It is the wrestling with a dilemma and discussing conflicting perspectives that is important, not the rules that might be developed from the discussion. In creating rules, the process is the point. Kohn stresses that rules in themselves are not valuable, but the conversation that gives rise to them is.

Kohn (2006) fears that the current structure of most classrooms makes it difficult for a community of learners to be established. He notes that the time restraints of many classrooms, especially those of the middle school and high school, make it difficult to establish the feeling of a community, in that a community cannot be built in forty-five-minute segments. Large classrooms with twenty to thirty students also limit the ability for teachers to get to know each individual student. However, the benefits of building a classroom community outweigh the obstacles in doing so. Schaps and Lewis (1997) found that community building includes the following benefits:

- significantly greater academic motivation and performance
- a liking for school
- empathy and motivation to help others
- an ability to resolve conflict
- greater enjoyment of class
- stronger commitment to key democratic values
- higher sense of efficacy
- increased altruistic behavior

Table 8.2 provides a listing of activities designed to build community within the classroom.

**Table 8.2**   Fifteen Ideas for Building Community Within the Classroom

1.  Believe in the importance of classroom community. Teachers act on their beliefs. If teachers believe in the concept, their actions will convey the same message to students.
2.  Greet students at the door. Check in with students each day to see what is going on in their lives. Don't just appear interested. Be interested.
3.  Assign "study buddies" who help each other to get organized, work on projects, encourage each other, solve problems, and provide peer feedback.
4.  Recognize each student for their uniqueness and the value they bring to the community. This should not be based on accomplishments, but on membership within the community.
5.  Teach perspective taking. Help students understand the sides to issues and the reasons others think and feel the way they do.
6.  Provide opportunities for discussion and debate. Lively debate and discussion are the foundation of a democracy.
7.  Play games. One of the best ways to develop good relationships is to have fun. Games can also be excellent ways to review class material.
8.  Help students find common threads. It is important that students learn about one another and to discover the ways they are similar and different. Games and activities should be developed to help students find the characteristics they share with others.
9.  Use literature to build community. Find common problems and characteristics with characters in books.
10. Conduct classroom meetings. Meetings can be used to share news, discuss academic issues, or resolve classroom problems.
11. Participate in service projects. Help students see that they are part of a bigger community and the contributions they can make to this bigger community. Achieving real goals builds a sense of community.
12. Have classroom jobs. Students who take on a variety of classroom jobs learn how people cooperate and depend on each other within a community.
13. Use cooperative learning. Providing students with an opportunity to work together not only promotes learning but also promotes a sense of community.
14. Use rituals and traditions. Developing rituals and traditions in which everyone participates helps to foster a feeling of comfort and belonging.
15. Share talents. Teach that it takes multiple talents and skills to make a community work. Discover the strengths and talents of each student, and provide them an opportunity to use these talents for the good of the classroom community.

*Sources:* Obenchain, Abernathy, and Lock (2003); Wolk (2003).

## STRATEGIES FOR WORKING WITH DIFFICULT STUDENTS

Disturbances and disagreements are inevitable in a classroom of twenty to thirty students. Kohn (2006) notes that more important than how a teacher deals with these disturbances and disagreements is how the teacher views a discipline situation. Classroom conflict and disagreements should be viewed as an opportunity to help students solve problems and grow. They can be viewed as an opportunity to help students become active participants in their own social and ethical development. Kohn contends, however, that overall misbehavior will diminish when conflict is used as a time to help students think about the feelings of others and to focus on the needs of the entire classroom. Kohn suggests that a more valuable way to view these situations is to see them as an opportunity for students and teacher to work out the problem together.

The success of problem solving depends on many factors, and Kohn provides the following ten suggestions for dealing with difficult students:

1. Develop positive relationships with students. These relationships must be ongoing so that when the teacher interacts with students, they trust the teacher, and they recognize that the teacher has the students' best interest in mind. Kohn (2005) suggests that just as the most effective parenting tool is unconditional love, the most effective discipline tool is unconditional teaching. Students must know that they are cared about and valued regardless of their behavior. Teachers might dislike the behavior, but they must never devalue the student.

2. Help students learn the skills needed to listen carefully, calm themselves, generate suggestions, and understand another's point of view. Many times students aren't reacting appropriately because they don't have the skills to do so. It is the teacher's responsibility to help students develop these valuable skills.

3. Diagnose what has happened and why. This requires that teachers ask lots of questions and carefully listen to the answer.

4. Analyze the teacher's own responsibility in creating the problem. Teachers must question their own practices. Sometimes situations can be resolved with a change in teaching strategies or a change in unrealistic classroom requirements.

5. Maximize student involvement in deciding how to resolve the situations. The process begins with asking the student, "What do you think you can do to resolve this problem?" The teacher should help the student to consider the appropriate options and the possible results of each option.

6. Help students develop authentic solutions to the problem. Too often students give the teacher the solution they think the teacher wants to hear. Refuse to accept pat answers, and force students to develop solutions that are unique to each situation.

7. Assist students in determining how to make restitution or reparations. This may require that students replace items, repair things that are broken, clean up messes they created, or apologize to the person they have wronged.

8. Check back later to see how the plan worked. Students may need to do more work to resolve the situation. In the best case, it provides the teacher with an opportunity to tell students how well they handled the situation.

9. Be flexible in dealing with situations. Sometimes a discussion might need to be delayed until everyone (students and teachers) has had time to calm down and reflect on the situation.

10. Remember that a "working with" approach to problem solving is more time consuming than the "doing to" approach typically taken by teachers. However, the payoff is greater as students learn problem-solving skills that will benefit them throughout their lifetime.

Every teacher will have to deal with students who are challenging. However, Kohn (2006) reminds teachers that the more challenging the student, the more important it is to cultivate a trusting relationship with the student.

## STRENGTHS AND WEAKNESSES OF BUILDING COMMUNITY

Perhaps the greatest strength of Kohn's ideas on classroom management is that they require teachers to consider their interactions with students. They emphasize the strong link between the way teachers talk to students and the way students behave in return. Morris (1996) considers the emphasis on creating a positive rapport between the student and teacher another important feature.

Although many agree philosophically with Kohn, they question how realistic their ideas are in handling typical discipline problems. Kohn has not provided a synthesized model for classroom management. Many of their ideas focus on curriculum and teaching, not discipline. For many teachers, the strategies are too broad to use in addressing the daily problems they encounter. In addition, Manning and Bucher (2001) suggest that many of the ideas presented by Kohn would be appropriate for middle school and high school students but may be inappropriate for younger students.

Some teachers question how to make Kohn's ideas work in classrooms where students have become accustomed to traditional discipline methods. The transition from traditional classroom practice to one in which the focus is on self-responsibility and self-discipline may be very difficult for students and time consuming for teachers.

## BUILDING COMMUNITY IN THE CLASSROOM

### Scenario

First-year teacher Patricia Sagasta had been determined to be different from the teachers she had had as a student. She wanted her students to understand why they should or shouldn't behave a certain way instead of only obeying rules to avoid punishment. So, at the beginning of the school year, she told her students that she wasn't going to establish a list of rules for them, but that they would deal with situations as they arose. Things had gone remarkably well the first four weeks of school and for the most part, Patricia was very proud of how her students had behaved. That was until she had to have a substitute teacher in the room.

After a night of fighting a stomach virus, Patricia called her principal and requested a substitute teacher. She was horrified the next day to find a note from the substitute, Ms. Stewart, saying that Patricia's class was unruly and that she would never again agree to teach that class. Before the students arrived for the day, the principal came by to say that she had been called to Patricia's classroom when several of the students had thrown spitballs at Ms. Stewart. Patricia was surprised and wondered what would have caused such unusual behavior from her students and what she should do to see that the behavior was never repeated.

After roll had been taken and the required reports had been sent to the office, Patricia asks the students to form a circle around her so they can have a class meeting. She begins by saying, "I understand that there were problems yesterday when we had Ms. Stewart as a substitute. I want to read the note left me by Ms. Stewart."

After reading the note, Patricia looks out at a sea of dropped heads. "Now, I think we need to do two things. One, we need to determine why this behavior occurred, and we need to think about the consequences of yesterday's actions."

Immediately, Kortnee's hand goes up. "Ms. Sagasta, I don't think it's fair that we all get punished. Some of us tried to do our work."

"Kortnee, I think you misunderstood me. I haven't said anything about punishment. But since you raised your hand, do you want to tell me why you think things got out of hand yesterday?"

"Well," Kortnee starts as she twists her hair around her finger, "Ms. Stewart wasn't nice like you. She started the day by yelling at us. She said she didn't know what we were supposed to be doing. She wouldn't let us go to the centers, and then she gave us a bunch of worksheets to do. We tried to tell her what we did each day, but she wouldn't listen, and it just made her mad."

Embarrassed, Patricia realizes that she has created part of the problem from the day before. Not expecting to have to miss the next day, the night before she had taken her plan book with her, and there had been no instructions for Ms. Stewart. "Well, class, I have to take responsibility for Ms. Stewart not knowing what she was to do. I took my plan book home, and there were no written plans for her. That is my fault. I should always have plans here in case of an emergency. I think I need to apologize to Ms. Stewart for not doing my job, and I need to make sure I either leave my plan book or I need to have alternative plans for a substitute."

The students look relieved to see that Ms. Sagasta is taking some of the blame. "However," Ms. Sagasta says, "do you think you should have acted as you did yesterday? Let's think of the consequences of your behavior yesterday. Can anyone think of the consequences?"

"Well, I guess we should miss recess today," offers Austin.

"Austin, I wasn't thinking about the consequences for you. I was thinking about the consequences for everyone. For example, how do you think Ms. Stewart felt last night? What do you think she thought about this class?"

Heads drop. Because no one answers, Ms. Sagasta calls on Kyah. "Kyah, if you had been Ms. Stewart, what would you have been thinking and feeling last night?"

"I guess I would have felt bad. I would have wondered if I should substitute-teach. And I would think that this class is bad. I don't think I would have liked us very much."

"Is that how the class wants Ms. Stewart to feel?"

Together the class answers, "No."

"All right, we have discussed how Ms. Stewart feels. How do you think Ms. Anderson thinks or feels?"

Immediately, the class realizes that the principal might now see the class differently. Payton raises his hand and says, "I don't want Ms. Anderson to think we are a bad class. We aren't a bad class. We are a good class."

"Payton, I agree. So we need to think how we can make sure Ms. Anderson sees you that way. All right, were there consequences for anyone other than Ms. Stewart or Ms. Anderson?"

Paige raises her hand. "Ms. Sagasta, do you feel bad about us? Do you not like us anymore?"

"Paige, I still like all of you, but I have to admit I was surprised by your actions. I'm not sure I trust you as much as I did. The class is going to have to win my trust back again."

"Ms. Sagasta, we are sorry. What if we write an apology to Ms. Stewart and to Ms. Anderson? Do you think that would fix things?"

"Well, Paige, I'm not sure everything can be fixed that easily, but I think it is a good first step. Why don't we divide into two groups; one group will write a note to Ms. Anderson, and the second group will write a note to Ms. Stewart."

"Ms. Sagasta, can we have three groups? I think one group should write a note to you."

Smiling, Ms. Sagasta says, "Yes, I think that is a fine idea. We will divide into three groups, and when you finish, you can read your notes to the class. Then if everyone agrees, we will send them around the room so everyone can sign them."

## Summary

Alfie Kohn builds on Haim Ginott's ideas, written some thirty years earlier, that suggested that communication, not rewards and punishments, is the key to effective classroom discipline. Kohn stresses that the ultimate goal of classroom management should be having students behave appropriately because they know it's the right thing to do and because they can understand how their actions affect other people. Therefore, Kohn stresses that the focus in classrooms must change from an emphasis on curbing negative behaviors to an emphasis on promoting positive ones. He stresses that effective classroom management requires the building of communities, and to do so, teachers must evaluate the manner in which they communicate with students, find alternatives to traditional punishments, and eliminate the focus on rewards and praise.

## Key Terminology

Definitions for these terms appear in the glossary.

## Chapter Activities

### Reflecting on the Theory

1. Robert Felts is a very angry, unreachable student. No matter what he is asked to do, he responds with a hostile comment. He calls his classmates names and seems to enjoy challenging and insulting his teachers. Most of his teachers have given up on him because he always has the last word in any confrontation. How would Kohn suggest that teachers work with Robert? Explain your reasoning.

2. In the opening scenario, Ms. Gaines questions why students should be rewarded for doing what is right. Does she have a legitimate concern? Do you agree that there is too much emphasis on extrinsic reward in today's classroom? Imagine a classroom in which no rewards are given. Would such a classroom be possible? Why or why not?

3. Kohn suggests that corporal punishment teaches children that aggression is acceptable. Does corporal punishment still have a place in modern classrooms? Would you be comfortable using corporal punishment to discipline your students? Why or why not?

### Developing Artifacts for Your Portfolio

1. Observe and document the interactions between a teacher and the teacher's students. Were the majority of the interactions positive? Were students praised? If so, what was the reaction to praise? What negative interactions did you observe? What positive interactions did you observe?

2. Create a specific plan for establishing a community in your classroom. What steps will you take to create this community?

### Developing Your Personal Philosophy of Classroom Management

1. Kohn suggests that "the ultimate goal of classroom management should not be on simple obedience but on having students behave appropriately because they know it's the right thing to do and because they can understand how their actions affect other people." Do you agree? How will you manage your classroom in such a way as to help students learn the "right" thing to do?

2. What strategies from "Building a Community" would you incorporate into your classroom-management plan?

## Resources for Further Study

For further information about Alfie Kohn, contact

www.alfiekohn.org

## Chapter References

Brandt, R. (1995). Punished by rewards? A conversation with Alfie Kohn. *Educational Leadership*, 53, 13–16.

Ginott, H. G. (1972). *Teacher and child: A book for parents and teachers*. New York: Collier Books.

Kohn, A. (1991). Caring Kids: The role of the schools. *Phi Delta Kappan, 72*, 494–506.

Kohn, A. (1993a). *Punished by rewards*. Boston: Houghton Mifflin Company.

Kohn, A. (1993b). Rewards versus learning: A response to Paul Chance. *Phi Delta Kappan, 74*, 783–787.

Kohn, A. (1994). The truth about self-esteem. *Phi Delta Kappan, 76*, 272–282.

Kohn, A. (1995). *The risks of rewards*. ERIC Digests–ERIC Clearinghouse on Elementary and Early Childhood: Office of Educational Research and Improvement, Washington, DC. (ERIC Document Reproduction Service No. Ed 376990.)

Kohn, A. (1996). *Beyond discipline: From compliance to community*. Alexandria, VA: Association for Supervision and Curriculum Development.

Kohn, A. (1997). How not to teach values. *Education Digest, 62*, 12–17.

Kohn, A. (2005). Unconditional teaching. *Educational Leadership, 63*, 20–24.

Kohn, A. (2006). *Beyond discipline: From compliance to community* (10th Anniversary Ed.). Alexandria, VA: Association for Supervision and Curriculum Development.

Manning, M. L., & Bucher, K. T. (2001). Revisiting Ginott's congruent communication after thirty years. *Clearing House, 74*, 215–219.

Morris, R. C. (1996). Contrasting disciplinary models in education. *Thresholds in Education, 22*, 7–13.

Obenchain, K. M., Abernathy, T. V., & Lock, R. H. (2003). 20 ways to build community and empower students. *Intervention in School and Clinic, 39*, 55–60.

Schaps, E., & Lewis, C. (1997). Building classroom communities. *Thrust for Educational Leadership, 27*, 14.

Wolk, S. (2003). Hearts and minds. *Educational Leadership, 61*, 14–18.

PEARSON
**myeducationlab**
The Power of Classroom Practice
www.myeducationlab.com

Go to the Topic: **Creating Positive Student–Student Relationships** in the MyEducationLab (www.myeducationlab.com) for your course, where you can:

- Find learning outcomes for **Creating Positive Student—Student Relationships** along with the national standards that connect to these outcomes.
- Apply and practice your understanding of the core teaching skills identified in the chapter with the Building Teaching Skills and Dispositions learning units.

# Discipline without Stress® Punishments or Rewards

## Objectives

Chapter 9 prepares preservice teachers to meet INTASC standards #1 (Content Pedagogy), #2 (Student Development), #5 (Motivation and Management), and #9 (Reflective Practitioner) by helping them to

- use knowledge about human behavior drawn from Discipline without Stress® Punishments or

Rewards to develop strategies for classroom management.

- learn how reward and punishment can be detrimental to student motivation.

- learn techniques for applying Discipline without Stress® Punishments or Rewards in the classroom.

- determine whether they will incorporate Marshall's concepts for classroom management into their personal discipline plan.

- learn to use classroom meetings to manage curriculum and discipline problems.

- use the principles of Discipline without Stress® Punishments or Rewards to deal with problem behavior.

## Scenario

Third-grader Reyes Quintero had always enjoyed being a Cub Scout until Ms. Hampton became the den leader. Ms. Hampton was always unprepared and allowed the boys to run wild rather than engaging the boys in a productive activity. If she did plan a project, she appeared clueless on how to manage the activity. Therefore, Cub Scout meetings usually ended in chaos.

Over the weekend, the boys were to have their first camping experience. Reyes had eagerly anticipated his first camping trip, but when the scouts arrived at the campsite, Ms. Hampton could not get the boys to help pitch the tents or participate in any of the activities she had planned. Frustrated, she took a seat and watched the boys run in a hundred different directions, with no one following directions. Finally, unable to contain himself any longer, Reyes stood on a picnic table, and yelled, "Stop! Stop! This is anarchy. We can't get anything done if you don't listen to Ms. Hampton. Stop acting like this."

Ms. Hampton watched in amazement as the boys not only stopped their misbehavior but also gathered around the picnic table. Once they were gathered, Reyes turned to Ms. Hampton and calmly asked her, "Now, what is it you want us to do?"

When the boys return home, Ms. Hampton ia eager to tell Reyes's parents what Reyes had done. His father quickly explains, "He has learned this at school. His teacher, Ms. Metcalfe, is using some new method of classroom management. Now, Reyes is always describing someone's behavior as anarchy or bullying. I will have to say, however, he is having a very good year. It seems to be working at home as well. The other day, he told his older brother that he was being a bully, and he needed to stop. It was the first time a situation between them hadn't ended in a screaming match and tears. Maybe you should talk to Ms. Metcalfe. She seems to really have her act together when it comes to managing her classroom."

## INTRODUCTION

If Ms. Hampton had taken the time to talk to Reyes's teacher, she would have learned that Ms. Metcalfe was using Marvin Marshall's classroom management strategy, **Discipline without Stress® Punishments or Rewards.** A relatively new classroom-management model, Marvin Marshall's Discipline without Stress® Punishments or Rewards was designed in order to teach students responsible behavior.

The model evolved through Marshall's personal search for a classroom-management plan that was proactive rather than reactive (Marshall & Weisner, 2004). His own teaching and administrative experiences have taught him teachers need a system of classroom management rather than a group of disjointed strategies. Too often, Marshall contends, good classroom management is viewed as a talent some teachers possess and others lack. He suggests that even talented teachers need a systematic plan to meet the needs of today's diverse students and that a systematic approach to classroom management allows all teachers to have a productive learning environment.

## Step-by-Step Discipline without Stress® Punishments or Rewards

To use Discipline without Stress® Punishments or Rewards in your classroom, you will need to do the following things:

1. Discuss Discipline without Stress® Punishments or Rewards with your administrator. Be confident that you have support for your plan.

2. Prepare to teach the concepts of the social development hierarchy. Lesson plans and materials should be prepared in advance.

3. Prepare forms to be completed by students whose behavior advances to the Guided Choices level.

4. Teach the vocabulary of the social development hierarchy. Provide for various learning styles in the classroom by providing multiple ways for understanding the concepts.

5. Check for understanding when misbehavior occurs. Reteach concepts that might be confusing.

6. Provide a form for students who continue to misbehave. Through guided choices students should have an opportunity to evaluate their behaviors and to make plans to change behaviors that do not meet the classroom standards.

7. Keep copies of the completed forms to send to parents in the event that students continue to display inappropriate behavior.

The philosophical basis for Discipline without Stress® Punishments or Rewards comes from what Marshall deems as a response to an important issue facing schools today. Marshall (1998a) notes that in previous generations students came to school with the social skills needed to be successful in the classroom and for the classroom to operate with few disruptions. Today's students, however, have grown up during a time when societal changes have allowed students to enter school without the needed social skills for classrooms to be productive. Therefore, it has become the school's responsibility to do what was once done in the home to help students develop social responsibility. Marshall maintains that behavioral standards must exist in any social relationship and that the classroom is no exception. Appropriate classroom behavior is a result of the awareness of appropriate standards of behavior. Therefore, the foundation of Discipline without Stress® Punishments or Rewards is a hierarchy of social development, which helps students increase self-responsibility, social awareness, and social responsibility.

According to Marshall (1998a) the teaching of social responsibility cannot occur in the traditional school environment of telling, punishing, and rewarding. Therefore, Discipline without Stress® Punishments or Rewards rejects the reward/punishment concepts of most classroom management models. Marshall notes that too often teachers and administrators try to motivate students by advising, cajoling, exhorting, rewarding, demanding, and punishing. However, these external approaches typically work only when the adult is present. They do little to motivate the student to display responsible behavior when the teacher or administrator is not present. The real power of teachers is in what students do when teachers are not available to supervise. The goal is that students will display appropriate behavior whether the teacher is present or not.

Marshall and Weisner (2004) stress that administrators and teachers have a hard time imagining a classroom in which they do not constantly tell students what to do, punish them if they resist, and reward them if they comply. However, Marshall suggests that these traditional methods of classroom management are coercive and manipulative and teach students they are not responsible for their own actions and choices. The focus of these methods is on external control.

For the same reason, Marshall has issues with rewards and incentives and notes that giving rewards for meeting expected standards of behavior conveys a false message. The practice of rewarding students for acting appropriately conveys the message that responsible behavior for its own sake is not good enough—that one needs to receive something in order to be motivated to act appropriately and responsibly. Again, the focus is on external motivators, rather than internal motivation for controlling and changing one's own behavior. To truly change behavior, Marshall stresses, it is important to tap into internal motivation.

Discipline without Stress® Punishments or Rewards is drawn from the theories of Steven Covey, Abraham Maslow, Douglas McGregor, William Glasser, and W. Edwards Deming. However, it is the philosophy and ideas of William Glasser (see Chapter 1 for a discussion of William Glasser) that has most shaped the system. Similar to Glasser's model of Choice Theory, Discipline without Stress® Punishments or Rewards encourages teachers to

- allow students to take responsibility for their own behavior.
- use a noncoercive approach to classroom management.
- spend little time determining the motivation for a behavior.
- teach students they choose their responses—regardless of the situation.
- view misbehavior as a teachable moment instead of a problem.
- ask questions that effectively guide students to reflect and self-evaluate.
- establish a safe environment for all students (Marshall and Weisner, 2004).

## THE THEORY

In order to move students from behavior based on personal desires and goals to one of increasing social responsibility, Marshall created a hierarchy of social development—a way to explain human social behavior in simple terms everyone would understand (Marshall, 1998a). The hierarchy is based on the ABCDs of social development: **A** = Anarchy, **B** = Bullying or Bothering, **C** = Conformity, and **D** = Democracy. The least desirable level is Level A (Anarchy) and the highest level is Level D (Democracy). Table 9.1 provides examples of the ABCD hierarchy.

**Table 9.1**   Discipline without Stress® Punishments or Rewards

| Corresponding Letter | | Level of Behavior | Description of Behavior |
|---|---|---|---|
| D | Acceptable Behavior | Democracy | Shows kindness to others |
| | | | Develops self-reliance |
| | | | Does good because it is the right thing to do |
| | | | Develops self-discipline |
| | | | *Motivation is internal* |
| C | | Cooperation/Conformity | Listens |
| | | | Does what is expected |
| | | | Complies |
| | | | Considerate |
| | | | *Motivation is external* |
| B | Unacceptable Behavior | Bullying/Bothering | Bosses others |
| | | | Bothers others |
| | | | Breaks classroom standards |
| | | | Responds to authority |
| | | | *Motivation is external* |
| A | | Anarchy | Noisy |
| | | | Out of control |
| | | | Unsafe |
| | | | *Motivation is external* |

*Source:* Marshall (2004).

## Anarchy

The lowest level of Marshall's hierarchy is that of **Anarchy.** Anarchy is the least desirable level of social behavior, and classrooms operating at this level are without social order or are in chaos. Students functioning at this level are noisy, fail to follow commands, and move throughout the classroom without permission. Anarchy is behavior in which there is no law or order, and anyone can do anything he or she wants to do without consideration for anyone else. Although individual students within classrooms may be behaving at the anarchy level, the entire classroom may also be in anarchy. This typically happens when teachers are unprepared or lack withitness. Substitute teachers and student teachers can also face classrooms in chaos because students operating at this level look for authority from the adults. If the teacher is hesitant to take control of the classroom, the students will take over the classroom. Some examples of classrooms and students operating at this level follow.

> First-year teacher, Jessica Malick, is starting to think she has made a poor career choice. If she allows her students to participate in any fun activities, she quickly loses control and the classroom erupts in chaos. Therefore, she has succumbed to the lure of worksheets and tries to keep the students busy by the threat of more handouts and increased homework. She hates coming to school each day and suspects her students do as well.
>
> When substitute teacher Michael Smith arrived at this assignment for the day, he was amazed to find a sea of ninth-graders moving around the room and totally ignoring his demands for them to take their seats. After thirty minutes of trying to get the students on-task, Mr. Smith walked to the office and suggested they send an administrator to take over for the day since he was going home.

## Bullying

The second level of Marshall's social development hierarchy is that of **Bullying** and **Bothering.** Students who operate at this level of social development bully other students and, in some cases, the teacher as well. They make up their own rules. They boss others, behave boisterously, break rules, violate the rights of others, and behave correctly only when the threat of punishment looms. Students who bully or bother only obey when authority figures are present. Bullying or bossing behavior impacts the entire classroom because little learning takes place when students are in constant fear of being bullied. Marshall (2004) notes that most children have no problem with the term "bullying," but that some teachers do. Therefore, "Bothering" is an alternate choice for these teachers.

If a bully prevails, irresponsible and provocative behavior will be repeated, and patterns will be learned that carry throughout life. Therefore, bullying behavior is not only detrimental to those being bullied but also for the bullies as well. Marshall (2004) provides the following suggestions for teachers who have students who bully or boss:

1. Never label or call a student a "bully." Focus on the behavior, not the character of the student.

2. Identify the behavior as "bullying or bothering behavior."

3. Help students take responsibility for behavior.

---

### Tips from the Field

I added "Bugging" and "Breaks classroom procedures" to Level B. I also added "A piling on" to Level A because I use a football analogy. Some students choose to tease other students. This is hurtful behavior. I explain to my students that in order to learn, they must (1) follow classroom procedures and (2) meet behavior standards.

Jim Mann
High School Teacher

Bullying occurs at all ages; however, bullying that occurs in the first grade will be different from bullying that occurs in the fourth grade, where name calling and similar activities are often more subtle. Some examples of students operating at the bullying/bossing level follow.

> First-grader Dwayne Watkins causes a constant disturbance in his classroom. Dwayne grabs whatever he wants to play or work with and if the other students resist, he hits and bites them.

> When ninth-grade teacher Tyrone Watkins comes in from hall duty, he finds April Richardson in tears. He walks over to April and gently touches her arm. "April, what is wrong? Are you feeling all right?" Wiping her tears away, April explains, "Jessica and Tammy are spreading rumors about me. They told everyone I got drunk after the ball-game last week. Why would they tell a lie about me? I thought I was their friend."

> Twelfth-grader Matt Darnell enjoys his reputation for giving teachers a hard time. He loves to argue and can waste an entire hour arguing over a missed point on a test or a statement he thinks is incorrect.

Marshall and Weisner (2004) stress that neither anarchy nor bossing/bullying is an acceptable level of classroom behavior. Students who display such behavior must come to understand their behavior is unacceptable and develop a means for changing the behavior.

## Cooperation/Conformity

Marshall (2004) identifies the next level of behavior on his hierarchy as **Cooperation/ Conformity.** This level of behavior is acceptable and desired as cooperation/conformity is as essential for a classroom to function as it is for a society to exist. Students operating at this level comply and cooperate with expected standards. The students are connected to the teacher and each other and involved with others in an appropriate manner.

Conformity is a result of accepting external influences. In a classroom, it is essential for classroom success for students to conform to the expected standards of behavior. Because conformity is a result of external influence, however, it is not at the highest level of the hierarchy.

Conformity can lead to unacceptable behavior if students are trying to seek the approval of peers. Marshall (2004) stresses that it is important for students to come to understand the external influences on their behavior and suggests that when they realize they are being controlled by external forces, they begin to feel liberated. Through awareness and discussions about the impact of allowing others to influence their decisions, adolescents can resist group temptations of an "antilearning" subculture. Understanding peer pressure helps young people to become more autonomous and to decide against engaging in socially irresponsible acts, both inside and outside of school.

Students have a strong need to conform—both for good and for bad behaviors. Some examples of students functioning at the cooperation/conformity level follow.

> Middle school principal Lane Blackwell enjoys watching his students as they get off the school buses and enter school. He is amazed at the way students dress; and the creative ways they approach the school dress code and how fast a trend sweeps through the school. Therefore, he is careful to watch what twins Tanner and Tyler Burkhart wear as they are the first to wear the latest fad. Fortunately, Mr. Blackwell has learned

that if he can talk to the two boys and explain why he feels what they are wearing is inappropriate, they will quickly change their style and comply with the school standards. By asking these two school leaders to comply, other students follow their lead and the dress code of the school as well.

Third-grade teacher Mattie Cook has established a weekly list of classroom tasks for her students. Each Monday, the students draw the tasks they will do for the week. By having her students take responsibility for many of the routine needs of the classroom, Ms. Cook has learned she has more time to work with students and that the students are learning to be responsible.

The students in Mr. Evans's class had enjoyed a presentation by a member of the local historical society. When the speaker gathered up her materials and prepared to leave, Mr. Evans turned to Logan and Lucas and asked the boys to help take the material to the speaker's car. The boys quickly jumped to their feet and helped the speaker.

## Democracy

The ultimate goal for any teacher or administrator is that students understand right from wrong and do something simply because it is the right thing to do (Marshall, 2004). As students grow, mature, cultivate manners, and develop values of right and wrong, the prompts for civility become internalized. Marshall refers to the highest level of his social development hierarchy as **Democracy.** It is at this level that students take responsibility for their own behaviors.

At the democracy level of the hierarchy, the motivation to be responsible is internal. Rather than relying on external motivators to influence their behavior, students derive their rewards from self-satisfaction. Rewards at this level come not from stickers, candy, and praise, but from self-satisfaction because one has acted responsibly. Democratic behavior is shown by the student who develops self-reliance, civility, and a sense of responsibility for the classroom. Students choose good behavior from a sense of self-evaluation and self-correction. Examples of students operating at the democracy level of behavior follow.

When fifth-grade teacher Lynn Morris heard a knock on her classroom door, she was surprised to see the head of the local school board and the principal. She learned the principal was giving the school board chair a tour of the school, and they were visiting each classroom. Before talking briefly to her guests, Ms. Morris turned to the classroom and asked if Carson would come to the overhead and continue with the lesson. Without hesitation, Carson and the rest of the students continued with their math lesson while Ms. Morris visited with her guests.

The principal of Northeast High School was very disappointed to learn that a few of his students had painted graffiti on their rival school's wall after a big loss. However, his faith in his student body was restored at midmorning when a group of students arrived at his office with a collection of money to buy paint and materials. They explained they would like to repaint the rival school's wall to make up for the bad behavior of some of their classmates.

The students in Mr. Evans's class had enjoyed a presentation by a member of the local historical society. When the speaker gathered up her materials and prepared to leave, Logan and Lucas quickly jumped to their feet and volunteered to help the speaker take the materials to her car.

*Class meetings provide a way for students to resolve classroom conflicts before they escalate.*

The last example above is identical to the last one for Cooperation/Conformity except that this time Logan and Lucas offer to help the speaker without being asked. Therefore, they took responsibility for their own behavior. Marshall (2004) notes that the primary difference between C and D behavior is motivation, not action. If a student cooperates and performs a task at the teacher's direction, the student is acting on Level C. The student has complied with the teacher's direction and, of course, the behavior is acceptable. However, if the student performs the task without being asked, then the student is operating at Level D. The motivation on Level C is external, but the motivation on Level D is internal. Marshall (2004) states that a critical component for growth and development is for students to understand the difference between Level C (external motivation) and Level D (internal motivation).

## THE PROCESS

Marshall (1998a) identifies three phases of Discipline without Stress® Punishments or Rewards:

1. Teaching vocabulary and concepts (proactive teaching)
2. Checking for understanding (effective questioning)
3. Using Guided Choices (if necessary, using authority without punishment)

## Teaching the Concepts

The process of implementing Discipline without Stress® Punishments or Rewards in a classroom begins by teaching the social development hierarchy. Marshall (2004) suggests that this process appeals to teachers because teaching is something teachers understand and embrace. During the initial learning phase, reference is made to the name of each level: anarchy, bullying, conformity, and democracy. However, after becoming familiar with the ABCDs of the social development hierarchy, the terms are no longer used and reference is made only to their letters.

The manner in which the concepts are taught will depend on the age of the students, their maturity level, and the subject matter. Just as no teacher would introduce a concept and assume students understand it, the same is true for teaching the social development hierarchy. Teachers must present the material in a variety of ways, drawing on as many learning modalities as possible. The key to teaching social development is to make the examples relevant to the community of learners (Marshall, 1998a). **Teaching the Concepts** requires more than just introducing and defining the vocabulary. Students must be actively engaged in constructing examples of each level specific to their situations. This is accomplished by engaging students in activities in which they relate their own experiences to the various levels. For example,

> To help her first-graders understand difficult concepts such as anarchy, bullying, conformity, and democracy, Ms. Myatt gives each student a sheet of paper with one of the terms written on the top. The students are to then draw a picture that they think identifies the term in some way. Students are then given an opportunity to share their work with the classroom.

### Tips from the Field

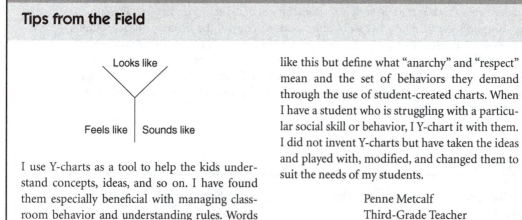

I use Y-charts as a tool to help the kids understand concepts, ideas, and so on. I have found them especially beneficial with managing classroom behavior and understanding rules. Words like anarchy and respect are relatively abstract to six-, seven-, and eight-year-olds. I still use words like this but define what "anarchy" and "respect" mean and the set of behaviors they demand through the use of student-created charts. When I have a student who is struggling with a particular social skill or behavior, I Y-chart it with them. I did not invent Y-charts but have taken the ideas and played with, modified, and changed them to suit the needs of my students.

Penne Metcalf
Third-Grade Teacher
East Manjimup Primary School
Western Australia

A third-grade teacher helps her students understand the social development hierarchy through literature. She reads, *Miss Nelson Is Missing* and has the students identify the levels of behavior displayed by the children in the story.

The students in Mr. Maynard's fifth-grade classroom are given large index cards. On the cards they are to write each of the four levels of social development and give examples of the behavior. The students then tape the index cards to the corners of their desks as a constant reminder of the social development hierarchy.

Ninth-grade teacher Jessica Morris has her class divide into teams and prepare a skit depicting each level of the social development hierarchy.

According to Marshall (1998a, 2004), teaching the social development hierarchy is the foundation of the entire strategy because it

- fosters communications. The vocabulary brings clarity to the different levels within the social development hierarchy.
- creates awareness of social responsibility as a value.
- encourages students to exercise self-control and individual responsibility.
- emphasizes that students choose their own level of behaviors.
- encourages students to see their role in maintaining an environment conducive to learning.
- helps students to distinguish between appropriate and inappropriate behavior.
- raises awareness for responsible citizenship.
- calls attention to the fact that students are constantly making choices and that students choose their own level of behavior.
- empowers students by allowing them to analyze and correct their own behavior.
- encourages students to go beyond simply showing acceptable behavior and to take more and more responsibility for themselves and their classmates.
- encourages mature decision making.
- focuses on labeling behavior, not people.
- fosters an understanding of internal and external motivators.
- leads to improved self-esteem.
- serves as the first part in a three-part strategy to create and maintain a positive, noncoercive learning environment at all times.

## Checking for Understanding

Marshall (1998b) notes that the first two elements of Discipline without Stress® Punishments or Rewards are based on the cognitive learning theory of teaching the concepts and then testing by checking for understanding. This is an important concept to understand as learning a new behavior is similar to learning new subject area content. Therefore, just as a teacher would not punish a student for struggling to learn new content, Marshall contends students should not be punished as they learn new behaviors.

**Checking for Understanding** is direct intervention for students who struggle with behaviors at the A or B level. It is used when students demonstrate socially unacceptable behavior by disrupting the class. This begins by establishing that the teacher is not going to punish students but is interested in having students develop self-control and social responsibility. Therefore, attention to inappropriate behavior is first brought to the student's attention through unobtrusive techniques such as proximity control and nonverbal means. Such means include the following:

- Establishing eye contact with the student. If necessary, looking at the disrupting student for a second or longer beyond normal sends an effective nonverbal message.

- Using facial expression. However, this should not be typical scowl of the "teacher look." A smile or nod can be just as effective.

- A change in voice, such as using a pause, inflection, or reducing.

- Moving to a new location in the room or moving into the student's space.

- Giving a signal for attention, such as raising hands or ringing a bell.

- Making a request such as "Thank you for your attention" or "Please ask yourself if what you are doing meets the standards of the class."

If the behavior continues, the teacher then uses questions to check for understanding. However, this is never done in a coercive or negative manner. The purpose is to guide the student in acknowledging the level of behavior, rather than to punish. Therefore, the dialogue is not confrontational. In this phase, students are not asked to describe the behavior, just the behavioral level of the behavior. Marshall (2004) notes the teacher has not given up authority by using this method as the person who asks the questions controls the situation. When students can make choices, however, regardless of how small they are, their dignity can be preserved and confrontations can be avoided.

The student is asked to reflect by identifying the level of chosen behavior. Because a level is referred to, rather than the student's behavior, the student feels no need to be defensive. It is not important to ask why the student did a certain behavior, because the teacher is encouraging awareness, not excuses. "Why" questions engender excuses, and as Marshall (2004) notes, many students do not know or understand why they behave as they do. Asking why gives the student an excuse not to take responsibility.

Although it is typically preferable to speak to students about misbehavior problems on a one-to-one basis, an advantage of the checking for understanding strategy is that the questioning can be done in front of the class without alienating the disruptive student. An additional advantage to the strategy is that instructional time is not wasted during the short teacher–student interchange because the levels of social development are being reinforced to the entire class. After the student acknowledges the level of behavior, the teacher continues with the lesson.

Marshall (2004) has found if teachers take sufficient time to teach the concepts and vocabulary of the social development hierarchy, the second element, checking for understanding, is required for only 15 percent to 20 percent of the students. In addition, he has found once students acknowledge the level of behavior, the misconduct stops. The majority of students, from kindergarten to about grade nine, apologize in addition to describing the level of behavior. The teacher does not ask a student to apologize. Marshall (2004) stresses the apology is offered as a natural byproduct of accepting responsibility and realizing that the behavior was not socially responsible.

> Seventh-grader Carson Ballesteros is having a hard time staying on-task. His teacher, Ms. Thornington, had given him a long look when she heard him tapping his pencil on the edge of his desk as he finished an assignment, and after a few seconds, Carson had stopped tapping his pencil. Now, she looks up to find him flipping paper wads at his friend Josh. Walking beside him, she quietly asks, "Carson, what level of behavior are you displaying?"
> Caught, Carson answers, "Level B."
> "Well, is your behavior helping you or Josh finish our assignment?"
> Carson drops his head and picks up his pencil so he can finish is work, "I'm sorry. I'll get back to work."

## Guided Choices

Marshall (2004) maintains that choice, self-control, and responsibility are so woven together one significantly affects the others. When a student makes a choice, self-control is enhanced. When they fail to choose, self-control is diminished. **Guided Choices** is the last part of Marshall's three-part strategy and is designed to provide choice to students and to foster responsible behavior. By using guided choices, the teacher maintains authority without being confrontational. Because the student has a choice, power and respect are retained and confrontations are avoided.

Guided Choices are used when students have acknowledged that their behavior is at the A or B level of the social developmental hierarchy, yet continue the behavior. During the second phase, Checking for Understanding, students were asked to acknowledge the level of their behavior. In Guided Choices, students are asked to go a step further and not only identify the level of behavior but also to evaluate the choices they are making. The strategy is to offer choices in the form of questions (Marshall, 2004). Rather than confronting and punishing, the teacher asks the student to complete a form that asks three questions:

1. What did I do?

2. What can I do to prevent it from happening again?

3. What will I do in the future?

Any form can be used for answering these questions as long as it fosters student thinking and reflection and it involves future planning.

Having students answer these three important questions shapes their thinking by the self-evaluation process. As students answer the questions they come to see they have choices in the behaviors they display. They learn that although they may have little control over the thoughts that spring into their minds or their initial emotions to these thoughts, they do choose their responses to both their thoughts and their emotions.

Through Guided Choices, students come to see the external forces controlling their behavior. Helping students understand they have a choice in how they respond to any situation helps them see they are in control of their actions and responses. It releases them from the external controls that may be influencing their behavior and prevents them from becoming victims. Marshall (1998a) states that teaching young people about choice-response thinking may be one of the most valuable thinking patterns a teacher can provide.

At the end of the class, the student and the teacher have a short discussion regarding the completed form. The teacher makes sure the student understands why it is necessary to complete the form. One way to show the student the teacher is interested only in the student's growth and not in punishment is for the teacher to ask the student what should be done with the form. Together they can decide if the student will keep the form as a reminder of the desired behavior or if the form should be thrown away. It is not necessary to keep the form as it has served its purpose in that it stopped the disruptive behavior and fostered self-evaluation (Marshall, 2004).

If a student continues to disrupt the classroom, a Self-Diagnostic Referral is the next stop. The self-diagnostic form requires a much deeper depth of analysis and may contain such questions as

- What happened that resulted in your being required to complete this form?
- What was the level of your behavior and did that behavior meet the standards of this classroom?
- Is this level of behavior helping you get the things you need from this class?
- On what level should you have acted to be socially responsible?
- What is your plan to show responsible behavior?
- What are your procedures to implement the plan?

Marshall (2004) stresses that students should feel they still have choices. Therefore, the form is handed to the student while asking in a noncoercive tone, one of the following questions: (a) "Would you rather complete the activity in your seat or in the rear of the room?" (b) "Would you like to complete the form now or at the end of this class?" (c) "Would you rather complete the activity in the classroom or in the office?"

The process changes if the student is required to complete a second self-diagnostic referral form. At this point, Marshall (1998a) suggests a copy of the first and the second forms be sent to the parents along with a note from the teacher. If a third referral becomes necessary, a rule of "three strikes and you are out" can reasonably be employed. Copies of all three self-diagnostic referrals should be mailed to the parent along with a second parent note indicating the teacher has exhausted every means to foster social responsibility and the student is being referred to the principal for further action.

Guided Choices fulfills four purposes:

1. It stops the disruption.
2. It isolates the student from the class activity.
3. It gives the disrupting student a responsibility-producing activity to encourage reflection.
4. It allows the teacher to return to the lesson promptly.

Marshall (2004) describes Guided Choices as a win-win situation. The teacher wins by using a nonconfrontational guidance approach that avoids stress. The student wins because dignity has been left intact. When disruptive behavior is thought of as a learning opportunity rather than as a punishment opportunity, everyone wins.

## PROMOTING A POSITIVE CLASSROOM ENVIRONMENT

To promote a positive classroom environment, Marshall suggests several strategies to complement Discipline without Stress® Punishments or Rewards. Specifically, he suggests teachers

- evaluate their instruction.
- conduct class meetings to promote democracy in the classroom.
- identify standards for appropriate behavior.
- use praise and rewards appropriately.

### Evaluating Instruction

Marshall (1998b) suggests that many students would rather be disruptive than stupid. Therefore, the classroom disruptions may be a result of problems with instruction or the lesson. The more the student understands the lesson, the less likely it is that there will be any disruption. So-called discipline problems often stem from faulty instruction. Good instruction reduces behavior problems. Lessons need to be planned so

1. students understand why the lesson is meaningful.
2. the lesson involves thinking on various levels.
3. students become actively involved in learning.

Therefore, when a student disrupts a lesson, the teacher needs to reflect on whether the disruption is related to curriculum, instruction, classroom management, or discipline. Differentiation can guide the teacher to the most affective resolution of the problem.

### Conducting Class Meetings

As mentioned earlier, the endeavors of William Glasser greatly influenced Marshall's work. One strategy initially advocated by Glasser that Marshall has incorporated into his theory is the use of classroom meetings. As early as 1969, Glasser suggested regular class meetings be held to decide how to best conduct the business of school. Glasser stressed that the cause of 95 percent of discipline problems in schools is because students feel that no one will listen to them. By having regular class meetings in which problems are aired, the majority of discipline situations are eliminated.

Marshall (2004) agrees that classroom meetings provide excellent opportunities for students to practice communication and socialization skills. Such meetings facilitate the

**Table 9.2**  Objectives for Class Meetings

- Improves communications skills of listening and speaking
- Provides opportunities for insightful, creative, and critical thinking
- Teaches the process of respectful interaction
- Promotes teamwork
- Increases social intelligence and empathy
- Fosters social skills
- Teaches trustworthiness and fairness
- Reduces anonymity
- Promotes feeling of acceptance and worthiness
- Builds trust and caring relationships between students and teacher and between all students
- Creates a sense of community
- Provides an avenue for students to talk about subjects that interest, affect, or concern them

*Source:* Marshall (2004).

solving of many classroom problems and engender both improved instruction and student learning. Class meetings can serve specific purposes such as instructional reflection, discussion of pertinent items, articulation and application of the values schools engender toward civility, character development, and problem solving. Table 9.2 outlines the many objectives of classroom meetings.

In classroom meetings the process is the point. During the process of discussing issues of interest and concern to both students and teachers, teachers develop a closer relationship with their students. Students benefit because they learn to listen attentively to classmates. The process fosters empathy as students learn to set aside their own desires, views, and values as they hear what others have to say.

Effective class meetings consist of three key parts in addition to rehearsing the procedures at the beginning and, on some occasions, summarizing at the end. The first part is a clarification of the topics to be discussed to ensure everyone understands the issues or topics. The second part, personalizing, gives participants the opportunity to relate the topic to their own knowledge and experiences. The third part provides an opportunity for the teacher to stretch the students' minds by applying the ideas to hypothetical questions or situations.

The role of the teacher during class meetings is to facilitate the discussion, not control the discussion. The teacher's role includes reviewing the procedures, posing some questions, monitoring participation, avoiding judgment, and concluding the session.

## Identifying Standards for Appropriate Behavior

Marshall (2009) does not advocate the use of rules in the classroom as he thinks they are counterproductive to producing the type of relationship desired in the classroom. He notes that rules are meant to control and can create adversarial relationships. He suggests rules can actually create problems in the classroom if

- rules are unclear.
- rules are perceived as unfair or are inconsistently enforced.
- rules cause students to look for loopholes around the rules.
- rules require consequences for when the rule is broken.

Instead of rules, which focus on *do's* and *don'ts*, Marshall (1998b) advocates a proactive approach that involves explaining standards and expectations as they connote a positive orientation. Expectations empower students and promote personal responsibility. They tap into internal motivation and foster commitment, rather than compliance.

## Using Praise and Rewards Appropriately

Although Marshall (1998c) agrees rewards can serve as great incentives, he stresses that they should not be used for expected standards of behavior as giving rewards for expected behavior is counterproductive to fostering social responsibility. Instead, he advocates the use of acknowledgments, recognition, and validation as they encourage and motivate without placing a value on the person. Acknowledgments simply affirm and foster self-satisfaction. They serve to give recognition to what the student has accomplished.

Unlike praise, which is often based on the desires of the adult, acknowledgments focus on what the student has done well. Praise often starts with a reference to oneself: "I am so proud of your grades," or "I like the way you are working." Such statements are viewed as patronizing. Acknowledgments focus on the actions which might include statements such as "Your grades show a great deal of effort," or "You are working hard on your project." It is a simple acknowledgment of the deed and does not carry an evaluation of the person.

## STRATEGIES FOR DEALING WITH DIFFICULT STUDENTS

Marshall acknowledges that some students will require special attention in order to help them become more responsible. At no point does he advocate punishing students, however, because he feels punishment (whether it is called punishment or consequences) is counterproductive to a positive teacher–student relationship (Marshall & Weisner, 2004).

Marshall (2004) states, "People pressured against their will keep the same opinion still" (p. 46). Too often teachers punish because they know nothing else to do, and punishment operates on the theory that young people must experience pain in order to grow into responsible adults. Clearly, punishment is ineffective with far too many young people and, at the best, is temporary and transitory. Punishment has little effect on fostering desired long-term changes because it deprives young people of taking responsibility for their own actions.

Instead, Marshall (2004) suggests that classroom disruptions should be seen as a teachable moment and as an opportunity to teach social responsibility. This doesn't happen in an atmosphere where students fear punishment. Social responsibility is learned with a guiding approach rather than a telling, punishing approach. Therefore, rather than punishment, Marshall (2010) suggests the following strategies for working with difficult students:

- Use positive language. The teacher should describe the behavior that is desired rather than focusing on undesirable behavior.

- Empower students with choices. Offering students more than one choice provides them with choices and ownership. This applies to class activities and course assignments.

- Ask reflective questions. Marshall stresses that since teachers can control students only temporarily, and because no one can actually change another person, asking reflective questions is the most effective approach to help students change their behavior.

- Teach impulse control. Students may not know how to stop impulsive behavior and must be taught how to redirect their impulses.

- Give clear, concise directions for transitions. Students with short attentions may have difficulty getting on-task. Reducing the time for transitions by giving clear directions will get all students on-task more quickly.

- Label distractions. Students may not know that their behaviors are distracting to their classmates and teachers. Labeling behavior as distractions increases the likelihood that students will stop and think about what they are doing.

- Ask for the difficult student's help. Explain that you don't have all the answers and need suggestions for how to stop the disruptive behavior.

- Put the difficult student in charge. Having responsibility will keep the difficult student on-task.

- Change behavior by asking the following four questions:
    - What do you want?
    - Is what you are choosing to do helping you get what you want?
    - If what you are choosing to do is not getting you what you want, then what is your plan?
    - What will you do to implement your plan?

## STRENGTHS AND WEAKNESSES OF DISCIPLINE WITHOUT STRESS® PUNISHMENTS OR REWARDS

Discipline without Stress® Punishments or Rewards is one of the fastest growing classroom-management models in the country. It has a large following because teachers and administrators appreciate the emphasis on self-discipline and personal responsibility. Realizing conventional classroom-management models that focus on rewards and punishments fail a great many students, teachers across the country are embracing Discipline without Stress® Punishments or Rewards.

## Tips from the Field

As you strive to create a classroom climate of respect, reward your students when they are following the expectations that the entire class has agreed upon. For example, give your students words of encouragement and praise—not only the generic comments like, "great answer," but also specific feedback such as, "I like the way you connected your answer to what we talked about yesterday. Great job!" When students know that you are focusing on what they are doing well instead of just looking for negative behaviors, they will meet and exceed your expectations!

Jessica Garner
Porter Ridge High School
Spanish Teacher
Indian Trail, North Carolina
2010 North Carolina Teacher of the Year

Conversely, there are those individuals who have concerns regarding the model. One concern is the use of standards or expectations rather than rules. They argue students will encounter rules throughout their lives and they need to understand there are consequences, sometimes severe, when students break society's rules.

Many argue Marshall overlooks some of the serious problems students have by suggesting they simply *choose* to act or respond in certain ways. They suggest teachers must try to understand why students misbehave in order to identify or treat the underlying causes of behavior. Students who are misbehaving as a result of child abuse, drug abuse, malnourishment, rejection, insecurity, loneliness, or emotional distress are not choosing to misbehave and need the intervention provided by caring, competent teachers.

There is an additional concern regarding the terms that make up the vocabulary of the social development hierarchy. Abstract terms such as anarchy, conformity, and democracy are very difficult for young children to comprehend. Perhaps the greatest concern is regarding the use of the term "bullying" to describe much of the misbehavior that occurs in the classroom. Bullying is a distinct behavior and an issue of much concern for parents, teachers, and administrators. Therefore, the second level of behavior on the social development hierarchy might be best described by a different term.

## DISCIPLINE WITHOUT STRESS® PUNISHMENTS OR REWARDS IN THE CLASSROOM

### Scenario

Eleventh-grade teacher Jason Stewart had just started going over notes with his history class when the door opened and Jamelia came in the room. Stopping, he smiled and motioned for Jamelia to go to her desk.

When Jamelia was late again a few days later, Mr. Stewart waited until she had taken her seat and asked, "Jamelia, what level of are you exhibiting when you arrive late to my class?"

Dropping her head, she answered, "I know. It is Level B. I'm sorry. I'll try to be on time from now on. I'm really sorry but—"

Before she could finish her statement, Mr. Stewart said, "It's not necessary to explain why. I just want to make sure you knew that being late did not meet the standards for our class."

A week passed before Jamelia was late to class again. When she entered, Mr. Stewart handed her a form to complete. "Jamelia, I would like for you to complete this form. Would you like to do it now or after class?"

At the end of class, Jamelia brings the completed form to Mr. Stewart. "Mr. Stewart, I am very sorry for coming late. I know when I'm late it disrupts the entire class when I enter the room." Mr. Stewart waits, so Jamelia adds, "But as I filled out this form, I think I thought of a plan to make sure it doesn't happen again."

Motioning for Jamelia to take the seat pulled beside his desk, Mr. Stewart asks, "I'm listening. What is your plan?"

"Well, I have homeroom over in Ms. Henderson's class in the B hallway. Then I have senior English with Mr. Frank in this wing. After English, I have gym. That means I either have to carry my history notebook and book through three periods or I have to go back to B hallway to my locker between gym and this class. By the time I leave the gym, go to the B hallway to my locker, and come all the way back over here, I'm late. If I take all my books to gym class, I have no place to put them. My gym locker will barely hold my clothes and my English book. I can't get the materials for your class in it as well. So, now do you understand why I'm late every day? I'm trying to get from gym to B hallway and then to your class in five minutes."

"I understand, but your lateness does not meet the standards for this class. There has to be a solution. Could we get a locker for you in this hallway?"

"I'm afraid that would just make me late to my afternoon classes. After fourth period, all my classes are in the B hallway. But I was thinking, maybe I could store my history book and notebook in here while I go to gym? I could bring them by on my way to English class and then I could come here after gym class without going to my locker. Would you mind storing my things?"

"No, that would be fine. In fact," he says, looking around the room and walking to a cabinet behind his desk, "you could put them in here. Come in between your homeroom and English class and put your books in this cabinet. Then you can come straight from gym class and be here on time." Mr. Stewart extends his hand to Jamelia, "I'm proud of you. I think you have developed a good plan."

Jamelia shakes his hand. "Thanks for helping me, and thanks for understanding my problem."

## Summary

Discipline without Stress® Punishments or Rewards is a proactive classroom management system that is quickly becoming the system of choice for many teachers. The positive and systematic approach appeals to new and veteran teachers. The program promotes the internal motivation to develop responsibly—both individually and socially. The system consists of three phases: Teaching the Concepts, Checking for Understanding, and Guided Choices. During the first phase, the vocabulary and concepts of the four parts of the social development hierarchy (Anarchy, Bullying, Conformity, and Democracy) are taught with students. During phase two, the teacher checks to determine if the students understand the hierarchy and reteaches it if necessary. When students continue to misbehave, the third phase, Guided Choices, is used to help students make appropriate choices and to take responsibility for their own behaviors.

## Key Terminology

Definitions for these terms appear in the glossary.

Anarchy   159
Bothering   160
Bullying   160
Checking for Understanding   166
Cooperation/Conformity   161

Democracy   162
Discipline without Stress® Punishments
   or Rewards   156
Guided Choices   167
Teaching the Concepts   164

## Chapter Activities

### Reflecting on the Theory

1. When fifth-grader Keith Garrett wasn't allowed to join in a game of kickball, he grabbed the ball and threw it over the playground fence. When his classmates complained, he taunted them by laughing. "I guess no one will play now."

   At which level of the social development hierarchy is Keith's behavior? How would Marvin Marshall suggest the teacher handle Keith's behavior?

2. Both Alfie Kohn and Marvin Marshall place little value on the establishment of classroom rules. Instead, they suggest teachers and students have discussion concerning classrooms expectations and standards of behavior. Where do you stand on the classroom rule issue? Are rules necessary? Is the creation of a set of classroom standards a more positive way of establishing expected behaviors in the classroom?

3. Rather than punishing a student for continued misbehavior, Marshall suggests the use of Guided Choices. Could the requirement of completing the questions be considered punishment by some students? Do you consider Guided Choices a valid way to handle misbehavior?

### Developing Artifacts for Your Portfolio

1. Develop a lesson plan for teaching the social development hierarchy. Write a lesson plan that introduces the concepts or one that focuses on one of the four categories.

2. Reflect on the different levels of the social development hierarchy you have observed in classrooms. Describe the behavior of the students, the level of behavior, and why you feel the behavior fell into each category.

### Developing Your Personal Philosophy of Classroom Management

1. What strategies from Discipline without Stress® Punishments or Rewards would you incorporate into your classroom-management plan?

2. Review the philosophy behind the development of Discipline without Stress® Punishments or Rewards. Does this philosophy match your personal philosophy of classroom management? Which parts would you reject? Why?

## Resources for Further Study

For more information about Discipline without Stress®Punishments or Rewards, contact

Marvin Marshall and Associates
P.O. Box 2227
Los Alamitos, CA 90720
714-220-0678
www.MarvinMarshall.com

## Chapter References

Glasser, W. (1969). *Schools without failure*. New York: Harper and Row.

Marshall, M. (1998a). *Fostering social responsibility. Fastback 428*. Bloomington, IN: Phi Delta Kappa Educational Foundation.

Marshall, M. (1998b). Fostering social responsibility and handling disruptive classroom behavior. *NASSP Bulletin, 82*, 31–39.

Marshall, M. (1998c). Rethinking our thinking on discipline: Empower—rather than overpower. *Education Week, 17*, 32, 36.

Marshall, M. (2004). *Discipline without stress®, punishments, or rewards*. Los Alamitos, CA: Piper Press.

Marshall, M. (2009). *Commonly used counterproductive approaches*. Retrieved March 12, 2010, from http://www.marvinmarshall.com/counterproductive_approaches.htm.

Marchall, M. (2010). *Simple strategies for dealing with difficult students*. Retrieved March 12, 2010, from http://www.marvinmarshall.com/pdf/dealing_with_difficult_students.pdf.

Marshall, M., & Weisner, K. (2004). Encouraging responsible student behavior. *Phi Delta Kappan, 87*, 498–507.

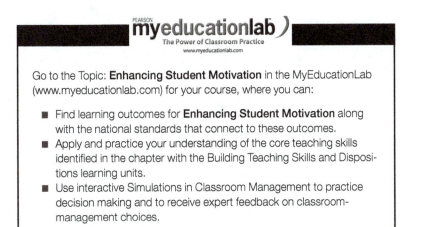

Go to the Topic: **Enhancing Student Motivation** in the MyEducationLab (www.myeducationlab.com) for your course, where you can:

- Find learning outcomes for **Enhancing Student Motivation** along with the national standards that connect to these outcomes.
- Apply and practice your understanding of the core teaching skills identified in the chapter with the Building Teaching Skills and Dispositions learning units.
- Use interactive Simulations in Classroom Management to practice decision making and to receive expert feedback on classroom-management choices.

# PART III
# Classroom Management as Instruction

Four models that have as their central focus the teaching of prosocial skills are presented in Part III: "Classroom Management as Instruction." The first model presented in Chapter 10 is Barbara Coloroso's Inner Discipline. Chapter 11 provides a review of Positive Behavior Support. Several approaches to teaching Conflict Resolution and Peer Mediation are presented in Chapter 12. Finally, Forrest Gathercoal's model, Judicious Discipline, is the focus of Chapter 13. The models presented in Part III share the following characteristics:

- A key to effective classroom management is teaching appropriate behavior and social skills.

- Effective classroom management does not focus on behavior at a particular moment, but on helping students develop positive interactions throughout their lifetime.

- Students must be taught to take responsibility for their behavior.

- The goal of classroom management is to establish habits of peacemaking.

- Teachers must help students learn to make ethical judgments and decisions.

- Teachers must ensure that students' rights are honored and respected.

- Classroom management is a form of guidance.

- Discipline comes from the self, not from outside authorities.

- Students must share in classroom responsibilities.

# Inner Discipline

## Objectives

Chapter 10 prepares preservice teachers to meet INTASC standards #2 (Student Development), #5 (Motivation and Management), #6 (Communication), and #9 (Reflective Practitioner) by helping them to

- evaluate the philosophical tenets upon which Inner Discipline is based.

- understand the basic principles of Reconciliatory Justice.

- learn the importance of communicating six critical life messages to students.

- evaluate classrooms to determine whether they are a jellyfish classroom, brick-wall classroom, or a backbone classroom.

- learn techniques for applying Inner Discipline in the classroom.

- differentiate between punishment and discipline.

- learn strategies for reducing bullying in classrooms and schools.

## Scenario

Entering the biology classroom, eleventh-graders Gus Beebe and Brenton Hatch are cutting up. As Gus playfully punches Brenton in the arm, Brenton falls backward into the lab experiment that has been placed on the table. Before either boy knows what is happening, broken beakers and lab equipment cover the floor. The sound of breaking glass gets the attention of the other students and Ms. Schallenberger.

"Brenton, are you cut or hurt?" Ms. Schallenberger asks as she reaches the boys.

"No, I'm not hurt." Looking around at the destroyed lab equipment, Brenton says, "Gee, Ms. Schallenberger, we're sorry. We didn't mean for this to happen."

"I know you were just joking around, but now we have a big problem—a problem we need to solve quickly. Go to the storage room and get what you need to clean up this mess. While I start class, I want you to clean up this area. Then I want you to sit at the table in the back of the room and think about three things. First, how do you intend to replace the broken equipment? Second, given that your lab equipment is broken, how are you going to do your assignment? Finally, I want you to think of how you are going to keep this from happening again. I want the answer to these three issues when class is over." Turning from the boys, Ms. Schallenberger announces that it is time for class to begin.

## INTRODUCTION

The first model presented as an example of Classroom Management as Instruction is Barbara Coloroso's theory, **Inner Discipline.** Like Ms. Schallenberger, Coloroso is more concerned with having students think about their behaviors and how their behaviors impact others than with providing punishments and consequences for inappropriate behavior. Coloroso (1994) sees the primary role of teachers as guiding students to make their own decisions and to take responsibility for their choices. The model is based on three key concepts:

1. Development of inner discipline is more important than traditional classroom control.

2. Problem solving is key to developing inner discipline.

3. Students must be taught *how* to think, not *what* to think.

---

### Step-by-Step Inner Discipline

To use Inner Discipline in your classroom, you will need to do the following things:

1. Create a classroom environment where students receive important life messages.

2. Establish classroom rules that prepare students for life, not just the classroom.

3. Approach misbehavior as a problem to be solved rather than a discipline issue.

4. Provide real-life consequences when consequences for misbehavior must occur.

5. Teach the concepts of Reconciliatory Justice.

**Table 10.1**  Coloroso's Critical Life Messages for Students

- I believe in you.
- I trust you.
- I know you can handle this.
- You are listened to.
- You are cared for.
- You are very important to me.

*Source:* Coloroso (1994).

Coloroso (1990) contends that through classroom instruction and positive teacher–student interactions, students are empowered to trust in themselves and to learn self-discipline. When students learn the supporting principles,

- I like myself.
- I can think for myself.
- There is no problem so great that it can't be solved.

they are buffered against life's evils such as drug abuse, sexual promiscuity, and suicide.

Coloroso (1994) stresses that empowering students begins with giving them a secure, safe, nurturing environment. Such an environment encourages creative, constructive, and responsible activity (Coloroso, 1997). In this environment, students are encouraged through the communication of one or more critical life messages. These critical messages, which appear in Table 10.1, can be communicated through the teacher's words or actions.

Coloroso suggests that these messages need no definition or explanation. If communicated in a caring, sincere manner, students will accept these messages and be empowered by them.

## THREE TYPES OF CLASSROOMS

Coloroso (1990) observes that schools and individual classrooms in these schools follow one of three models. According to Coloroso, classrooms can be described as jellyfish classrooms, brick-wall classrooms, or backbone classrooms.

The **jellyfish classroom** has no structure. Like a jellyfish, the teacher's expectations are constantly shifting. In such classrooms, punishments are arbitrary and inconsistent. Therefore, students are never quite sure of how they are to act or respond. Students cannot predict whether they will or will not be punished for violations to classroom policy, because punishment is based on gender, ethnicity, or some other personal characteristic rather than on a fixed discipline plan. If there are rules, they are vague and contain phrases like "Be kind" or "Be thoughtful" without giving students a clear meaning of what is expected of them.

---

### Tips from the Field

I want to build a relationship with my students. One way of doing this is through dialogue journals (5"-by-7" spiral notebooks) where students can write about anything they wish, and they put it in a basket on my desk. I take a few home each night and write personal notes to the students, asking them about what they write or praising them for something in class. I also hold weekly class meetings where we discuss problems in class and work out solutions. I stress that we are a community.

Colleen King
First-Grade Teacher
Parkview Elementary School
Carpentersville, Illinois

---

The **brick-wall classroom** is a dictatorship in which rules are rigid and unbending. Like a brick wall, teachers are unyielding in how they handle the classrooms. Individual needs or motivations are not considered when giving consequences for inappropriate behavior. Rules are used to control or manipulate students, and all power is in the hands of the teacher. Often, the students are controlled by physical threats, humiliation, and bribes. In the brick-wall classroom, students are told *what* to think, not taught *how* to think.

The **backbone classroom** provides a consistent structure that is flexible and functional. Students are listened to and learn to respect themselves and others. Students learn to accept their own feelings and to act on these feelings in a reasonable way. In the backbone classroom, students are given second chances, because mistakes are viewed as opportunities to learn. The goal is to teach students how to problem-solve and to think before they act (Coloroso, 1994). Teachers model the desired behaviors by

- acknowledging their own feelings and labeling them.
- admitting that they are angry, hurt, or afraid, and by modeling appropriate ways to express these feelings.
- making assertive statements about themselves.
- acknowledging students' feelings as real and legitimate without passing judgment on those feelings.
- teaching students how to handle their own problems.

## DISCIPLINE IN THE BACKBONE CLASSROOM

The focus of teachers in backbone classrooms is on discipline rather than on punishment. Coloroso (1990, 1994, 2001) stresses that contrary to popular belief, discipline is not synonymous with punishment. To Coloroso, there is a clear distinction between punishment and discipline. Coloroso describes punishment as punitive actions that

- are adult oriented.
- require judgment.

- impose power from without.
- arouse anger and resentment.
- invite more conflict.

Such actions include physical isolation, embarrassment and humiliation, shaming, emotional isolation, grounding, and brute force. Under the guise of discipline, physical and emotional violence toward children is allowed and legitimized. However, Coloroso stresses that teachers should never rely on such actions to promote the positive behaviors teachers desire in their students.

According to Coloroso (1994), discipline differs from punishment because discipline involves real-world consequences or interventions or a combination of both. Discipline deals with the reality of the situation, not with the power and control of the teacher. Discipline gives life to a student's learning in a way that punishment cannot because it

- shows children what they have done wrong.
- gives them ownership of the problem.
- gives them ways to solve the problems they created.
- leaves their dignity intact (Coloroso 1997, 2001).

Discipline allows students to make legitimate choices and to face the consequences of these choices. **Real-world consequences,** according to Coloroso (1994), either happen naturally or are reasonable consequences that are intrinsically related to a student's actions. Although natural consequences are often the greatest learning tool, if the natural consequences are life threatening, morally threatening, or unhealthy, the teacher must intervene and provide real-world consequences that are safe and appropriate.

With real-world consequences, actions and consequences match. Coloroso suggests that teachers use the acronym RSVP to determine whether a consequence is appropriate:

**R**  Is the consequence *reasonable?* For example, it is reasonable to expect students who leave their lunch table dirty to return to the cafeteria and clean up their mess. It is *not* reasonable to require them to clean the entire cafeteria. The first consequence requires students to be responsible for their own behavior, whereas the second punishes them rather than teaches a life lesson.

**S**  Is it *simple?* Many times, when consequences are given, other people are inconvenienced by the consequences. For example, requiring students to miss recess while they complete homework is a simple consequence. Requiring students to come to school on Saturday morning requires coordination among the teacher, the parents, and other school personnel. Although such a consequence might be reasonable, it is not simple.

**V**  Is it *valuable* as a learning tool? Any time a consequence is given, the teacher must analyze the lesson to be learned. In the first two examples, students are taught that they must be responsible for their behaviors. If in the first example, however, the teacher had required the students to write "I will not leave the lunch table dirty" a hundred times on the chalkboard or in their notebooks, the students would have learned little.

## Tips from the Field

After seven years of teaching in both public and private schools, I have learned that if students respect you and know in their hearts that you respect them, management will fall into place. Respect and consistency are the keys and starts from the minute they walk in the door. By consistently showing them that you respect them enough not to degrade or yell at them in front of their peers, they will respect you. I can't emphasise this enough.

Bridget Cantrell
Third-Grade Teacher
Santa Fe Trail Elementary School
Independence, Missouri

**P**   Is it *practical?* Does the consequence take time away from the goal of the class? Often, consequences prevent students from being involved in the classroom and learning the required material. For example, Coloroso (1990) points out that students who are tardy are often required to leave the classroom to retrieve a tardy note. The result is that they are even later to class and have missed even more of the required material. Such a consequence is not practical, because it is counter to the goal of the classroom.

Regardless of how reasonable the consequences of inappropriate behavior are, students will try to get teachers to back down or give in on punishments they hand out. They use what Coloroso calls the three cons—begging, bribing, weeping, wailing, and teeth gnashing; showing anger and aggression; and sulking—to get teachers to change the consequences. However, if the consequences meet the four conditions outlined above, such tactics on the part of student should be ignored.

## RULE SETTING IN THE BACKBONE CLASSROOM

Although Coloroso is less concerned with rule development than with helping students to become productive classroom citizens, she recognizes that rules are necessary in all areas of society. Coloroso (1997, 2001) proposes that rules should be simple, clearly stated, and related to life's expectations. She suggests that such expectations, whether at a job or as a student, fall into four categories:

- Show up on time.
- Be prepared.
- Do assignments.
- Respect your own and others' life space.

When students choose to break or ignore these rules, they must learn that choices have consequences. However, these consequences should be designed to teach rather than to punish.

## PROBLEM SOLVING IN THE BACKBONE CLASSROOM

Coloroso (1994) considers problem solving a key to helping develop inner discipline. Therefore, it is the teacher's responsibility to help students develop problem-solving skills. The age of the students will determine the teacher's involvement in the process of problem solving. If the student is in middle school or high school, the teacher may simply be a "sounding board" for the student who is reviewing several options for solving the problem. If the student is in elementary school, the teacher may need to suggest solutions or actively intervene if the student is not mentally, emotionally, or physically capable of solving the problem. The goal for all students is to develop problem-solving skills that will serve them for their entire lifetime.

Coloroso stresses that before beginning the process of solving a problem, it is critical to know who "owns" the problem. Who is involved in the problem will also determine the amount of involvement by the teacher. If the problem is between a student and the teacher, the teacher must be involved in the solution. If the problem is between a student and another student, the teacher may act as facilitator who helps the students develop a plan for solving the problem. This empowers students by sending them a message that says, "You have a problem; I know you can solve it" (Coloroso, 1990 [film]).

Coloroso (1994) provides six steps to teaching problem solving.

1. *Identify and define the problem.* Part of defining the problem is allowing students to discuss their feelings. Students need to realize that everyone has the right to be happy, concerned, joyful, sad, angry, or frustrated. The critical issue, therefore, is not what students are feeling, but how they *handle* those feelings. Students must learn that although they cannot always control situations, they can control their *reactions* to situations.

   In defining the problem, it is important to help students get to the root problem. Often the focus is on the result of a problem rather than the actual problem itself. For example, if Eric goes to sleep in each class, having Eric move around the classroom or get a drink of water may temporarily solve the problem. This action, however, does not solve the fact that Eric is not getting enough sleep at night. The solution may need to involve parents, other students, other faculty members, and administrators. Students alone cannot solve some problems.

2. *List possible solutions.* Encourage students to consider every possible solution and to brainstorm without passing judgment. Allow students time to think about possible solutions.

3. *Evaluate the options.* Students should first list the options and then consider the consequences of these options. The teacher is there to guide, to support, to encourage, and to help students think through each solution carefully. If the option creates a

*What some students might consider teasing may feel like bullying to the victim.*

bigger problem, nothing has been resolved. As students evaluate the options, they must be conscious of the effect of the solution on others and ask

> Is it unkind?
>
> Is it hurtful?
>
> Is it unfair?
>
> Is it dishonest?

4. *Choose one option.* Although there may be several ways to solve a problem, students must decide on the plan of action they will follow. In some cases, multiple steps may be needed to resolve the issue. Teachers should help students prioritize the steps that must be taken. It is helpful to start with a goal that is achievable in a relatively short period of time to provide for reinforcement of the effort.

5. *Make a plan.* If the plan involves several steps, it is important to have students act on one step and report the result. It may then be necessary to revise the plan if the original solution is not working.

6. *Reevaluate the problem and the student.* Coloroso (1994) stresses that this is an important missed step in problem solving, but that it is important in the learning process. This review should include a discussion of the causes of the problem and how to avoid them in the future.

**Table 10.2** Reconciliatory Justice in the Classroom

| Three Parts of Reconciliatory Justice | Classroom Example |
|---|---|
| **Restitution**—Concept of "if you break it, fix it." Restitution involves fixing the damage done to another's property. | On a field trip to the children's museum, friends Seth Goodowens and Ricardo Woodfine started to play-fight. As they pretended to throw punches at each other, Seth moved backward to avoid a play punch and fell into a display case. Fortunately, only the glass broke (none of the valuable artifacts inside). Seth and Ricardo agreed that they should pay to replace the broken glass from their allowance. |
| **Resolution**—Identifying the steps to prevent the situation from happening again. | In order to participate in future field trips, both boys had to prepare a contract to be signed by each of the boys, their parents, and their teacher describing the behavior they would display on the next outing. |
| **Reconciliation**—Healing the hurt caused by the event so that all parties can heal. | Each boy decided to write an apology letter to both the director of the children's museum and to their teacher. In the letter to the museum, they offered to volunteer at the museum for six Saturday mornings. |

*Source:* Colororo (1994).

Coloroso (2001) states that the six-step problem-solving model allows for **Reconciliatory Justice**—Restitution, Resolution, and Reconciliation. Restitution involves fixing the damage that has been done to another person's property. Resolution requires identifying and correcting the deeper issues causing the situation. Reconciliation is the process of helping those hurt by the situation to heal. Through this process, students are taught to fix problems they create, to prevent situations from happening again, and to heal with people they have harmed. Table 10.2 provides examples of Reconciliatory Justice.

The process of Reconciliatory Justice can be enhanced by students providing an **Apology of Action** (Northeast Foundation of Children, 1998). Students, and many adults, often find an apology empty and realize that they feel no better after receiving an apology. This is especially true when feelings have been hurt. An Apology of Action allows the offender to make amends in some tangible way. In addition to the apology, the offender completes an action to ease the hurt feelings. This process gives the student who has done the offense an opportunity to do something to make amends, and it gives students who have been hurt the opportunity to stand up for themselves and assert their needs. The most important guideline is that the action must be related to the hurtful behavior. The process of finding an action to relieve the hurt feelings gives the offender a chance to really feel the pain of the one who was hurt, and it provides a way for the relationship to be healed.

## CLASS MEETINGS IN THE BACKBONE CLASSROOM

Many classroom problems can be solved through the six-step problem-solving model. If the problem is more complex or affects several people, a class meeting may be needed to find a solution.

Coloroso (1990) notes that much stress and tension can build in an average school day and, if unresolved, can cause students to be tired, irritable, and unable to concentrate. The class meeting is an excellent way to reduce this stress and tension.

Class meetings are wonderful vehicles for teaching democracy. Coloroso (1997) stresses that students learn democracy through experiences. To learn democracy, students must participate in activities that allow them to resolve conflicts in a nonaggressive manner.

Coloroso (1994) states that there are three basic requirements for class meetings:

1. The problem must be important and relevant to the entire class.

2. The teacher must be willing to provide nonjudgmental leadership.

3. The meeting must be handled in such a way that all feel willing to share and students feel it is safe to express their feelings.

---

### Tips from the Field

When visiting a school in Scotland, I learned about a program to prevent bullying in schools. Friends against Bullying (FAB) is designed to reduce the amount of bullying among students by dealing with bullying behavior and teaching students ways of dealing with bullying by other students. From kindergarten to eighth grade, students are encouraged to report incidences of bullying. Students who bully meet with the principal, counselor, and parents in order to discuss needed changes in behavior. Students who are bullied participate in counseling sessions to learn to be assertive in order to stop future bullying. When all members of the school—students, teachers, administrators, staff, and parents—treat bullying as a serious problem that must be stopped, the incidences of bullying are greatly reduced.

Deborah Newman
Seventh-Grade English/Reading Teacher
Wassom Middle School
Fort Campbell, Kentucky

## STRATEGIES FOR DEALING WITH DIFFICULT STUDENTS

Since writing her first book on classroom management, Coloroso's attention has turned to the prevention of bullying. This interest is in response to a growing number of students who report they have been bullied each year. The National Center for Educational Statistics (2009) reports that in 2007, 32.2 percent of all students reported they had been bullied. Youth Violence Project (2009) shows that bullying increased from 1999 to 2005 with a reported increase of 7 percent for sixth-graders and 6 percent for tenth-graders. Bullying is a serious matter, with serious psychological and social consequences for both those who are being bullied and those doing the bullying. The victims perceive school as a threatening place and experience adjustment difficulties, feelings of loneliness, and a desire to avoid school. The bully is reinforced for inappropriate behavior, leading to even more violent and aggressive behavior in the future. For both the bully and the victim, bullying can have lifelong effects.

Unlike schools in many European countries, schools in the United States have made little or no attempt to deal with the problem. Ross (1996) suggests that one reason that school administrators have ignored bullying is that the gravity of weapon-related violence in schools makes the problem of bullying seem incidental. But research shows that bullying can be an antecedent of such violence and that dealing with the problem of bullying in the early grades can reduce acts of violence in middle school and high school. Some school personnel are unaware of the extent of bullying, and others believe the myth that children "picking on" or teasing one another is a normal part of childhood. They also may believe that children should resolve these conflicts themselves. Students who are bullied typically feel that adult intervention is ineffective or fear that telling adults will only bring more harassment. The net result of all these points of view is that schools become environments where bullies flourish and victims deteriorate.

According to Bullock (2002) bullying refers to repeated, unprovoked, harmful actions by one child or children against another. The acts may be physical or psychological. Physical bullying, or **direct bullying,** involves face-to-face confrontation, open attacks, (including physical aggression), and threatening and intimidating gestures. It includes hitting, kicking, pushing, grabbing toys from other children, and engaging in very rough and intimidating play. Direct bullying tends to increase through the elementary school years, peak in middle school, and decline during the high school years.

Psychological bullying, or **indirect bullying,** includes name-calling, making faces, teasing, taunting, and making threats. Indirect bullying is less obvious and less visible and includes exclusion and rejection of children from a group. Ross (1996) notes that indirect bullying is a more subtle form of bullying, often involving a third party and resulting in social isolation, rumor spreading, and scapegoating.

With students' increased use of the Internet, a new type of bullying has emerged—**cyberbullying.** Cyberbullying involves the use of technology to intimidate, threaten, stalk, ridicule, humiliate, taunt, and spread rumors about victims (Coloroso, 2008). The harm caused by cyberbullying can be greater than the harm caused by other bullying because

- cyberbullying can be extremely vicious.
- cyberbullying continues 24/7 and provides no escape for the victim.

- rumors related through cyberbullying can be distributed worldwide.
- cyberbullies can remain anonymous.

Students who engage in bullying behaviors seem to have a need to feel powerful and in control. They derive satisfaction from inflicting injury and suffering on others. They have little empathy for their victims and often defend their actions by saying that their victims provoked them in some way. Many of these students have been taught to strike out physically as a way of handling problems. Students who regularly display bullying behaviors are generally defiant or oppositional toward adults. Studies of bullying show that bullies' antisocial behavior is not limited to school but continues in other settings and into adulthood. Approximately 60 percent of boys who were classified by researchers as bullies in grades six through nine were convicted of at least one crime by the age of twenty-four, compared with only 23 percent of the boys who were not characterized as bullies or victims (Fox, Elliott, Kerlikowski, Newman, & Christeson 2003).

Bullock (2002) notes that students who are bullied are often younger, weaker, and more passive than the bully. The victims appear anxious, insecure, cautious, sensitive, and quiet, and they often react by crying and withdrawing. They are often lonely and lack close friendships at school. They may lack social skills and friends, and thus are often socially isolated. Many of these students have physical characteristics that promote teasing. Without adult intervention, these children are likely to be repeatedly bullied, putting them at risk for continued social rejection, depression, and impaired self-esteem.

Recently, more emphasis has been placed on the third party in bullying situations—the bystander. Hyman, Kay, Tobori, Weber, Mahon, and Cohen (2006) stress that "bullying is fundamentally a group process; the behavior of peers are crucial for its survival" (p. 869). Bystanders are students who stand around and watch bullying take place without intervening, or too often, encourage the bully. Therefore, teachers must not only act to change the behavior of bullies and those who are bullied but also the behavior of those who idly watch and do nothing to prevent the bullying from occurring. Coloroso (2008) stresses that when bullying is challenged, it stops.

Boatwright, Mathis, and Smith-Rex (1998) and Ross (1996) suggest that teachers do the following to create a classroom atmosphere that prevents or lessens bullying incidents:

- Provide opportunities for students to talk about bullying and why it is inappropriate and unacceptable behavior. Students must discuss the harm that bullying can cause and the things they can do to reduce the amount of bullying that occurs in a classroom.
- Develop a classroom plan and make sure students know what to do when they see a bullying incident.
- Help students develop a set of rules about bullying, with the goal of reducing bully–victim problems.
- Provide cooperative learning activities in which small groups of students work on a common goal, with the evaluation of the activity focusing on the performance of the group.
- Attend to students' behaviors throughout the day (recess and lunchtime) to prevent bullying incidents.

- Act immediately when bullying is reported. Students must understand that bullying will not be tolerated.

- Learn the signs of a student who may be a victim of bullying. These include avoiding certain situations, people, or places. Students who are bullied often exhibit changes in behavior, such as being withdrawn and passive, being overly active and aggressive, or being self-destructive. Teachers may notice a drop in grades and signs of learning problems. Students who are bullied often have unexplained physical symptoms such as stomach pains and fatigue.

## STRENGTHS AND WEAKNESSES OF INNER DISCIPLINE

There are no research data to verify the effectiveness of Inner Discipline, but many accept its validity. This is because they agree with the philosophical tenets on which Inner Discipline is based:

- Students are worth the effort it takes to make them responsible, resourceful, and caring individuals.

- Teachers shouldn't treat children in ways they wouldn't want to be treated.

- Intervention techniques must not only work but must also leave a student's dignity intact (Coloroso, 2001).

For teachers who share these tenets, Inner Discipline is an effective classroom-management model.

However, some wonder whether the consequences Coloroso proposes are actually punishments presented in a different format. Others argue that the process of dealing with each student individually and taking the time to help him or her discover the solutions to problems is a time-consuming one. Many teachers argue that this process takes valuable time away from the main responsibility of the teacher—classroom instruction. Others see this process as necessary to developing self-discipline and personal responsibility.

## INNER DISCIPLINE IN THE CLASSROOM

### Scenario

As sixth-grade social studies teacher Elizabeth Shepherd begins class, she notices that Saki is standing at her desk with tears streaming down her face. Moving to her, she asks, "Saki, what is wrong?"

"I can't find my homework. I did my homework last night and put it in my back-pack, but now I can't find it." Going through her things again, she says through her tears, "I have to find it. I worked hard on my homework." Then noticing that her best friend, Jana, is laughing, she turns, "Jana, did you take my homework? This isn't funny."

Jana stops laughing. "I don't have it. I swear, I didn't take it."

"Well, you were laughing because I lost it. What kind of friend does that? You aren't my friend. I hate you." Then, realizing what she has said, Saki runs from the room.

Calmly, Ms. Shepherd says, "Students, your daily review is on the overhead. I want you to start on it immediately while I check on Saki. Ms. Champion is here if you have questions."

After a brief search, Ms. Shepherd finds Saki in the girls' restroom. Putting her arm around Saki, she says, "Saki, wash your face and then let's go somewhere we can talk."

When Saki becomes calmer, Ms. Shepherd questions her. "I've never seen you act this way before. Now tell me what's wrong."

"I'm trying to make an A in this class. I made a B the last six weeks, and my parents put me on restriction. I'm not allowed to use the telephone for six weeks. Now, I've lost my homework, and I'll lose those points. And I said those awful things to Jana, and she won't be my friend anymore. I can't do anything right." She started to sob again. "I mess everything up."

"Well, let's think how you can fix this. I think you have an A in my class with or without your homework. The homework only counts for five points, so it isn't a big concern. But if you did the homework, I would like to give you the grade. Is there any way to get your homework to me today?"

"I could call my mom. Would you take it if she brought it to you after school today?"

"Yes, I would. In fact, maybe your mother and I need to talk about your grades. I think you are doing very well in my class. I would like to talk to her about that. Do you want to call her, or do you want me to?"

"No, I will call her. But, what am I going to do about Jana? I told her I hate her. I shouldn't have done that."

"Well, let's think for a minute. If Jana had said that to you, what would you want her to do?"

"I would want her to apologize and tell me she didn't mean what she said." Saki's face brightened. "I need to tell Jana that. I know we have class now, but could I talk to Jana for just a minute and then call my mother?"

"Yes, I will send Jana to talk to you. I'm going back to class. After you talk to Jana, go to the office and call your mother. Then you need to come back to class. We will talk at the end of the class about what your mother said."

## Summary

Barbara Coloroso's classroom-management model, Inner Discipline, is based on three key concepts: (1) Developing inner discipline in students is more important than maintaining traditional classroom control; (2) problem solving is key to developing inner discipline; and (3) students must be taught *how* to think, not *what* to think. Coloroso describes classrooms as jellyfish classrooms, brick-wall classrooms, or backbone classrooms and stresses that it is only in the backbone classroom that students learn to accept their own feelings and act on these feelings in a reasonable way. The focus of teachers in backbone classrooms is on helping students make legitimate choices and to face the real-world consequences of these choices. Recently, Barbara Coloroso has turned her attention to the issue of bullying and has written *The Bully, the Bullied, and the Bystander.*

## Key Terminology

Definitions for these terms appear in the glossary.

Apology of Action   189
Backbone classroom   184
Brick-wall classroom   184
Direct bullying   191
Cyberbullying   191

Indirect bullying   191
Inner Discipline   182
Jellyfish classroom   183
Real-world consequences   185
Reconciliatory Justice   189

## Chapter Activities

### Reflecting on the Theory

1. When Ms. Fowler's fourth-period class returned from lunch, two of the students discovered that money had been taken from their backpacks. Deciding to watch the room more carefully when the students were at lunch, Ms. Fowler returned to the room early to discover Brad searching through a student's purse.

   How can Ms. Fowler use Reconciliatory Justice to resolve the problem with Brad? Would you be comfortable using Reconciliatory Justice to resolve this problem? Why or why not?

2. Coloroso shares many ideas with several other theorists presented in this text. Which of Coloroso's ideas have been presented in other theories? What appear to be the major differences in Coloroso's theory and others you have studied?

3. Consider how Ms. Schallenberger handled the situation with Brenton and Gus in the beginning scenario. Do you think the situation was handled appropriately? Should Brenton and Gus be punished for their behavior?

4. How are the consequences described in Coloroso's model different than traditional punishment? Are "real-world consequences" just punishments with a different name? Explain your answer.

### Developing Artifacts for Your Portfolio

1. Analyze the interactions between a teacher and students you have observed. Provide examples of four different interactions you observed. What did these interactions say about the relationship between student and teacher?

### Developing Your Personal Philosophy of Classroom Management

1. Review the philosophical tenets of Inner Discipline. Which of these match your personal philosophy of classroom management? With which do you disagree? Why?

2. Coloroso introduces the concept of Reconciliatory Justice in the classroom. What value do you see in Reconciliatory Justice? How could you use Reconciliatory Justice in your classroom?

## Resources for Further Study

For more information about Inner Discipline, contact

Barbara Coloroso
Kids are Worth It, Inc.
P.O. Box 621108
Littleton, CO 80162

## Chapter References

Boatwright, B. H., Mathis, T. A., & Smith-Rex, S. J. (1998). *Getting equipped to stop bullying: A kid's survival kit for understanding and coping with violence in the school.* Minneapolis, MN: Educational Media Corporation.

Bullock, J. R. (2002). Bullying among children. *Childhood Education, 78,* 130–134.

Coloroso, B. (1990). *Winning at teaching—without beating your kids.* Video. Littleton, CO: Kids are Worth It.

Coloroso, B. (1994). *Kids are worth it!: Giving your child the gift of inner discipline.* New York: William Morrow.

Coloroso, B. (1997). Discipline that makes the grade. *Learning, 25,* 44, 46.

Coloroso, B. (2001). *Parenting and teaching with wit and wisdom.* Littleton, CO: Kids are Worth It.

Coloroso, B. (2008). *The bully, the bullied, and the bystander* (updated edition). New York: HarperCollins.

Fox, J. A., Elliott, D. S., Kerlikowski, R. G., Newman, S. A., & Christeson, W. (2003). *Bullying prevention is crime prevention.* Washington, DC: Fight Crime: Invest in Kids.

Hyman, I., Kay, B., Tobori, A., Weber, M. Mahon, & Cohen, I. (2006). Bullying: Theory, research, and interventions. In C. Evertson & C. Weinstein (Eds.), *Handbook of classroom management: Research, practice, and contemporary issues.* Mahwah, NJ: Lawrence Erlbaum Associates.

The National Center for Educational Statistics. (2009). *Indicators of school crime and safety: 2009.* Retrieved March17, 2009, from http://nces.ed.gov/programs/crimeindicators/crimeindicators2009/tables/table_11_1.asp.

Northeast Foundation of Children. (Winter 1998). Apology of action. *Responsive Classroom Newsletter, 10,* 1–3.

Ross, D. M. (1996). *Childhood bullying and teasing: What school personnel, other professionals, and parents can do*. Alexandria, VA: American Counseling Association.

Youth Violence Project. (2009). *Violence in schools*. Retrieved March 17, 2009, from http://youthviolence.edschool.virginia.edu/violence-in-schools/national-statistics.html.

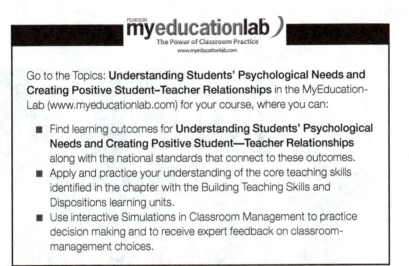

Go to the Topics: **Understanding Students' Psychological Needs and Creating Positive Student–Teacher Relationships** in the MyEducation-Lab (www.myeducationlab.com) for your course, where you can:

- Find learning outcomes for **Understanding Students' Psychological Needs and Creating Positive Student—Teacher Relationships** along with the national standards that connect to these outcomes.
- Apply and practice your understanding of the core teaching skills identified in the chapter with the Building Teaching Skills and Dispositions learning units.
- Use interactive Simulations in Classroom Management to practice decision making and to receive expert feedback on classroom-management choices.

# Positive Behavior Support

## Objectives

Chapter 11 prepares preservice teachers to meet INTASC standards #1 (Content Pedagogy), #3 (Diverse Learners), #4 (Instructional Strategies), #5 (Motivation and Management), #7 (Planning), and #9 (Reflective Practitioner) by helping them to

■ use knowledge regarding human behavior drawn from education and psychology to develop strategies for preventing problem behavior and for teaching prosocial skills to students.

■ understand the history of the Positive Behavior Support movement in the United States.

■ create a classroom environment that promotes responsible behavior and academic achievement.

■ understand the three-tier approach to changing student behavior.

■ use the elements of Positive Behavior Support to deal with inappropriate behaviors outside the classroom.

■ use the principles of Positive Behavior Support to deal with problem behavior.

## Scenario

Approximately a month before the school year began, veteran teacher Theresa Sagasta pulled into the parking lot of Fort Fulton Middle School. She realized that if her interview went well, she would be working in the eighth school in her twenty-five-year career as a teacher. As a military wife, she and her family relocate every three to four years. Therefore, every few years, Theresa goes through the interview process and learns a new school and new procedures.

Entering the building, she was greeted by principal Stan Ellis. "Ms. Sagasta, it is a pleasure to meet you. Your credentials are impressive. Come into my office and let's have a cup of coffee and talk."

Theresa and Stan spent the next thirty minutes reviewing Theresa's experience teaching math at the middle school level. Since Theresa had spent numerous years teaching at military installations, she was interested in how Fort Fulton Middle differed from her previous teaching assignments.

Leaning back in his chair, Stan laced his fingers across his impressive belly. "Well, I think you are going to find that Fort Fulton is very different in how we handle discipline problems. Our focus is on preventing problems and helping students make good decisions rather than on consequences. So, Theresa, my primary concern is if your classroom-management philosophy will fit into our school."

Before Theresa could answer, Stan asked her a question. "Can you estimate how many students you referred to the office last year?"

Theresa hesitated, worried that her answer might cost her the job. "I'm not sure. I try to handle things in my own classroom and use the office as my last resort." She paused. "I would guess I sent about thirty-five students to the office last year. I probably averaged one student a week."

Stan leaned forward. "That doesn't sound like a lot, but if every teacher in this school sent thirty-five students a year to the office, we would have almost six hundred students being referred to the office. Before we changed to our current classroom-management plan, we were seeing close to a thousand students a year. In fact, seeing students referred by teachers was all my assistant principal had time to do. After we changed to our current plan, we dropped the number of referrals seventy-five percent."

"That's amazing," Theresa said. "How have you done this?"

"Two years ago we adopted Positive Behavior Support as our classroom-management system. Are you familiar with this system?"

Hesitating, Theresa said, "No, I've been at schools that had a schoolwide system, but I don't believe it was Positive Behavior Support. Can you tell me more?"

"Why don't I do this?" he said, reaching for a notebook. "In this notebook, we have outlined all the expectations, rules, and procedures we expect at Fort Fulton. Why don't you read through the manual and let's meet again tomorrow to discuss the program."

Wanting to put closure on the job, Theresa said, "I'm sure I will be able to abide by any procedures you have established. One thing I have learned is to be flexible."

"I don't doubt that you can be. But one thing you have to understand is that Positive Behavior Support can't work unless everyone employed at the school agrees to the same expectations and treat students in a certain way. I find that veteran teachers are actually more hesitant to adopt the plan than new teachers. Sometimes, it means you have to give up procedures you have used for years and the mind-set you have concerning classroom management. So, I want you to feel comfortable regarding how we manage behavior before accepting the position. I also have to be confident that you are willing to follow our procedures." Walking Theresa to the door, he said, "We will talk tomorrow. Hopefully you will find that Fort Fulton is a good fit for you, and we will find that you are a good fit for Fort Fulton."

Three weeks later, Theresa is decorating her classroom at Fort Fulton and eagerly awaiting the school year.

## INTRODUCTION

Like Fort Fulton Middle School, over 7,000 schools have adopted **Positive Behavior Support** (PBS) as their primary schoolwide classroom-management plan (Newcomer, 2009). The movement to incorporate PBS as schools' primary management plan began in 1997 when the amendments to the Individuals with Disabilities Education Act (IDEA) became law and required that schools use positive behavioral support and functional behavioral assessment with students with significant behavioral disabilities (Sugai et al., 2000). When school administrators across the country discovered that the techniques used to reduce the behavior of the most difficult students in their schools could also be used to change the behavior of students without disabilities, the PBS movement began.

PBS is a perfect blend of old and new theories and based on the belief that when environmental factors are controlled, behavior can be changed. A product of over twenty-five years of research in behavioral science, PBS incorporates positive reinforcements and functional behavior analysis. To prevent behavior problems, rules and procedures are developed and taught to students. Therefore, PBS centers less on controlling behavior and more on enhancing the quality of life for students by teaching them the skills to interact appropriately in a multitude of settings and situations. The strategies and interventions used in PBS have been validated through years of research as approaches to eliminate challenging behaviors and replace them with prosocial skills (Cohn, 2001).

## THE THREE-TIER APPROACH TO BEHAVIOR SUPPORT

The PBS model focuses on preventing behavior problems rather than reacting to them. In schools that use the PBS model, administrators and faculty spend time creating learning environments to support social and academic development (Trussell, 2008). Rather than spending hours disciplining students, the same hours are spent teaching students rules and procedures, reminding students of how to act in both the classroom and other school spaces, teaching prosocial skills to those students who have problems interacting with classmates, and conducting functional behavior analysis for those students who have more serious behavior problems (Lewis, Newcomer, Trussell, & Richter, 2006).

Sugai et al. (2000) state that although students with serious behavior issues represent only 1 percent to 5 percent of a school's enrollment, often they can account for more than 50 percent of the behavioral incidents handled by office personnel and consume significant amounts of faculty and administrators' time. To reduce the number of incidents and the tremendous amount of time spent dealing with problem students, schools and school districts that use PBS create a system of discipline management that provides consistent expectations for all aspects of the school. The foundation of this system is a three-tier approach to the prevention of discipline problems. The **three-tiered approach** of PBS has been validated in the reauthorization of IDEA in 2004 (Trussell, 2008). Figure 11.1 provides an analysis of the three-tier process.

The first level of the three-tier approach is **primary prevention** which focuses on preventing the development and frequency of behavior problems (Jones, 2008). At the

**Figure 11.1**

Three-Tiered Approach to Behavior Support

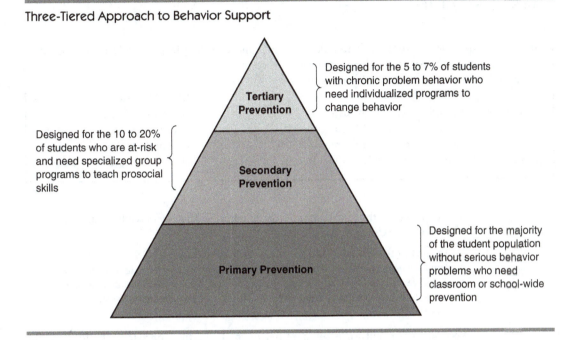

Designed for the 5 to 7% of students with chronic problem behavior who need individualized programs to change behavior

Tertiary Prevention

Designed for the 10 to 20% of students who are at-risk and need specialized group programs to teach prosocial skills

Secondary Prevention

Primary Prevention

Designed for the majority of the student population without serious behavior problems who need classroom or school-wide prevention

primary tier, these schools create a foundation of support to prevent problem behavior and academic failure for all students. This preventive approach can decrease the frequency of problem behaviors and reduce the development of more serious problems with students at risk (Newcomer, 2009). PBS research indicates that the preventative measures used at the primary tier are sufficient for eliminating disruptions by 80 percent to 90 percent of students (Sugai et al., 2000).

Primary prevention focuses on structuring the school environment so problems do not occur in the first place. This structuring begins with the creation of rules and procedures for how students are to interact in all areas of the school. This is followed by the close supervision by faculty and adminstratiors to ensure that students abide by school rules and routines. Primary prevention also includes the creation of incentives to reward compliance with rules. These incentives can be provided in individual classrooms or in all areas of the school. Primary prevention includes the establishment of effective instructional processes because discipline problems are often the by-product of ineffective instruction (Newcomer, 2009).

During her first faculty meeting at Fort Fulton, Theresa was given an envelope of play dollars. Stan explained that at Fort Fulton, these dollars are called Eagle Eyes in honor of the school mascot, the eagle. The faculty members were encouraged to distribute the dollars to students when they were found to be following rules or committing a good deed. The dollars could be used to pay for entrance to special events or saved to be used at the end of the nine-week term to purchase items donated by local businesses.

## Tips from the Field

In my second-grade classroom, effective class-room management begins with consistent communication with my students' parents. By informing parents of behavior expectations and student responsibilities, my students are held to high standards that extend beyond the walls of our classroom. This is one more piece of evidence that informing, involving, includ-ing, and investing in parents leads to student success.

Kevin M. Grover
Second-Grade Teacher
D.W. Lunt School
Falmouth, Maine
2010 Maine Teacher of the Year

Jennifer Bambara, the teacher in the classroom next to Theresa, raised her hand. "How often should we give students dollars?"

"At the first of the term, I would distribute them on a daily basis," Stan explained. "As students become accustomed to our rules, you should make the distribution more random. We want to establish good habits and for students to see the value in following the rules. I also want to encourage each of you to establish an award system for your classroom."

**Secondary prevention** is the next tier of the three-tier approach. The focus of the secondary prevention is to respond to the 10 percent to 20 percent of students who will require support beyond the primary level (Lewis et al., 2006). Secondary prevention can occur in the classroom or through school intervention. It includes individualized behavior-management programs and targeted group interventions.

When students consistently display problematic behaviors, they are referred to the schoolwide team for intervention. In most cases, these interventions are designed to teach these students the prosocial skills needed to be successful in the classroom and in their relationships with peers. These prosocial skills are taught in the same way as academic skills, and behavioral deficits are addressed by teaching functional replacement behaviors. The focus is on teaching students the skills to self-monitor their behavior. As these students display appropriate behaviors, their improved behaviors are acknowledged by faculty and administrators. In addition, the positive feedback they receive from their peers reinforces the newly learned behavior. Lewis et al. (2006) notes that when effective secondary systems are in place, students who display precursors to chronic challenging behaviors are referred, and through early interventions can learn to be productive students and effective class-room citizens.

During the weekly schoolwide PBS meeting, guidance counselor Francis Mitchell reads the list of students who had been referred by their teachers for the school's weekly skillstreaming classes. "Theresa Sagasta has referred Kaitlin Jordan for our afternoon skillstreaming classes. Theresa describes her as immature and states that the other students don't want her in their groups because she acts so immature. I've checked with her other teachers, and they agree with Theresa's assessment. I plan on calling Kaitlan's mother so we can arrange for a conference about Kaitlan's behavior and the benefits of our program. I've asked Theresa to be there to talk about specific examples of Kaitlan's behavior that are problematic."

**Tertiary prevention,** the final tier, focuses on students who exhibit patterns of behaviors that are dangerous, highly disruptive, and/or impede learning (Jones, 2008). These students make up 5 percent to 7 percent of the student population and have not responded to primary and secondary preventions. These students will need intense, individualized functional-based interventions (Lewis et al., 2006). Cohn (2001) has found that using functional-based analysis with these students doubles the rate of success for interventions.

As the semester continued, Theresa became increasingly concerned about Madison Vaughn. Madison began the school year as a good student who displayed few behavior problems. As the year progressed, however, both her academic performance and behavior deteriorated. To Theresa, it appeared that Madison wanted to get into trouble and actually relished the idea of being referred to the office. The sweet girl who always complied was evolving into someone who openly defied her teachers. Theresa talked to Madison's mother, but she insisted that she had seen no behavior change at home. The behavior Madison displayed in other teachers' classrooms was much like what she displayed in Theresa's.

After exhausting all she knew to do to help Madison, Theresa referred her to the schoolwide PBS team. The guidance counselor talked again to Madison's mother about any changes in Madison's health or home life. She learned that like many of the students in the school, Madison's father had been recently deployed. Her mother, however, did not think that was the source of Madison's problems, because they had been through deployments before.

The guidance counselor spent one day following Madison to her classes to observe her interactions with teachers and her peers. She reviewed Madison's previous records and talked to all of Madison's teachers. She also brought Madison into her office to see if she could explain her behavior. Madison refused to participate until they began

## Step-by-Step Positive Behavior Support

To use Positive Behavior Support in your classroom, you will need to do the following:

1. Discuss incorporating Positive Behavior Support with your administrator. Be confident that you have support for your plan.

2. Review your classroom policies, rules, consequences, and procedures to determine if they create the classroom environment you desire.

3. Evaluate your actions and interactions. Are you the model you desire?

4. Incorporate the three-tier approach to prevent behavior.

5. Create a system of positive reinforcements to change student behavior.

talking about her father. Finally, Madison asked, "If I'm bad enough, you will have to have my father come home, right?"

Surprised, the guidance teachers said, "Well, no. That's not what usually happens. We have never asked a father to come home because a student was bad."

Suddenly, Madison began to cry. "But I heard that one of the high school kids' father had to come back because he got in so much trouble. If I'm bad enough, you should make my father come home."

The guidance counselor reached over and put her hand on Madison's shoulder. "Madison, is this what this has been about? Were you hoping to bring your father home by being bad?"

Through her tears, Madison explained that she hadn't wanted her father to be deployed and had hoped she could bring him home. Over the next few weeks, Madison and her mother met regularly with the counselor, and Theresa watched as Madison returned to her old behavior.

## SCHOOLWIDE APPROACH TO PBS

The principles of PBS can be used by an individual teacher or by an entire school. However, they are most effective when adopted by a school or school district. This ensures that students are getting consistent messages from all faculty, administrators, and staff. A shared vision of the appropriate way to prevent inappropriate behaviors ensures that faculty and staff training is consistent and that all stakeholders are in agreement regarding how they approach problem solving (Carr et al., 2002).

*In the Positive Behavior Support plan, students who consistently display problematic behaviors are referred to a schoolwide team for intervention.*

In schools where PBS is adopted as their classroom-management model, a leadership team is established to guide all processes of the schoolwide PBS. An initial task of the team is to find consensus among stakeholders of what will be the desired student behavior and to express these as the school's expectations. Many schools develop an expectation matrix to make sure that the expectations are applied to all aspects of the school. Table 11.1 provides an example of such a matrix. The leadership team also identifies ways to acknowledge students who meet these expectations. Incentives for positive behavior can range from individual to group rewards.

School teams who adopt PBS understand that time is needed to teach rules and procedures to students. However, they feel that the time spent in preventing behavior problems results in less time responding to discipline problems. It is the belief of those adopting schoolwide PBS that if the number of students sent to the office for behavior problems can be reduced, the administrative staff can spend the time they saved in working one-on-one with students who need additional interventions. Therefore, part of the training for faculty is in helping teachers and supervisory staff differentiate between the behaviors that they should manage and the behaviors that warrant a referral for administrative involvement. In order to assure consistency among faculty, the leadership team develops scripted lessons based on direct instruction for teachers to use.

Schools adopting schoolwide PBS must collect data to determine if adopted practices are having the desired results (Lewis et al., 2006). On a school-wide level, PBS relies on accurate and reliable discipline referral data to understand the behaviors occurring within a school. An analysis of data allows the leadership team to identify problem areas of the school, brainstorm interventions, and reward the students exhibiting the expected behavior. The data are then shared with the staff, students, and families.

> Each Monday at noon, the Fort Fulton PBS leadership team has a working lunch. As the team settles into their places, Stan hands out the agenda. "Folks, as you can see, we have a lot to cover today. So, we need to get started as soon as possible. Phillip, you have the results from our most recent analysis of office referrals. Do you want to share your findings?"
>
> Assistant Principal Phillip Richardson passes out a report showing the week's referrals. "As you can see, our referrals were up this past week, but almost all of them are coming from two new bus drivers. I don't think they are familiar with our PBS program and our expectations for student behavior. I called Joe Miller at the transportation office to discuss a time we can provide training for all the new drivers. I also want to recommend that next week we ask all faculty to spend part of their morning going over our expectations for bus behavior with students. Does anyone have any questions?"

## Non-Classroom PBS Strategies

PBS is most effective when it is not only used in classrooms but extends to areas of the school where large numbers of student congregate, where social interactions among students occur, and in areas that have minimal adult supervision. These areas of the school present a different set of management challenges from the classroom. Prevention is the key to reducing problems and includes removing unsafe objects, eliminating obstructed views,

**Table 11.1**  Sample School Expectations Matrix

| School Expectations | Be Ready | Be Responsible | Be Respectful |
|---|---|---|---|
| Classroom | ■ Bring all needed supplies to class.<br>■ Have homework completed at the beginning of class.<br>■ Be on time.<br>■ Be in assigned seat.<br>■ Dress appropriately.<br>■ Focus on directions given. | ■ Stay actively involved during the entire class period.<br>■ Use time wisely.<br>■ Ask for help when needed.<br>■ Take care of the materials and work space.<br>■ Organize our own personal belongings and materials. | ■ Listen while someone else is talking.<br>■ Use property as it was intended to be used.<br>■ Leave others' belongings alone.<br>■ Leave work area clean and neat.<br>■ Keep your hands to yourselves.<br>■ Use appropriate, non-offensive vocabulary and gestures. |
| Hallway | ■ Have hall pass with you.<br>■ Have only conversations that can be heard at an arm's length.<br>■ Move toward class at the warning bell.<br>■ Walk. | ■ Talk without using profanity or offensive language.<br>■ Listen for the warning bell and go to class.<br>■ Refrain from horseplay. | ■ Leave room for people to come and go down the hallway.<br>■ Keep hands and feet to yourselves.<br>■ Pick up what you drop.<br>■ Help keep hallway clean. |
| Cafeteria | ■ Have money/number ready to pay.<br>■ Get utensils/all food items before being seated. | ■ Clean up area after eating.<br>■ Use arm's length voices.<br>■ Keep food on trays.<br>■ Walk to line up and return to class appropriately. | ■ Speak politely.<br>■ Allow your classmates their personal space.<br>■ Use good table manners.<br>■ Use school and personal property appropriately. |
| Restroom | ■ Use the nearest facility.<br>■ Go directly to and from the restroom.<br>■ Use during break time. | ■ Notify staff of problems.<br>■ Use facilities as intended. | ■ Use restroom supplies appropriately.<br>■ Use trash receptacles.<br>■ Be mindful of other people's privacy. |

altering traffic patterns, or adjusting schedules to reduce the number of students in a particular area. To encourage compliance of rules and procedures, some schools make posters of pictures of students complying with school rules and procedures and display these posters in non-classroom settings. Effective management of non-classroom areas requires four processes: **precorrection, active supervision** by faculty and staff, positive reinforcement, and modeling (Newcomer, Colvin, & Lewis, 2009).

Precorrection procedures are used to make adjustments before a student has a chance to respond inappropriately. Teachers use precorrection when they anticipate the occurrence of problem behavior. During precorrection, faculty or administrators remind students of the expected behavior and provide reinforcement for correct behavior. Newcomer (2009) identifies the following two objectives of precorrecton: (a) elimination or reduction of problem behavior and (b) establishment of an expected behavior to replace the problem behavior. Precorrection is essential when students are transitioning from the classroom to non-classroom settings.

The second strategy to prevent problems in non-classroom settings is active supervision by administrators, faculty, and staff. Active supervision extends the concept of proximity control to areas outside the classroom. When students know that faculty and administration are present and available, students display appropriate behavior. It is for this reason that many schools require teachers to stand outside their doorways during class change. Visual scanning of areas where students gather and have social interaction prevents much of the misbehavior that can occur.

Increasing the amount of positive teacher-to-student interactions is the third strategy for improving behavior in non-classroom situations. Basic principles of human behavior suggest that behavior is largely a product of the environment and that appropriate behavior is more effectively shaped by positive consequences than negative consequences. Therefore, high rates of interaction between teachers and students are needed in non-classroom areas.

Finally, it is important that teachers model the behavior they desire. When students are told they cannot talk in certain areas of the school complex and in assemblies and, yet, teachers huddle and have conversations in these areas, students receive mixed messages. Teachers must model the behavior they expect of students.

> Because the referrals from bus drivers had increased, the administrative team at Fort Fulton felt that more attention should be paid to preventing such incidents. They began by having posters made of students displaying the appropriate behavior in the bus loading zones and on the buses. These posters were displayed in the exit hallways. Teachers were asked to have class meetings and to discuss with students the rules and procedures for loading buses and for riding the buses. Finally, as a precorrection, each faculty took a few minutes before releasing students to the buses to review the school expectation for bus behavior.

## Classroom Strategies

Newcomer (2009) notes that the most crucial setting for implementing PBS is the classroom. Although PBS is most effective when it is a schoolwide initiative, teachers in schools without a schoolwide program can still use the principles of PBS as their classroom-management

### Tips from the Field

I keep track of responsible student conduct by assembling a three-ring notebook and placing one page per student inside at the beginning of the year. On the first day of school, I show the students their blank page and challenge them to keep it blank for the whole school year. Here's how it works. When a student breaks one of our rules, that student must go to the behavior notebook and write a brief account of what transpired. If I agree with the assessment, I sign it and date it. This page is sent home with the report card at the end of the marking period. A big point is made of the fresh start for all at the beginning of the next marking period. If a student has a blank page all year, I send home the original blank page with a heartwarming note of praise for good behavior all year long.

Maribeth Petery
Fourth-Grade Teacher
Clay Elementary School
Ephrata, Pennsylvania

model. To be effective, teachers should use **classroom universals** identified to support PBS. Classroom universals are those organizational and teacher instructional practices that are essential in preventing the occurrence of problem behaviors while simultaneously increasing academic achievement. There are three classroom universals to be used with PBS:

1. Identification and instruction of rules and routines. Although classroom rules and expectations should reflect the unique characteristics of an individual classroom, they must be linked to and reflect the greater schoolwide expectations. By linking back to the language of the schoolwide expectations, students learn how classroom expectations fit into the school context. As with the schoolwide expectations, these rules are taught in the first few weeks of school and reviewed on a regular basis.

2. Establishment of the physical structure of the classroom. This would include the arrangement of student desks and the equipment that must be used by students. It also includes the posting of classroom rules. In successful classrooms, procedures have been developed and practiced for how students should be doing their work, turning in papers and homework, and exiting the classroom.

3. The use of instructional strategies that promote positive student–teacher interactions. Teachers using the PBS model are trained in how to use wait time, prompts, and instructional talk to create a positive learning environment. Newcomer (2009) states that "Instruction may be the most critical antecedent for appropriate student behavior" (p. 9). This implies that by using engaging, structured instructional practices, teachers can improve student task engagement and reduce the occurrence of problem behaviors.

Schoolwide PBS programs often overlook the important role of the classroom teacher, and the training of teachers in prevention techniques often receives the least amount of attention. The results are inconsistencies in implementation of the schoolwide PBS. Therefore,

## Tips from the Field

When we started PBS we saw a tremendous improvement in behavior—especially in office referrals. The added bonus that we had not anticipated was that it seemed to change the whole climate of our school. Teachers were no longer barking at students to "pull cards," but rather looking for good things students were doing that they could reward. Our faculty seemed happier, and so did the kids. The biggest area of help was in the transition areas (hallways, bus duty, etc.), and in places like bathrooms and cafeterias. Procedures for how to act in those areas were demonstrated and practiced by each class and teacher. Businesses donated hundreds of dollars for T-shirts and prizes. Since our mascot was the panther, students were given Paw cards for good behavior. Each Paw card is worth a point toward prizes in our Paw Store. Weeks before the store opened, there were posters displayed all over the school with pictures of the prizes—everything from pencils to bicycles and video games. This really motivated the students to try extra hard to get "caught" following our schoolwide rules, which are Be ready . . . Be responsible . . . Be respectful.

Amy Whitworth
Chair of PBS Team
Pleasant View Elementary School
Pleasant View, Tennessee

each classroom in the school should have agreed upon classroom universals, and teachers should be trained in their implementation.

> During the first few weeks at Fort Fulton, Theresa was invited to attend a workshop on the relationship between instructional practices and student behavior. As a veteran teacher, Theresa felt she understood how her behavior impacted her students, but during the workshop she realized that there were numerous things she could do to improve her practices. She started to post a daily agenda so that she and the students would stay on-task. She assigned students tasks so that less time was wasted passing out papers and graded work. She kept a chart to make sure she had some positive interaction with each student every day. She soon realized that all these strategies not only improved behavior but also increased academic achievement.

## STRATEGIES FOR DEALING WITH DIFFICULT STUDENTS

The PBS approach to dealing with difficult students requires a substantial shift in thinking regarding behavioral interventions and about the students who present very difficult problem behaviors. Bambara, Nonnemacher, and Kern (2009) note that PBS requires "letting go entrenched beliefs and practices and accepting those that emphasize prevention rather than consequences, individualization rather than standard disciplinary interventions and inclusion rather than exclusion" (p. 173). Therefore, the response to difficult students is not on how to punish the student but on how to help students change their behavior and learn new skills.

The third tier of the three-tier approach, tertiary prevention, is used with this population of students. The most common intervention is the functional behavior analysis. This approach is required for students with identified disabilities but has been shown to be successful with all students. This process is described in detail in Chapter 2.

## STRENGTHS AND WEAKNESSES OF POSITIVE BEHAVIOR SUPPORT

Research shows that PBS is effective in assisting students with challenging behaviors. In fact, research also shows that when PBS strategies are implemented schoolwide, children with and without disabilities benefit (Cohn, 2001). Cohn notes that PBS research conducted over fifteen years has shown that PBS is effective in promoting positive behavior in students and schools. In schools that implement systemwide interventions, there is a reported increase in time engaged in academic activities and improved academic performance.

In addition, Cohn found that schools that employ schoolwide interventions for problem behavior prevention indicate reduction in office referrals of 20 percent to 60 percent. With this reduction, less time is spent in dealing with discipline issues that could have been prevented and more time is devoted for serious issues.

The major criticism of the PBS model for many teachers is that implementing PBS is a time-consuming issue. Much time must be spent reminding students of rules and procedures. Teachers must be trained in the consistent application of the principles behind PBS if it is to be effective. Bambara et al. (2009) found that principal support is critical if teachers are to be successful in implementing PBS.

Marshall (2009) criticizes PBS on a more philosophical level. Noting that PBS is an outgrowth of B. F. Skinner's work with pigeons, rats, and other animals, he questions its use with students. He recognizes that it has worked with some special needs students but criticizes administrators who determine that the program should be used with the entire school population. Kohn (2006) agrees and states that PBS is just "old Skinnerian wine in shiny new bottles" (p. 138). He contends that PBS is old behavioral techniques applied at a schoolwide level.

## POSITIVE BEHAVIOR SUPPORT IN THE CLASSROOM

### Scenario

As Theresa returned from winter break, she stopped by the office to get her mail and to say hello to the school secretary. Handing Theresa three file folders, the school secretary said, "You will be getting three new students today. Their parents came by during the break to get them registered."

Theresa was accustomed to the constant change in the enrollment in her classroom. Two students had left at Thanksgiving and three more had told her good-bye on the last day of class before winter break. Being part of a military family, she understood the emotions that come with leaving and entering a new school. Therefore, she made an extra effort to see that each student who left her classroom would take positive memories of their time with her, and she tried to make every student feel welcome.

The constant change in demographics had seemed a challenge when she first started using the PBS model. Because the teaching of rules and procedures is so critical to the success of PBS, she feared she would constantly have to reteach as new students entered her room. However, she quickly learned that because of the schoolwide adoption of PBS, a system was in place to teach students and their parents regarding the school's expectations. Each Monday afternoon, an orientation was conducted for new students and their parents. The teachers of new students were asked to attend and to meet after the group meeting to explain specific classroom rules and procedures.

Between first and second period, Theresa was at the door, supervising the movement of students in the hall, when a new face appeared at her door. Reaching out to shake his hand, she said, "You must be Devin. I heard you will be joining my class today. Let me show you where you will sit." Leading Devin to his desk, Theresa continued, "I have assigned you a seat beside Jake. If you have any questions about how to do something, a class rule, or a procedure, ask Jake. Once I get everyone settled, I will come back to get to know you better."

## Summary

In 1997 Positive Behavior Support (PBS) became an important aspect of most schools' classroom-management system when the amendments to the Individuals with Disabilities Education Act (IDEA) became law and required that schools use positive behavioral support and functional behavioral assessment with students with significant behavioral disabilities. Since then, over 7,000 schools have adopted PBS as their primary management plan as research found that the strategies used for students with severe behavior problems were effective with the general population of students.

The foundation of PBS is a three-tier approach to the prevention of discipline problems. The first level of the three-tier approach is primary prevention, which focuses on preventing the development and frequency of behavior problems. The second tier, secondary prevention, includes individualized behavior-management programs and targeted group interventions. Tertiary prevention, the final tier, focuses on students who exhibit patterns of behaviors that are dangerous, highly disruptive, and or impede learning interventions

## Key Terminology

Definitions for these terms appear in the glossary:

## Chapter Activities

### Reflecting on the Theory

1. In Ms. Resnik's sixth-grade class, students frequently get into arguments. Most of these altercations begin when one student calls another student a derogatory name. When she intervenes, Ms. Resnik usually hears, "I was only kidding." How can Ms. Resnik use Positive Behavior Support to change the behavior of her sixth-grade students?

2. Some have suggested that Positive Behavior Support is a luxury that schools cannot afford during a period when high-stakes testing determines what will be presented in schools. Do you agree or disagree?

3. Bambara et al. (2009) note that PBS requires "letting go entrenched beliefs and practices and accepting those that emphasize prevention rather than consequences, individualization rather than standard disciplinary interventions and inclusion rather than exclusion" (p. 173). What does this mean? What are the entrenched beliefs that teachers have regarding the appropriate ways to deal with problem students?

### Developing Artifacts for Your Portfolio

1. In the classrooms you have observed, what were the prevalent social skills that students appeared to be lacking?

2. Consider one procedure you will have in your classroom. Write a lesson plan for teaching this procedure to your students.

### Developing Your Personal Philosophy of Classroom Management

1. Review the philosophy behind the development of Positive Behavior Support. Does this philosophy match your personal philosophy of classroom management? How or how not?

2. Positive Behavior Support is based on the assumption that it is the responsibility of the classroom teacher to provide instruction in the social skills required for a productive life. Others would argue that the teaching of these "life" skills is the responsibility of the family and community. What is your stand on this issue? Explain your reasoning.

3. Will you be incorporating Positive Behavior Support in your classroom? Why or why not? Are there some strategies that you will definitely incorporate into your classroom-management plan? Why?

## Resources for Further Study

Further information about Positive Behavior Support and resources for its use in the classroom can be found by contacting

**OSEP Center on Behavior Interventions and Support**
http://www.pbis.org

## Chapter References

Bambara, L. M., Nonnemacher, S., & Kern, L. (2009). Sustaining school-based individualized positive behavior support: Perceived barriers and enablers. *Journal of Positive Behavior Interventions, 11,* 161–176. doi 10. 1177/1098300708330878.

Carr, E. G., Dunlap, G., Hormer, R. H., Koegel, R. L., Turnbull, A. P., & Sailor, W. (2002). Positive behavior support: Evolution of an applied science. *Journal of Positive Behavior Interventions, 4,* 4–16.

Cohn, A. M. (2001). Positive behavior supports: Information for educators. *NASP Resources.* Retrieved December 30, 2009, from www.nasponline.org/resources/fastsheets/pbs_fs.aspx.

Jones, F. (2008). *Tools for Teaching* implements PBIS level II: Secondary prevention in the classroom. *Education World.* Retrieved October 12, 2009, from http://www.educationworld.com/a_curr/columnists/jones/jones038.shtml.

Kohn, A. (2006). *Beyond discipline: From compliance to community* (10th anniversary edition). Alexandria, VA: Association for Supervision and Curriculum Development.

Lewis, T. J., Newcomer, L. L., Trussell, R., & Richter, M. (2006). Schoolwide positive behavior support: Building systems to develop and maintain appropriate social behavior. In C. Evertson & C. Weinstein (Eds.), *Handbook of classroom management: Research, practice, and contemporary issues.* Mahwah, NJ: Lawrence Erlbaum Associates.

Marshall, M. (2009). Commonly used counterproductive approaches. Retrieved December 26, 2010, from http://www.marvinmarshall.com/counterproductive_approaches.htm.

Newcomer, L. (2009). Universal positive behavior support for the classroom. *PBIS Newsletter.* Retrieved October 12, 2009, from http://www.pbis.org/pbis_newsletter/volume_4/issue4.aspx.

Newcomer, L., Colvin, G., & Lewis, T. J. (2009). Behavior support in nonclassroom settings. In W. Sailor, G. Dunlap, G. Sugai, & R. Horner (Eds.), *Handbook of behavior support.* New York: Springer. doi: 10.1007/978038709632221.

Sugai, G., Horner, R. H., Dunlap, G., Heineman, M., Lewis, T. J., Nelson, C. M., & Wilcox, B. (2000). Applying positive behavior support and functional behavioral assessment in schools. *Journal of Positive Behavior Interventions, 2,* 131–143.

Trussell, R. P. (2008). Classroom universals to prevent problem behaviors. *Intervention in School and Clinic, 43,* 179–185. doi: 10:1177/1053451207311678.

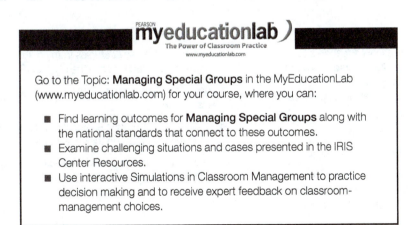

CHAPTER

# 12

# Conflict Resolution and Peer Mediation

## Objectives

Chapter 12 prepares preservice teachers to meet INTASC standards #3 (Diverse Learners), #5 (Motivation and Management), and #9 (Reflective Practitioner) by helping them to

■ understand the basic principles behind **conflict resolution** and peer mediation.

■ evaluate approaches to conflict resolution.

■ learn how conflict resolution and peer mediation can be used to reduce conflict based on differences in gender, sexual orientation, class, ethnicity, and physical and mental abilities.

■ learn how to apply strategies from conflict resolution and peer mediation in the classroom.

■ understand the basic reasons for conflict within a classroom.

■ evaluate the appropriateness of using a conflict-resolution approach in their classrooms.

■ use the principles of conflict resolution to deal with problem behavior.

## Scenario

Third-grade teacher Jennifer Cunningham is helping Allison with her math when she hears a loud crash at the computer center. When she reaches the computer center, she finds the chair overturned, Jamil on the floor, and Sean standing over Jamil. Helping Jamil to his feet, she asks, "Do you guys want to tell me what is going on here?"

Obviously upset, Sean quickly explains. "It was my time to use the computer, but Jamil wouldn't move. I pushed him to get him out of the chair, and the chair turned over. I wasn't trying to hurt him."

Jamil turns to Sean. "I'm not hurt, but you had no business pushing me. I was going to let you use the computer as soon as I finished my game."

Ms. Cunningham stops the argument. "Okay, let's talk about this. Sean, which of our rules did you break?"

"Not to touch anyone without permission."

"And what is the consequence for breaking this rule?"

"I have to get detention after school."

Turning to Jamil, Ms. Cunningham asks, "And Jamil, you weren't following our procedures for computer use, were you? What is the consequence for not following our procedures?"

"I lose my next turn at the computer, but Ms. Cunningham, I only needed a few more minutes. Sean should have waited. He shouldn't have pushed me."

Not wanting to be the only one at fault for the situation, Sean quickly says, "You always hog the computer. It's not fair. You're selfish."

"All right, boys, that's enough. I'm more concerned about your relationship with each other than who is at fault or who should be punished. Now, I want to give you a chance to work this out between you. Are you willing to go to the Peace Corner and resolve this problem?"

In unison, the boys say, "Yes, Ms. Cunningham."

"Good. When you have finished, come see me and tell me how you plan to keep this from happening in the future."

# INTRODUCTION

Resolving classroom problems through conflict resolution and peer mediation has become an accepted part of many schools' discipline plans. Peterson (1997) found that by 1995 there were 5,000 such programs in U.S. schools, and the number rises each year. In some cases, conflict resolution and peer mediation are used by an individual teacher, such as Ms. Cunningham, as a means of teaching social skills and resolving classroom conflicts. In other cases, it is a schoolwide approach, in which participation, support, and resources extend beyond a single classroom.

Donna Crawford and Richard Bodine developed one of the earliest and best known approaches to conflict resolution. They consider conflict as an inevitable part of life and suggest that learning how to respond to it constructively is essential for peaceful schools and successful lives. As Bodine, Crawford, and Schrumpf (1994) note: "Conflict is a natural, vital part of life. When conflict is understood, it can become an opportunity to learn and create. The challenges for students in conflict are to apply the principles of creative cooperation in their human relationship" (p. 51).

Crawford and Bodine (1996, 2001) view conflict resolution as a viable alternative to traditional classroom-management programs because they found that much of classroom misbehavior is actually unresolved conflict. Johnson and Johnson (2006) agree and suggest that, "all discipline problems are conflicts, but not all conflicts are discipline problems" (p. 830).

## Step-by-Step Conflict Resolution and Peer Mediation

To use Conflict Resolution and Peer Mediation in your classroom, you will need to do the following things:

1. Evaluate the sources of conflict in your classroom and determine your contribution to the issues.

2. Determine what conflicts you can eliminate in your role as teacher.

3. Teach conflict-resolution skills to students through direction instruction or through an integrated curriculum.

4. Provide opportunities for students to practice conflict management skills with your assistance.

5. Conduct class meetings to resolve classroom-wide conflicts.

Conflicts evolve into discipline problems when teachers manage the issues arising from conflicts without dealing with the problems that created the misbehaviors in the first place. Students learn little about alternative ways of dealing with their misbehavior when their behavior is controlled by traditional management methods of punishment such as time-out, detention, suspension, and expulsion. Therefore, conflict-resolution education moves away from the focus on punishment and has the following goals:

- to create a safe learning environment where incidents of aggression and violence are reduced

- to create a constructive learning environment where students feel safe to express ideas and feelings

- to enhance student social and emotional development by giving them the tools to deal with values different from their own

- to create a constructive conflict community where social justice is the cornerstone of thought (Jones, 2007)

## CAUSES OF CLASSROOM CONFLICT

As Bodine and others (1994) stress, conflict is a part of life, and without conflict there would be no personal growth or social change. It is important that students learn effective ways of dealing with the types of conflict they will encounter throughout their lives. In fact, Girard and Koch (1996) note that conflict is part of the hidden curriculum in schools and exists in classrooms, lunchrooms, hallways, and on the playground. Kreidler (1984) suggests that the causes of classroom conflicts reflect those of society and typically revolve around issues of needs, values, and resources.

Many of the conflicts in the classroom center on the desire to meet basic needs, including the need for power, friendship and affiliation, and self-esteem and achievement. Bodine et al. (1994) note that conflict resolution is extremely difficult when students perceive that others are threatening their psychological needs. It is important for teachers to understand that conflicts over unmet psychological needs are often played out against the backdrop of limited resources. Students appear to be in conflict over physical things when in reality, the need may be much deeper and more fundamental. If psychological issues are left unresolved, the conflict will appear again and again.

Conflicts may arise over limited resources (time, money, property) and are typically the easiest to resolve. The goal is to teach students that cooperating rather than competing for scarce resources is in their best interests.

Conflicts involving different values (beliefs, priorities, principles) tend to be more difficult to resolve than those about resources. When students' values are challenged, they feel threatened. Conflicts over values involve the use of words such as *honest, equal, right,* and *fair.* Through effective conflict resolution, however, students can learn that resolving a values conflict does not mean that they have to change or realign their values. Often, agreeing that each person views the situation differently is the first step toward resolution. If students can learn to accept each other's differences in beliefs, they will be able to deal with the issue in conflict rather than focusing on their differences.

The diversity of today's classrooms provides an arena for conflict as students learn and play with students from backgrounds different from their own (Crawford & Bodine, 1996). This diversity may lead to misunderstandings or misperceptions of the intentions, feelings, needs, or actions of others. Reactions to differences often take the form of prejudice, discrimination, harassment, and hate crimes. Conflict-resolution education programs provide a framework for addressing these problems by promoting respect and acceptance through new ways of communicating and understanding. Although complex, these conflicts can be resolved by increased awareness, understanding, and respect.

Kreidler (1984) suggests that sometimes the classroom teacher is the source of conflict in the classroom. Teachers who create a highly competitive atmosphere will have classrooms

## Tips from the Field

I learned a wonderful technique for solving classroom problems from my cooperating teacher during my student teaching. She used a method called "Having a Bone to Pick." My cooperating teacher made copies of skeleton bones and placed each child's name on a bone. Her name also appeared on a bone. These were placed on a bulletin board. Whenever a student had a problem with another child or with the teacher, they went to the board and "picked a bone." At the end of the day, she allowed fifteen minutes for resolving issues. If a student had picked the bone of another student, they went to a quiet location to work out their differences. If a student had picked the teacher's bone, he or she came to the teacher's desk to discuss the issue. This discipline plan teaches children to resolve their problem in a diplomatic way and prevents small issues from escalating.

Candida Phelps
Special Education Teacher
Rivermont Elementary School
Hixson, Tennessee

full of conflict. When teachers favor one student or group of students, tension and jealousy are created. Too often, teachers place irrational or impossible expectations on students. Students often feel that rules are inflexible or that consequences are not applied equally. All of these teacher-created situations create an atmosphere of fear and mistrust.

## RESPONSES TO CONFLICT

According to Bodine et al. (1994), responses to conflict can be categorized into three basic groups: soft responses, hard responses, and principled responses. In both soft and hard responses, students negotiate from these positions, either trying to avoid or win a contest of will.

**Soft responses** usually come from students who are friends or students who want to keep peace in the classroom, school, or neighborhood. In many cases, the students want to agree, and they negotiate softly to do so. Avoidance is a common response and is achieved by withdrawing from the situation, ignoring the conflict, and denying emotions. Accommodation is another response that offers protection from aggression by other students. With both avoidance and accommodation, resentment grows and eventually feelings of disillusionment, self-doubt, fear, and anxiety about the future develop. For example, consider a typical middle school situation in which avoidance is the chosen response:

> When Callie Davis transferred to Chapman Middle School, she was pleased when Shauna, one of the more popular girls in the eighth grade, wanted to be her friend. Now, Callie fears that Shauna just likes her so that she can borrow Callie's clothes. Every time Shauna comes to Callie's house, she asks if she can borrow a blouse or pair of jeans. Callie's wardrobe is slowly being emptied, but she is afraid that if she confronts Shauna, Shauna will not only stop being her friend, but she will also lose the circle of friends she has made through Shauna.

In contrast to soft responses are **hard responses** to conflict, in which adversaries war until one is victorious. Hard responses to conflict are characterized by confrontations that involve threats, aggression, and anger (Bodine et al., 1994; Kreidler, 1984). In hard responses, pressure is applied as those in conflict try to have their own way. Hard responses typically result in one of two outcomes. One outcome is that the more aggressive student wins, and the other loses. The second outcome involves a lose-lose situation in which the desire to hurt or get even with the other student provokes vindictive actions. Consider how a hard response results in a lose-lose situation for Demario and Ryan.

> Demario Wamble dreads riding the school bus because he has become the target of bullying by Ryan Poole. On the first day of school, Ryan made Demario move so Ryan could sit closer to his friends. Now, making Demario move each morning has become a game for Ryan. No matter where Demario sits, Ryan decides he wants to sit where Demario is sitting and threatens Demario until he relinquishes his seat.
>
> After weeks of such treatment, Demario is plotting revenge. On the ride to Ryan's stop, Demario hides thumbtacks in the seat. Carefully avoiding the sharp points, Demario can't wait until Ryan once again threatens him and makes him relinquish his seat.

**Principled responses** to conflict are proactive rather than reactive. Students who use principled responses have developed communication and conflict-resolution skills (Bodine et al., 1994). Principled responses to conflict are characterized by each student seeking to understand the other while trying to be understood. Principled negotiators are skilled, active, empathetic listeners. Principled negotiators focus on the interests of both sides and strive to create situations in which each person wins. The following example shows how Jade and Leigh use a principled approach to resolve their differences.

> For the last few days, tension has been mounting in Mr. Merriwether's class. Best friends Jade and Leigh are no longer speaking to each other, and the other students have begun to take sides in the dispute. Taking the girls aside, Mr. Merriwether learns that Jade has accused Leigh of telling a secret that Jade shared with Leigh. Realizing that the girls want to remain friends, he suggests that they participate in peer mediation. After one session with the peer mediator, the girls put aside their disagreement and become friends once again. Mr. Merriwether is pleased when peace returns to his classroom.

The three types of responses to conflict produce different outcomes. The actions students choose when they are involved in a conflict will either worsen or lessen the problem. Soft positional bargaining is considered a lose-lose approach to conflict. Students do not deal with the root of the problem, and eventually both students lose. In hard positional bargaining, a win-lose situation is created that can be self-destructive as well as destructive to the opponent. Only through a principled approach, such as conflict resolution or peer mediation, can issues be resolved in a peaceful, productive manner.

## PRINCIPLES OF CONFLICT RESOLUTION

Crawford and Bodine (2001) propose that conflict resolution offers an alternative approach to classroom management that brings the disputing parties together, provides them with the skills to resolve the dispute, and expects them to do so. Because there are different approaches to conflict resolution, Kreidler (1984) recommends that teachers consider the following when choosing a conflict-resolution technique.

- *The age and maturity level of the students involved.* Younger students may need adult intervention to help in the resolution of the problem. If one of the students is angry and poses a danger to others, the teacher's presence is needed to ensure the safety of all involved.

- *The time and place appropriate for intervention.* Conflict resolution requires time for those in conflict to express feelings and to consider solutions. Such negotiations cannot take place quickly or in a public forum. In some cases, students may need a cooling-off period before beginning negotiations.

- *The type of conflict.* Whole-class problems may require a group meeting, whereas issues between individual students may be resolved by the students or through the use of a mediator.

The type of intervention used must meet the specific needs of those involved. There are three basic types of conflict resolution available for use by students and teachers: mediation, negotiations, and consensus decision making (Crawford & Bodine, 1996, 2001).

The most commonly used and best known method is **mediation.** Mediation is a problem-solving process in which conflicting students meet face-to-face to work together to resolve the dispute assisted by a neutral third party (Bodine et al., 1994). Mediation can take place within the classroom setting or in the context of a schoolwide program available to all students.

Essential to the success of the mediation process is the mediator who orchestrates the prescribed step-by-step procedure, asking questions and ensuring that those in conflict hear each other. Although the role of mediator can be filled by the teacher, the principal, or another adult, it is best filled by a fellow student or students who have been trained to be peer mediators. Peer mediation has the advantage of demonstrating to students that they have the ability, by communicating and cooperating, to resolve their differences without adult intervention. When peer mediators are used, they should be selected from groups who represent the general student population in terms of race, gender, achievement, and behavior. Bodine and colleagues (1994) stress that students as young as third grade have the ability and sophistication to serve as co-mediators in such a program.

In **negotiations,** conflicting students work together, unassisted, to solve their dispute. Negotiation can be a powerful tool, especially within a classroom in which all of the students have been trained in conflict resolution. Bodine et al. (1994) suggest that classrooms have a negotiation center or "peace corner" where students in conflict sit face-to-face to conduct the negotiation while other classroom activities proceed concurrently.

The final option available to teachers is **consensus decision making.** This is a group problem-solving strategy in which all parties affected by the conflict collaborate to create a plan of action that all parties can and will support. Crawford and Bodine (2001) suggest this strategy of group problem solving when conflict affects the entire class. The vehicle for group problem solving is the class meeting.

The purpose of such class meetings is to solve a problem rather than to determine who is to blame or who should be punished. Through the process, an agreement is reached that is

## Tips from the Field

I use a small plastic bucket to address the issue of tattling. I decorate the bucket with a sad face, a nose, eyes, and some big ears. After I discuss tattling with the class, I tell my students that if they want to tattle, they must write their concern on a piece of paper and place it in Mr. Bucket. This has been a great help in stopping the tattling because kids don't get my attention. Later, I read what is placed in Mr. Bucket and then decide if anything needs to be addressed.

Kirk Ver Halen
Gifted and Talented Teacher
Elisha M. Pease Elementary School
Dallas, Texas

acceptable to the group. This may mean that the decision will be the best resolution of the conflict for the group as a whole but may not be the best solution for individual students.

Classroom teachers facilitate group problem solving through class meetings. To begin, teachers review the process and list key issues to be resolved. The focus is on the *process,* and the teacher is there only to ensure that all the steps in the process are completed rather than to lobby for a particular outcome. Teachers can provide their points of view by asking questions. Teachers restate agreements as they occur and help the class develop a plan for solving the problem.

## THE CONFLICT-RESOLUTION PROCESS

Crawford and Bodine (2001) propose that the steps in conflict resolution should be taught to all students, not just those with disruptive behaviors. The problem-solving process incorporates the following steps (see Table 12.1).

**Table 12.1** Steps in the Conflict-Resolution Process

|  |  |
| --- | --- |
| **Step 1: Set the stage** | Each day a conflict develops on the playground as Pedro Salcedo and Clayton Vassey struggle to see who will be the leader of whatever game is being played. Both boys are good athletes and both feel they have the right to be team leaders. Their constant bickering is ruining everyone's fun, and little gets done during the limited recess hours. |
| **Step 2: Gather perspectives** | During mediation with their teacher, Sara Kurita, Pedro and Clayton are encouraged to tell their side of the conflict. It was agreed that only one boy could talk at a time and when one boy finished, the other boy had to repeat what he had just heard. |
| **Step 3: Identify interests** | During the discussion, it became obvious that while each boy wanted to be the leader, both Pedro and Clayton realized that they were not being fair. |
| **Step 4: Create options** | One option suggested by the boys was that they would take turns being leader. |
| **Step 5: Evaluate options** | While the plan seemed fair to them, Pedro and Clayton realized that other students might want to be the leader as well. They decided that the fair way to handle the problem was for all the students to take turns being the leader, and once a student had a turn, the student could not be leader again until everyone had had a turn. |
| **Step 6: Generate agreement** | Because their plan involved the entire class, Pedro and Clayton decided they should present their plan to the class for approval. At the end of the session, the boys shook hands, pleased with their ability to solve the problem. |

## Step 1: Set the Stage

Whether the method of conflict resolution is mediation, negotiation, or group problem solving, all participants must agree to participate and cooperate to solve the problem. If at any point the participants indicate a lack of desire to cooperate, the process ends. Without cooperation, the process is futile.

In conflict resolution, it is important that ground rules be set. Doing so begins with a review of the steps involved in conflict resolution. Determining the need for confidentiality is essential. With elementary-age students, strict confidentiality may not be required; however, it becomes increasingly important as the age of those in conflict increases and the issues in dispute become more personal and sensitive. All parties must agree that there will be no name calling or put-downs. All must view themselves as partners in trying to solve the problem. When all agree to the ground rules, the process can begin.

## Step 2: Gather Perspectives

During conflict resolution, all students have an opportunity to express their opinions and to be heard. If one student has requested mediation, that student should be the first to describe the problem. The mediator alternates between those in conflict, asking for clarification and summarizing each person's point of view, until all issues have been heard. It is important that the mediator use open-ended questions rather than questions that can be answered with "yes" or "no."

In this step, mediators must help participants deal with problems of perceptions and emotions. When dealing with problems of perception, it is important to remember that conflict is not necessarily based on reality but in how students *perceive* the situation (Bodine et al., 1994). It is ultimately each student's perception that defines the problem. Understanding each other's perceptions opens the way to resolution.

Emotionally charged students may be more ready to fight than to work together cooperatively to solve the problem. Fear can be played out through a show of anger. Having students identify both their own emotions and those of the other side opens the way to understanding.

Bodine et al. (1994) suggest that as mediators work with the students they should be careful to address the following:

- **Attend** to the nonverbal behaviors so that all can fully understand what everyone is thinking and feeling.

- **Summarize** or restate facts by repeating the most important points, organizing interests, and discarding extraneous information. In summarizing, the mediator acknowledges emotions by stating the feelings each person is experiencing.

- **Clarify** by using open-ended questions and statements to obtain more information and ensure understanding.

## Step 3: Identify Interests

The mediator asks participants to explain what they want from the process. Critical to the success of the process is the determination of shared interests. Shared and compatible interests are the building blocks for resolving the conflict.

*It may be necessary for the teacher to act as the mediator as students learn to resolve conflict.*

The goal is to separate the students from the problem by focusing on interests rather than on positions (Bodine et al., 1994). Understanding the difference between positions and interests is crucial because interests, not positions, define problems. Students should come to see themselves as working side by side and attacking the problem rather than each other.

## Step 4: Create Options

Creating options involves a brainstorming process. Because evaluation hinders creativity, the process of *generating* options is separate from the process of *evaluating* options and from creating an agreement. This step allows students the opportunity to design potential solutions without the pressure of deciding which is the best decision. Brainstorming is used to separate inventing from deciding.

## Step 5: Evaluate Options

Using group problem solving, evaluation options are divided into two parts. The first part establishes criteria for evaluating options. The second part is the actual evaluation of options. The following must be considered as the participants evaluate the option:

Does the option help everyone involved?

Is the option fair?

Can the option solve the problem?

Can the group do it?

Does the option violate school rules or policies?

## Step 6: Generate Agreement

After those in conflict have discussed the available options, the mediator asks students to make a plan of action describing what they will do.

# ADDITIONAL APPROACHES TO CONFLICT-RESOLUTION EDUCATION

Four additional approaches to conflict-resolution education exist. The first is the **conflict curriculum approach.** Using this approach, students receive instruction in a separate course, distinct curriculum, or daily or weekly lesson plan. Instruction is provided in listening skills, critical thinking, and problem solving, which not only resolves classroom problems but also enhances all learning.

The second is the **integrated curriculum approach.** In this approach conflicts found in literature, social studies, science, and other subject matter are used to teach students how to resolve conflict. Rather than teaching conflict resolution as a separate curriculum, the integrated curriculum approach integrates training in conflict resolution into the existing curriculum. Stevahn (2004) notes that the integrated curriculum approach not only enables students to learn, use, and develop more positive attitudes toward conflict resolution, it also enhances academic achievement. The process starts with teachers examining the content of existing curricula and identifying where conflict occurs. This process is valuable because teachers no longer have to choose between teaching interpersonal skills and academics. The two are accomplished simultaneously.

The **peaceable classroom** is the third approach to conflict-resolution education. It is possible to develop a peaceable classroom in any school (Bodine et al., 1994). The peaceable classroom is a warm and caring community in which five qualities are present:

1. **Cooperation:**  Students learn to work together and trust, help, and share with each other.

2. **Communication:**  Students learn to observe nonverbal clues, communicate accurately, and listen actively.

3. **Tolerance:**  Students learn to respect and appreciate other students' differences and to understand how prejudice impacts the classroom.

4. **Positive emotional expression:**  Students learn self-control and to express feelings of anger and frustration in ways that are not aggressive or destructive.

5. **Conflict resolution:**  Students learn the skills for responding creatively to conflict in the context of a supportive, caring community.

Peaceable classrooms are the building blocks of the **peaceable school,** the last approach to conflict-resolution education. Crawford and Bodine (2001) describe the peaceable school approach as a whole-school methodology that builds on the peaceable classroom approach by using conflict resolution as a system of operation for managing

---

### Tips from the Field

In order to have PEACE in our classroom, we will have

> P—Pride in our class and what we accomplish. We will come to class prepared and ready to learn.
>
> E—Expectations of excellence for ourselves and others.
>
> A—Acceptance of our differences. We will be tolerant and learn from each other.

C—Consideration for others' feelings. "Please," "thank you," and "I'm sorry" will be said often by the teacher and students.

E—Enthusiasm and excitement about what we will learn.

Poster found in classroom in Dublin, Ireland.

---

the entire school. Using this approach, the adults and students involved learn and use conflict-resolution principles and processes. In the peaceable school, students learn about peacemaking in the social context of the classroom and the school. In the peaceable school, interactions between students, between students and adults, and between adults are designed to value human dignity and build self-esteem.

## STRATEGIES FOR WORKING WITH DIFFICULT STUDENTS

Thornton, Craft, Dahlberg, Lynch, and Baier (2002) note that when students are faced with social situations for which they are emotionally and cognitively unable to handle, they can respond with aggression and violence. When teachers teach students the skills to resolve conflict, they equip students with the skills they need to deal with difficult social situations. If the training occurs in the early grades, the chances of successfully preventing aggressive attitudes and behaviors in the future are improved. Training in early grades builds better communication skills and facilitates peer relationships.

Schools can approach the teaching of conflict-resolution skills on two levels (Thornton et al., 2002). The first are programs that are preventive in nature and are designed to teach all students pro-social skills. These preventive programs can be taught by classroom teachers who have been trained to incorporate these skills into their traditional curriculum.

Although violent students may be positively influenced by nonviolent participants, students with high levels of aggression need special attention. Therefore, the second type of school programs is reactive in nature and is designed to deal specifically with those students who have displayed aggressive behavior. Separate programs for aggressive students are critical because interventions designed for the general student population may fail to impact students at risk for aggression. Aggressive students need to have skill building in impulse control, problem solving, anger management, assertiveness, and empathy. The goal is that these difficult students will develop skills that prevent them from resorting to aggression when faced with uncomfortable situations. Programs for this population of students are often conducted by other school personnel because students may be hesitant to disclose hostile or sensitive emotions to their own teachers.

Thornton et al. (2002) note that programs for students who display aggressive tendencies must take into account the environment where participants live and the circumstances they face. Often these students come from homes where aggression is the norm and from neighborhoods where risk factors such as poverty, drug or alcohol abuse, and divorce are commonplace. Programs must address these issues if they are to be effective.

## STRENGTHS AND WEAKNESSES OF CONFLICT RESOLUTION

With students exposed to a daily diet of talk shows on which the participants yell and scream at each other rather than actively work to resolve conflicts, it is critical that students learn that there is another way to resolve conflicts. Crawford and Bodine's conflict-resolution model is an important alternative because it invites participation and expects those who choose to participate to plan for more effective behavior.

An additional strength in Crawford and Bodine's model is that faculty and students work and learn together while supporting one another. Conflict resolution and peer mediation promote academic and social growth, in that they increase skills in listening, critical thinking, and problem solving—skills basic to all learning.

School-based conflict-resolution programs reach every child in the school. They are critical in changing the total school environment and creating a safe community that promotes nonviolence. When youth experience success with negotiation, mediation, or consensus decision making in school, they are more likely to use these conflict-resolution processes elsewhere in their lives.

Unfortunately, conflict-resolution programs, whether classroom or schoolwide, require additional time and planning on the part of teachers and administrators. Many teachers contend that they simply don't have the extra time needed to implement the plan.

Others note that conflict resolution works only if all participants are willing to cooperate and be actively involved in reaching a solution. If one of the parties in the conflict refuses to participate, then the process fails and more traditional discipline methods have to be implemented.

The benefits of teaching students to resolve conflicts are numerous. These skills not only enhance the lives of individual students but also improve the overall school climate a well. Table 12.2 provides a listing to the benefits of teaching conflict resolution to students.

**Table 12.2**   Benefits of Teaching Students to Resolve Conflicts

- Students who can resolve conflict constructively are healthier psychologically.
- Students who can resolve conflict constructively develop socially and cognitively in more healthy ways.
- Students who can resolve conflict constructively are happier more of the time.
- Students who can resolve conflict constructively have more positive and supportive interpersonal and intergroup relationships.
- Students who can resolve conflict constructively have a greater sense of meaning and purpose in life.
- Students who can resolve conflict constructively are more engaged with the school and its academic program.
- Students who can resolve conflict constructively make more friends and have stronger relationships.
- Students who can resolve conflict constructively have more successful careers.
- Students who can resolve conflict constructively achieve higher academically.
- Students who can resolve conflict constructively show more empathy and less prejudice.

*Source:* Heydenberk and Heydenberk (2007); Johnson and Johnson (2006).

## CONFLICT RESOLUTION IN THE CLASSROOM

## Scenario

When Karen Aquino's sixth-grade class won Stapleton Middle School's Accelerated Reader contest, she never dreamed that winning would cause a major conflict in the classroom. As part of their prize, the class had been given a field trip to a location of their choosing. Where the class would spend their free day had become the issue of daily battles between the boys and the girls.

The boys want to go a professional ballgame. The girls want to go to a mall and to a movie. Because they can't agree, a class meeting is called to resolve the issue. After the students gather in a circle and Ms. Aquino has reviewed the ground rules, she asks, "Who wants to start?"

Benjamin raised his hand and says, "We think we should go to a professional baseball game. There are more boys than girls, so the majority should win."

"So, you are suggesting that the majority should win and that the minority, the girls in this case, should just go along, whether they are happy or not?"

Several of the girls raise their hands, and Ms. Aquino calls on Kayla. "All the boys ever want to do is play ball. Whenever we have free time, they start a ballgame, and they don't want the girls to play. We are tired of being left out. Besides, the girls read more books, and that is why we won. We wouldn't have this prize if it weren't for the girls, so we should be the ones to decide where we go."

Daniel is recognized. "I guess I can see the girls' point of view, but none of the boys want to go to a mall. Is there anything the girls would like that is outside?"

Several of the girls want to speak, but Ms. Aquino calls on Lindsey. "Well, I would like to go to a park or to the zoo. Then the girls could picnic and the boys could play ball. I like the idea of being outside. We are inside all the time at school. On our free day, we should do something different."

"Could we do both?" Kimree asks. "I know that the zoo has a picnic area and a playground. I like the idea of going to the zoo. I would vote for that."

"I think we are making progress," Ms. Aquino notes. "Let's see if we have any consensus. How many of you think the idea of going to the zoo and having a picnic at the park is a good idea?" Several students hesitate, looking around the group to see how their friends will vote. Slowly hands go up, and in seconds every hand is up. "Wonderful: I think we have reached an agreement that will please everyone. I'm proud of your willingness to work through this problem."

## Summary

Conflict resolution and peer mediation are accepted parts of many schools' discipline plans. Donna Crawford and Richard Bodine propose that conflict resolution offers an alternative approach to classroom management that brings the parties of a dispute together, provides them with the skills to resolve the dispute, and then requires them to use these skills to resolve the problem. There are three basic types of conflict resolution available for use by students and teachers: mediation, negotiation, and consensus decision making.

## Key Terminology

Definitions for these terms appear in the glossary.

Conflict curriculum approach   224
Conflict resolution   215
Consensus decision making   220
Hard responses   218
Integrated curriculum approach   224
Mediation   220

Negotiations   220
Peaceable classroom   224
Peaceable school   224
Principled responses   219
Soft resposes   218

## Chapter Activities

### Reflecting on the Theory

1. A committee of faculty, administrators, and parents at Liberty High School are reviewing the school's zero-tolerance policy. They incorporated the policy two years earlier as a response to an increase in the number of fights they were seeing between students. However, in most cases the fights were the result of misunderstandings and could easily have been

resolved before punches were thrown. They fear that a reversal in the zero-tolerance policy will send a message that violence is tolerated, but they also realize that the policy creates more problems than it resolves.

How could the establishment of a conflict-resolution program at Liberty High School provide an alternative to their zero-tolerance policy?

2. This chapter presents three approaches to conflict resolution. Do you consider all three equally effective, or is there one you would be more comfortable implementing? Why?

3. In the first scenario, Jamil and Sean agreed to negotiate. Should they still face the consequences for their behavior at the computer center? Why or why not?

## Developing Artifacts for Your Portfolio

1. Consider conflicts you have observed between students. What were the causes of these conflicts? What could the teacher have done to prevent these conflicts? Develop a plan to resolve conflicts in your classroom.

## Developing Your Personal Philosophy of Classroom Management

1. One of the criticisms of conflict resolution is that it requires a great deal of time and planning by the classroom teacher. Do you think the benefits of conflict resolution are sufficient to offset the time commitment by the teacher? Is this an approach you will use in your classroom? Why or why not?

2. Do you feel that conflict resolution is a solution to all conflicts that occur in schools? Are there types of students or students of certain grade levels who might not respond to conflict resolution? Are there types of conflict that must be dealt with by teachers and administrators rather than by students? Explain your answer.

## Chapter References

Bodine, R. J., Crawford, D. K., & Schrumpf, F. (1994). *Creating the peaceable school: A comprehensive program for teaching conflict resolution. Program Guide.* Champaign, IL: Research Press.

Crawford, D. K., & Bodine, R. J. (1996). *Conflict resolution education: A guide to implementing programs in schools, youth-serving organizations, and community and juvenile justice settings.* Washington, DC: U.S. Department of Justice, Office of Juvenile Justice and Delinquency Prevention, and U.S. Department of Education, Office of Elementary and Secondary Education, Safe and Drug-Free Schools Program.

Crawford, D. K., & Bodine, R. J. (2001). Conflict resolution education: Preparing youth for the future. *Juvenile Justice, 8,* 21–29.

Girard, K., & Koch, S. J. (1996). *Conflict resolution in the schools—A manual for educators.* San Francisco: Jossey-Bass, Inc.

Heydenberk, R. A., & Heydenberk, W. R. (2007). The conflict resolution connection: Increasing school attachment in cooperative classroom communities. *Reclaiming Children and Youth, 16,* 18–22.

Johnson, D., & Johnson, R. (2006). Conflict resolution, peer mediation, and peacemaking. In
     C. Everston & C. Weinstein (Eds.), *Handbook of classroom management: Research, practice,
     and contemporary issues.* Mahwah, NJ: Lawrence Erlbaum Associates.

Jones, T. S. (2007). Combining conflict-resolution education and human rights education:
     Thoughts for school-based peace education. *Journal of Peace Education, 3,* 187–208.

Kreidler, W. J. (1984). *Creative conflict resolution.* Glenville, IL: Scott, Foresman.

Peterson, G. J. (1997). Looking at the big picture: School administrators and violence reduction.
     *Journal of School Leadership, 7,* 456–479.

Stevahn, L. (2004). Integrating conflict resolution training into the curriculum. *Theory into
     Practice, 43,* 50–58.

Thornton, T. N., Craft, C. A., Dahlberg, L. L., Lynch, B. S., & Baier, K. (2002). *Best practices of
     youth violence prevention: A sourcebook for community action* (rev.). Atlanta, GA: Centers for
     Disease Control and Prevention and National Center for Injury Prevention and Control.

PEARSON
# myeducationlab )
The Power of Classroom Practice
www.myeducationlab.com

Go to the Topic: **Creating Positive Student–Student Relationships** in
the MyEducationLab (www.myeducationlab.com) for your course, where
you can:

- Find learning outcomes for **Creating Positive Student–Student
  Relationships** along with the national standards that connect to
  these outcomes.
- Apply and practice your understanding of the core teaching skills
  identified in the chapter with the Building Teaching Skills and
  Dispositions learning units.

# Judicious Discipline

CHAPTER 13

## Objectives

Chapter 13 prepares preservice teachers to meet INTASC standards #3 (Diverse Learners), #5 (Motivation and Management), and #9 (Reflective Practitioner) by helping them to

- understand the basic principles behind Judicious Discipline.

- understand how Judicious Discipline helps all students, regardless of backgrounds, abilities, and behaviors, to feel that they are a part of the school community.

- evaluate the rights of students guaranteed by the United States Constitution.

- establish class rules based on compelling state interests.

- learn that all classroom-management strategies must protect students' due process.

- evaluate the balance between individual rights and responsibilities.

- learn the appropriate application of Judicious Discipline in the classroom.

- use the principles of Judicious Discipline to deal with problem behavior.

**231**

## Scenario

The student council at John F. Kennedy Middle School is struggling to develop a new dress code. The members of the council agree that the way many of their classmates dress is offensive, but they are hesitant to place too many restrictions on the student body. Frustrated, Aaron says, "I still think we have no right putting restraints on what someone wears. How about our right to free speech? Isn't the way we dress one of the ways we express ourselves? Doesn't the Constitution protect our personal rights even if we are students?"

Mr. Reedy, the student council sponsor, tries to explain. Remembering a line he learned from one of his education classes, he says, "Aaron, students don't leave their personal rights at the schoolhouse door. Of course you have your rights, but the rights of an individual student can't interfere with the rights of others. Therefore, we have to carefully balance our decisions to ensure that the rights of an individual student don't interfere with the rights of all the other students to learn or to participate."

Shaking her head in confusion, Kennisha says, "I don't think this group is smart enough to figure this out. How does a school ever manage to balance the rights of a thousand individuals with the needs and interests of the entire student body?"

## INTRODUCTION

Kennisha's question is a good one, and one that administrators, teachers, and school boards struggle with on a daily basis as they strive to establish and maintain a learning environment that ensures freedom, justice, and equality. Forrest Gathercoal (2004) addresses these issues through his classroom-management model, **Judicious Discipline.** According to Gathercoal (2004), it is critical that students and educators understand that students' constitutional rights consist of three foundational principles:

- **Freedom**—Students have the right to be themselves and the right to express themselves through their behavior and opinions.

- **Justice**—Students have the right to school rules and consequences that are fair to everyone. They have the right to due process if accused of breaking a school or district rule.

- **Equality**—Students have the right to an equal opportunity. This does not mean that students are treated the same, but that that each student has an opportunity to succeed.

Noting that one of the most important jobs of educators is the teaching of citizenship, Gathercoal proposes that Judicious Discipline teaches citizenship by requiring educators and administrators to acknowledge and respect students as citizens. Gathercoal suggests that citizenship is best learned when educators teach students about their individual rights and allow students to exercise their rights within the school and its classrooms.

Judicious Discipline is both a philosophy and a framework for classroom management and school discipline. Forrest Gathercoal (2001) describes Judicious Discipline as "a management style based on the synthesis of professional ethics, good educational practice, and students' constitutional rights and responsibilities" (p. 15). Judicious Discipline allows teachers to move beyond punishments and rewards to the development of personal responsibility and moral behavior. One of the primary aspects of Judicious Discipline is that unlike reward and punishment models for classroom discipline, Judicious Discipline teaches citizenship skills that can be transferred from school to community and from today to tomorrow. It is a model that prepares students for life outside the classroom.

Gathercoal (2001) stresses that a classroom-management model such as Judicious Discipline is needed for two reasons. One is the increasing diversity in our classrooms. The constitutional framework of Judicious Discipline ensures equality that cuts across cultural, ethnic, and religious lines. F. Gathercoal (2004) contends that Judicious Discipline helps all students, regardless of backgrounds, abilities, and behaviors, realize that they have a valued place in the school community. Through Judicious Discipline, intolerance and prejudices can be replaced with concern for others, feelings of self-worth and confidence, a sense of belonging, and a cooperative attitude.

The second reason for the need for a classroom model with an emphasis on student rights is the shift from "*in loco parentis*" to the realization that students "no longer shed their constitutional rights at the schoolhouse gate" (F. Gathercoal, 2001, p. 51). Until 1969, court decisions historically supported the concept of **in loco parentis,** which granted to educators the same legal authority over students as that of parents. Early courts' decisions applied the same "abuse tests" used for parents to educators, and unless abuse was evident, courts rarely interceded. *In loco parentis* has been replaced by language that addressees the constitutional rights and responsibilities of students. F. Gathercoal (2001) notes that today "our public schools and classrooms have become, in fact, microcosms of the United States of America" (p. 51).

Judicious Discipline is an approach to classroom management that provides educators with a foundation for teaching citizenship. This is primarily done through daily student–teacher interactions. Educators using Judicious Discipline become role models who practice the values of a democratic society through the professional and ethical relationships they establish with all members of their learning community (McEwan, P. Gathercoal, & Nimmo, 1999).

Judicious Discipline is unique because the constitutional language that is used promotes reasoned decision making and a peaceful school climate. P. Gathercoal & Nimmo (2001) describe Judicious Discipline as a citizenship approach, based on the U.S. Bill of Rights, that teaches students about their rights and responsibilities for living and learning in a democratic society.

---

## Step-by-Step Judicious Discipline

To use Judicious Discipline in your classroom, you will need to do the following things:

1. Determine to treat all students with respect and to assure that they are provided justice, freedom, and equality.

2. Study the First, Fourth, and Fourteenth Amendments to determine student rights.

3. Review these amendments with students and discuss their rights as citizens of a democracy.

4. Teach that rights are balanced with responsibilities through compelling state interests.

5. Teach the concept of Time, Place, and Manner.

6. Work with students to create classroom rules using compelling state interests.

7. Solve classroom issues through class meetings.

8. Resolve individual discipline issues through logical consequences and problem solving.

## THE BILL OF RIGHTS

The foundation of Judicious Discipline is the U.S. Bill of Rights. The Bill of Rights, the first ten amendments to the U.S. Constitution, were written to protect three basic human values: freedom, justice, and equality. F. Gathercoal (2004) notes that it is important for students to understand that in our nation's constitutional democracy, individual rights are as important as the needs and interests of the majority. Three of those amendments—the First, Fourth, and Fourteenth—specifically apply to schools. Teachers who practice Judicious Discipline teach students the concepts of these three amendments and how they apply in the school environment.

### The First Amendment

> Congress shall make no law respecting an establishment of religion or prohibiting the free exercise thereof; or abridging the freedom of speech or of the press; or of the people peaceably to assemble, and to petition the government for a redress of grievances.

According to F. Gathercoal (2004), the First Amendment protects freedom of speech, freedom of expression, freedom of press, freedom of religion, and the right to assemble peacefully. Until the late 1960s, the courts rarely applied the First Amendment to students. However, during the years following the Vietnam War, numerous judicial decisions related to matters concerning free speech were litigated. In addition, issues concerning student rights to publish and distribute material on school premises have been raised in the court. However, it has been matters related to church-state and school relationships that have been most troublesome for courts to resolve.

### The Fourth Amendment

> The right of the people to be secure in their persons, houses, papers, and effects against unreasonable searches and seizures, shall not be violated, and no warrants shall issue but upon probable cause, supported by oath or affirmation, and particularly describing the place to be searched, and the persons or things to be seized.

### Tips from the Field

The 1970–1971 school year was my first as a teacher. I taught in an urban high school and was having discipline problems. I noticed that Joe Geremia, a science teacher down the hall, never seemed to have discipline problems so I asked him for advice. He replied, "If you need to discipline a student, take the student outside the door of your classroom. This accomplishes two things. First, it gives you both some time to calm down. Second, it means that the student no longer has to "save face" in front of the class when you tell the student what you plan to do about the behavior." This advice has served me well the past three and a half decades.

Burt Saxon
Advanced Placement (AP) History
Hillhouse High School
New Haven, Connecticut
Connecticut Teacher of the Year 2004–2005

This amendment addresses situations in which it is necessary for teachers and administrators to take property from students. Effective school management requires school personnel to adhere to guidelines similar to those law-enforcement officers have to follow when taking property from students. The Fourth Amendment protects students' property at school and requires teachers and administrators to have reasonable cause to search lockers or desks (F. Gathercoal, 2004).

## The Fourteenth Amendment

All persons born or naturalized in the United States, and subject to the jurisdiction thereof, are citizens of the United States and of the state wherein they reside. No state shall make or enforce any law which shall abridge the privileges or immunities of citizens of the United States; nor shall any state deprive any person of life, liberty, or property, without due process of law; nor deny to any person the equal protection of the laws.

F. Gathercoal (2004) notes that two phrases of the Fourteenth Amendment have had a significant impact on public education. The first, known as the "due-process clause," provides the legal basis for reasonable rules and a fair process for balancing student rights. Educators

*The constitutional framework of Judicious Discipline ensures equality that cuts across cultural, ethnic, and religious lines.*

who understand and are able to apply the concepts of due process to student conflicts are viewed as just and fair. In order to have the right to appeal, courts require that there be a state action. Therefore, only students in public schools enjoy due process. Administrators and teachers must understand that every rule or decision made in a public institution is subject to review by another person, board, or court and that all rules and decisions made in public schools are appealable.

The last clause, known as the "equal-protection clause," serves as the constitutional foundation for prohibiting all forms of discrimination. The Fourteenth Amendment provides equal protection under the law and protects against discrimination based on sex, race, national origin, disabilities, age, or religion.

## COMPELLING STATE INTERESTS

Providing a balance to the individual rights held by students are four time-tested public-interest arguments crafted in the courts for the precise purpose of limiting constitutionally protected freedoms (F. Gathercoal, 2004). These arguments are well grounded in legal principles and history and are the line of reasoning that allows for individual rights. Authority for denying people their civil rights comes from Article I, Section 8 of the Constitution, which reads, in part, "The Congress shall have power to provide for the common Defense and General Welfare of the United States." This general-welfare clause acts as the legal foundation for legislative bodies representing the needs and interests of the majority.

This legal concept is commonly referred to as "compelling state interests," and simply means that in some cases the welfare and interests of the majority are more compelling than the rights of an individual. These compelling interests give educators all the legal authority they need to create and carry out fair and equitable school rules (F. Gathercoal, 2004; Larson, 1998). Legally speaking, if educators can demonstrate a compelling state interest, the rights of students can be denied.

The following four **compelling state interests** assure that the needs and interests of the majority are balanced with the rights and needs of individuals:

1. **Property Loss and Damage:** An interest that acts as steward for the care and appropriate use of individually and state-owned property.
2. **Threat to Health and Safety:** An interest that serves a fundamental purpose of government to protect the health and safety of students who attend public schools.
3. **Legitimate Educational Purpose:** An interest that legitimizes administrators', teachers', and the educational institution's license to make arbitrary decisions that are based on sound educational practice and the mission of the school.
4. **Serious Disruption of the Educational Process:** An interest empowering schools with the professional responsibility to deny student rights that seriously disrupt student activities (P. Gathercoal & Nimmo, 2001).

School rules and policies based upon these four compelling state interests are upheld in court. Educators not only have a legal *authority* to deny student constitutional rights, but it is also their professional *responsibility* to prohibit student behaviors if those behaviors are detrimental to the welfare of the school (P. Gathercoal & Nimmo, 2001).

## Figure 13.1

Principles of Judicious Discipline

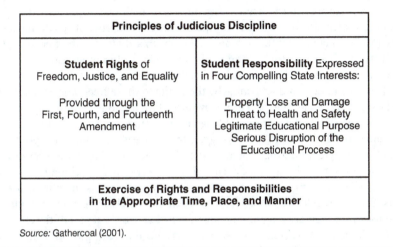

| Principles of Judicious Discipline | |
|---|---|
| **Student Rights** of Freedom, Justice, and Equality | **Student Responsibility** Expressed in Four Compelling State Interests: |
| Provided through the First, Fourth, and Fourteenth Amendment | Property Loss and Damage Threat to Health and Safety Legitimate Educational Purpose Serious Disruption of the Educational Process |
| **Exercise of Rights and Responsibilities in the Appropriate Time, Place, and Manner** | |

*Source:* Gathercoal (2001).

## TIME, PLACE, AND MANNER

When students are taught about the need for balancing their rights with the rights and interests of society, they come to understand that there is always an appropriate time, place, and manner for exercising their individual rights. McEwan et al. (1999) note that Judicious Discipline teaches students to examine their actions critically by looking at their behaviors in light of the "appropriate time, place, or manner" criteria.

Judicious Discipline is composed of ten basic principles. The principles of individual freedom, justice, and equality provided by the First, Fourth, and Fourteenth Amendments are balanced with the four compelling state interests—property loss and damage, legitimate educational purpose, health and safety, and serious disruption. Providing the bridge between individual rights and the needs of the majority are the questions of reasonable time, place, and manner. Figure 13.1 shows the balance among these principles.

## IMPLEMENTATION

Because the concepts presented in Judicious Discipline are counter to the typical behavior-management approaches presented in schools, it is critical for teachers to provide classroom instruction about the concepts of Judicious Discipline (McEwan et al., 1999). F. Gathercoal (2001) stresses that such activities should begin on the first day of school, in order to communicate trust in students' abilities to reason and to act appropriately.

P. Gathercoal and Nimmo (2002) stress that implementing Judicious Discipline takes time. Teachers can't begin using the model without teaching the basic concepts of Judicious

Discipline to students. Students have to know and practice the language and concepts embedded in Judicious Discipline, and they must develop their own expectations for civil living around the framework of democracy.

Teachers incorporating Judicious Discipline into their classroom structures begin by introducing students to the rights encompassed in the concepts of freedom, justice, and equality (McEwan et al., 1999). Students are taught that they have the freedom to express themselves in their speech, their clothing, their writing, and in other aspects of their lives. However, it is also made clear to students that a free society only functions successfully when all citizens understand and abide by the limits to those freedoms. Students then develop classroom and school expectations by rewording the four compelling state interests into positive behavioral statements and language they understand.

P. Gathercoal and Nimmo (2001) suggest that the teacher define each positive behavioral statement by conducting a democratic class meeting. From the first day of class through the rest of the school year, class meetings can serve as the lifeblood of a democratic community. Class meetings are important, in that they create a sense of enfranchisement for students. Paul Gathercoal (2000) stresses that democratic class meetings provide students with a sense of value and belonging, and are therefore an essential part of the effective operation of all Judicious Discipline classrooms. Class meetings can give students a feeling of significance and eliminate most of the reasons students resort to "power struggles." Landau and P. Gathercoal (2000) stress the following key elements of democratic class meetings:

- Teachers and students determine who can call a class meeting and when meetings should be held.

- All students and the teacher should be seated so that everyone can see the faces of the others in the class meetings.

- The teacher sets the ground rule that individual names will not be used during the class meetings. The purpose is to discuss issues rather than individuals.

- The teacher reminds students of the expectation that they will stay on the topic and avoid sharing personal information during the class meetings.

- Students should never be coerced to participate in the class meeting.

- Each student and teacher should be encouraged to have a class-meeting journal. Immediately following each meeting, both teachers and students should take a few minutes to record their thoughts about what took place.

- Students and the teachers should write down the goals they set for themselves after or during the class meetings.

McEwan (1991) stresses that Judicious Discipline is not designed to supplant other discipline models or to be used alone. She feels that Judicious Discipline is most successful when used with other student-centered discipline approaches. Judicious Discipline is designed to be integrated into these other approaches by specifically framing the decision-making process of management in the language of human rights and responsibilities. Rudolph Dreikurs's model, Logical Consequences, is often used as a complementary piece to Judicious Discipline.

## DEVELOPING RULES

After a classroom discussion of the rights and responsibilities of students, classroom rules are developed together. However, F. Gathercoal (2004) notes that it is not the rules that keep students in school and behaving appropriately, but rather the philosophy and attitude with which educators approach rules that convince students that they belong. The philosophy upon which all rules and decisions are based is critical to whether school will be an inviting and safe place for students.

The four compelling state interests are the basis for classroom rules (McEwan, 2000). See Table 13.1 for examples of rules developed from the four compelling state interests. Educators should work with students to develop rules that emphasize the behavior desired and empower students to think for themselves. As students learn to think and act using the four compelling interests, the language used in the classroom moves from autocratic talk to democratic talk. Involving students when creating rules gives the students a feeling of responsibility. Rules should be written clearly for the educational level of those affected. It is imperative that students fully understand the meaning of

**Table 13.1** Turning Compelling State Interests into Classroom Rules

| Compelling State Interests | Corresponding Classroom Rules |
|---|---|
| 1. **Property loss and damage** | Treat all school property with respect. Use equipment and school property appropriately. Respect others' possessions by not taking items belonging to others. |
| 2. **Legitimate educational purpose** | Take responsibility for learning. Bring needed materials to class. Be organized and prepared for class. Bring books, pencil, and paper to class every day. |
| 3. **Health and safety** | Act in a safe and healthy way. Report incidences where you or others are bullied. Teasing or harassment is not tolerated in this classroom. Fighting and play fighting are unacceptable. Racist, sexist, threatening, and/or derogatory remarks will not be tolerated. Weapons, or items that can be physically dangerous to school, will not be tolerated. |
| 4. **Serious disruption of the educational process** | Respect the rights and needs of others. No interfering with the teaching and learning of others. Raise your hand before you speak during a classroom lesson. Have permission before leaving your seat. Never talk when the teacher is talking. |

## Tips from the Field

Part of our curriculum is a discussion of the Constitution and the Bill of Rights. To help students understand rights and responsibilities, I have them create a Bill of Rights for our classroom. Students are put in groups and draft a Classroom Bill of Rights. We then review each group's contribution and create a final version for our classroom. The following is a copy of last year's Classroom Bill of Rights.

> *We, the students, have the right to*
> *Teachers who will not discriminate against us according to our race, gender, age, religion, size, background, or social class;*
> *Be provided desks, textbooks, resources, and other necessities;*
> *A safe uninterrupted learning environment;*

> *Use the bathroom in an emergency;*
> *Be notified of our current grade;*
> *Express our opinion without offending others;*
> *Be informed and responsible for all assignments and accept the consequences of not completing it or not handing it in at the appropriate time.*

When completed, all students sign the Classroom Bill of Rights and it is posted for all to see.

> Kevin White
> Eighth-Grade Social Studies Teacher
> Coopertown Middle School
> Coopertown, Tennessee

rules in order to meet the adequate-notice requirement of the Fourteenth Amendment. Consider how the students in Ms. Stafenau's fifth-grade class develop rules from the four compelling state interests.

"Class, now that we have discussed the four compelling state interests, we are going to use these interests to develop our class rules. I want to divide you into groups and have each group suggest rules that we might want for our class that relate to the compelling state interests you are assigned."

After the groups discussed possible rules for their classroom, Ms. Stafenau asked each group to report. "Wade, your group had the compelling state interest of Health and Safety. What rules did you develop?"

As Wade listed each rule, he also wrote the rule on the whiteboard. "We developed the following four rules:

Be careful with your words.

Walk when inside the school or classroom.

Keep hands and feet to yourself.

Use classroom equipment safely."

"Your group did an excellent job. I noticed that you expressed the rules in positive terms. We may want to consider this for all our rules. Nina, your group had the compelling state interest of Property Loss and Damage. What rules did your group develop?"

Nina came to the front of the classroom. "Our group had one rule similar to the first group: 'Be careful with classroom equipment.' We could only think of two other rules. They are

Ask permission before using someone else's things.

Treat school property with respect."

"Very good. Seth, your group had Serious Disruption of the Educational Process. What rules did your group develop?"

"Well, we said ours as don'ts," Seth explained as he came to the front of the room, "but they can be changed if you want. Here are our rules:

Don't touch anyone without permission.

Don't make noise while others are working.

Don't use bad language.

Don't talk when someone else is talking."

As Seth returned to his desk, Ms. Stafenau explained, "Well if we decide to write our rules in positive terms rather than negative, I think we can easily change what you wrote. All right, our last group is Karlisa's. What rules did you develop for Legitimate Educational Purpose?"

"We developed three rules. They are

Come to school prepared to learn.

Bring needed materials to class.

Work quietly and on time."

Reviewing the students' work, Ms. Stafenau said, "All of you did a great job. Now let's decide if we will keep all the rules or select the ones we think will best serve our class."

## DEVELOPING CONSEQUENCES

Judicious rules necessitate judicious consequences (Larson, 1998). One important concept of the Judicious Discipline model is that it focuses on teaching appropriate behavior, not punishing inappropriate behavior. When students misbehave, teachers act as mentors, viewing students' problems as an educational opportunity. When a problem does occur or a rule is broken, Judicious Discipline advocates approaching the situation as a teachable moment.

Teachers begin by asking questions. Behavior questions should be approached by asking general questions of inquiry and concern in an effort to encourage students to talk about their perceptions of the event. It means approaching the problem from the perspective of the student with the intent of getting to the heart of the problem and understanding the student's point of view. F. Gathercoal (2004) stresses that questions have a way of "softening the blow" to those who might be in the wrong and allowing

## Tips from the Field

I teach my students about the "productive hum" level of sound in the room. I get the students in small groups to demonstrate what it sounds like. I tell the students that this is the sound level you'd find in most offices. People aren't silent. They're interacting, but they're respectful of each other's need to keep the noise level down so people can think and work.

James F. Linsell
Eastern Elementary School
Sixth-Grade Social Studies
Traverse City, Michigan
2002 Michigan Teacher of the Year

them to save face and recover. By asking leading questions and listening carefully, the underlying issues begin to emerge. The students then have the opportunity to tell about the situation, recalling what happened, explaining perceptions of the situation, making predictions about what is likely to happen, and suggesting possible choices based on recollections and predictions. The question/reflecting process is important, because, as F. Gathercoal (2001) states, "Good communication lies not in the words we use, but in the spaces between the words. The longer the spaces, the more we are sharing power with our students" (p. 120).

Consequences should flow logically from the student's misbehavior and not be designed to punish students. Therefore, Gathercoal is an advocate of logical consequences that are tied directly to the behavior. When rules are broken, the discussion needs to center around two important questions: What needs to be done now? What can we learn from this? Consider the questions Mr. Davis asks a student who has vandalized the school.

When Springlake High School principal Paul Davis saw the graffiti written on the back wall of the gym, he feared he knew who had written "Coach Greene is unfair. Coach Greene sucks." The day before, basketball coach Joel Greene had cut tenth-grader Bastian Borowik from the team. A review of the campus surveillance video confirmed that sometime during the night, Bastian had used spray paint to express his anger on the back wall of the school.

Within minutes of the opening of school, Bastian sat in the principal's office. After showing Bastian the incriminating evidence, Mr. Davis asked, "Bastian, do you want to tell me why you did this?"

Defensively, Bastian responded, "You are always talking about our rights. Well, don't I have the right to say what I want? What happened to free speech?"

"You absolutely have the right to free speech, and there were several ways you could have expressed your anger over being cut from the team. If you had written a letter to the school paper or come to talk to me, those would have been appropriate actions. If you wanted to walk with a sign around school stating that you think the coach is unfair, you would have had my permission. But you didn't consider two other things when considering your rights. First, one of our compelling state interests is protection of school property. Now, the back wall of the gym will have to be repainted. Second, remember that there is an appropriate time, place, and manner in which to do everything. You went about this in the wrong manner. We have a game tonight. Your classmates aren't going to be happy to have what you wrote on the wall of the gym displayed during our game. So, we have to think what you need to do next. What do you think? How do we fix this? What do we do now?"

Bastian dropped his head. Embarrassed by his own behavior, he thought of what he could do to make up for the problems he had created. Finally, he said, "First I need to apologize. I need to apologize to Coach Greene, and I need to apologize to the school. I think I should apologize to Coach Greene in private, but I will apologize to the school when you make the morning announcements, if that is all right."

"I think that is a good way to start. What are we going to do about the wall?"

"I'll repaint the wall. If I start this morning, do you think it will be done by tonight? I guess we need to call my parents and tell them what I've done. I may need their help in buying the paint I need."

"I think you are developing a good plan. I'm going to leave you alone so you can call your parents. We will talk again after you get off the phone."

There are two important aspects in determining consequences for each student's misbehavior. The first is understanding the real nature of the problem, and the second is taking into account individual differences among students (McEwan, 2000). By definition, judicious consequences are designed to take into account individual differences among students in order to meet the emotional and learning needs of each person involved. Because consequences are educational by nature, students who misbehave simply may have different ways of learning from their mistakes. As a result, different consequences are necessary. Age and the mental, emotional, and physical condition of the students being punished are factors that must be considered when determining reasonable consequences.

Judicious consequences are never malicious, cruel, or excessive. The primary goal of a consequence should be on restitution, not shame (Landau, 2008b). Therefore, the following discipline methods should be avoided when using Judicious Discipline:

- demeaning students
- judging or lecturing students on their behaviors
- comparing students
- criticizing students
- demanding respect
- refusing to apologize
- accusing students of not trying
- asking students why they misbehave

- getting into a power struggle
- becoming defensive
- losing control
- intimidating students
- punishing the class for one student's misbehavior
- acting too quickly without information
- believing that all students should be treated equally

Conferences, community service, apology, and restitution are among the many appropriate options available. It is most important for educators using Judicious Discipline to be flexible about consequences because what is most appropriate for one situation may not be for another. F. Gathercoal (2001) notes that this flexibility helps to avoid the mistake of being locked into predetermined responses that fail to meet the needs of the individual student or the student body as whole.

## STRATEGIES FOR DEALING WITH DIFFICULT STUDENTS

Busse (2008) states that she often hears that Judicious Discipline cannot work with students who have severe behavior problems, because they are incapable of controlling their behavior. However, through her work with students with behavior disorders she found that Judicious Discipline can be used. She notes that her students adapt to the model quickly because it makes sense to them; they see it as not some "made up" system. Busse's students see Judicious Discipline as fair because they understand that it provides for due process in decisions made about their behaviors.

Before consequences are provided, teachers must determine what is in the best interest of the student and what are the goals of consequences. Teachers first need to evaluate their behaviors and the environment. What, if anything, should be changed to prevent problems in the future? Then, teachers must determine what students can learn that will prevent the problems in the future. Landau (2008b) suggests that teachers use the following consequences when working with difficult students:

- conferencing with teachers and parents to determine an agreed upon consequence
- requiring an apology from the student
- providing a "time-out" so the student has time to cool down and gather his or her thoughts
- assigning in-school suspension with the intent that the student will receive one-to-one attention from a caring teacher
- providing counseling with a professional to resolve personal issues that might be the cause of the behavior

# STRENGTHS AND WEAKNESSES OF JUDICIOUS DISCIPLINE

Judicious Discipline is the only model for school and classroom management that is based on principles of democracy and operates at the principled level of moral development. Since its introduction in the 1980s, those using it have found that Judicious Discipline

- empowers students to be strong in character.
- encourages higher-order thinking skills through real social situations as students are invited to describe, explain, predict, and make reasoned choices.
- minimizes classroom stress and anxiety for both students and teachers because of the environmental emphasis on human rights and individual dignity.
- serves as a real-life model for the same system of rules and responsibilities under which students will live when they leave school.
- teaches students accountability, self-efficacy, tolerance, cooperation, and mutual respect.
- promotes fairness and consistency by balancing individual freedom, justice, and equality with the needs and interests of society.
- contributes to a decrease in dropout rates, in acts of violence in and around schools, and in referrals to the office, while also resulting in an increase in any levels of daily attendance (F. Gathercoal, 2001; P. Gathercoal & Nimmo, 2001).

Most important, Judicious Discipline does not wait for problems to occur. Teachers who use this constitutional framework for classroom rules and decisions teach students to resolve classroom conflicts peacefully in a democratic forum.

However, not everyone will find Judicious Discipline as a workable model for their classrooms. If teachers do not believe that students have the ability to think and behave responsibly, a democratic model will not work for them. F. Gathercoal (2001) notes that much of the success of Judicious Discipline comes from the teacher's ability to trust the students, teaching them the concepts of rights and responsibilities, and acting in ways consistent with civil responsibility. To teach one thing and do another is abuse of power and is disrespectful to the human rights of the students.

It is time consuming to use an approach such as Judicious Discipline. P. Gathercoal and Nimmo (2001) found that teachers need time to make Judicious Discipline work. Converting to a democratic school community takes time, because students and teachers are not accustomed to reacting in this manner. It takes time to process new perceptions and expectations. Grandmont (2003) found that many teachers found it hard to find logical consequences to discipline problems and would revert to filling out referral forms and more traditional forms of punishment.

Finally, there are students who may not be cognitively or emotionally able to respond to an approach like Judicious Discipline (Larson, 1998). Students who are emotionally unstable or who suffer from physiological disorders may not respond to the principles of

Judicious Discipline. Grandmont (2003) found that the model simply did not work for very difficult students. For Judicious Discipline to be effective, students must have reached a level of moral development that allows them to understand socially agreed-upon standards of individual rights. This will lessen its effectiveness with very young children and those who are not cognitively able to process these ideas.

## JUDICIOUS DISCIPLINE IN THE CLASSROOM

### Scenario

Realizing that many of the sixth-grade students entering Westover Middle School had never been taught using a classroom-management plan like Judicious Discipline, the sixth-grade teachers spend much of the first week of classes discussing student rights and responsibilities. After spending time the first day providing an overview of Judicious Discipline, Ms. Umayam spends the second day discussing the issues related to the First Amendment.

Reading the First Amendment to the class, Ms. Umayam asks, "All right, what rights does this amendment give to you as individuals?"

Heather raises her hand and says, "Well, as a citizen I have freedom of speech. But does this mean I can say anything I want to anyone, including a teacher?"

"Well, having personal rights doesn't give us total freedom to do anything we want. Remember what we talked about yesterday. If your rights interfere with those of the majority and are in conflict with one of the compelling state interests, then your rights might be limited. Can anyone think of an example?"

Brittney answers, "Well, if I stood in the middle of the hall and yelled, 'Run! Run!' I might cause chaos. That might be a threat to health and safety."

"Exactly! In addition to considering the compelling state interests, we have to consider the proper time, place, and manner for our actions. So yelling 'run' in a crowded hallway might never be appropriate, or it might be the right thing to do if there was some immediate danger in the hall. So we have to always remember that our personal freedoms have to be balanced with the compelling state interests and with whether it is the appropriate time, place, and manner for our actions."

### Summary

Administrators, teachers, and school boards struggle daily to establish and maintain a learning environment that ensures justice and equality for all students. Forrest Gathercoal addresses these needs through his classroom-management model, *Judicious Discipline*.

Judicious Discipline is both a philosophy and a framework for classroom management and school discipline and is composed of ten basic principles. The principles of individual freedom, justice, and equality provided by the First, Fourth, and Fourteenth Amendments are balanced with the four compelling state interests—property loss and damage, legitimate educational purpose, health and safety, and serious disruption. Providing the bridge between individual rights and the needs of the majority are the questions of reasonable time, place, and manner. Landau (2008a) describes Judicious Discipline as a framework for ensuring the permanent value of all students.

## Key Terminology

Definitions for these terms appear in the glossary.

Compelling state interests   236             Judicious Discipline   232
*In loco parentis*   233

## Chapter Activities

### Reflecting on the Theory

1. In the middle of Mr. Lee's discussion of noun/verb agreement, Deidre England exclaimed, "Yuk, there's chewing gum stuck to the bottom of this desk." After class, Mr. Lee was disappointed to find chewed gum stuck to several of the desks. He thought he had been fair to all students when he allowed students to chew gum in his class. Now, he is considering disallowing all gum chewing.

   How could Mr. Lee use the principles of Judicious Discipline to resolve this problem?

2. There are those who suggest that Judicious Discipline can work only when it is a schoolwide plan and will not be effective for an individual classroom. Do you agree? What problems could develop if Judicious Discipline were used only in an individual classroom rather than by an entire school?

3. Give an example of when the rights of an individual student should come before the rights of the student body as a whole.

### Developing Artifacts for Your Portfolio

1. What rules could you develop for your class based on the four compelling state interests?

2. Judicious Discipline teaches students to examine their actions critically by teaching them to examine their behaviors in light of the "appropriate time, place, or manner" criterion. Develop an activity to help students understand this concept.

### Developing Your Personal Philosophy of Classroom Management

1. Judicious Discipline requires a great deal of time and planning by the classroom teacher. Do you consider the benefits of Judicious Discipline sufficient to offset the time commitment by the teacher? Why or why not?

2. Consider the age and maturity level of the students you will be teaching. Would Judicious Discipline be an effective classroom-management tool to use with these students? Why or why not?

## Resources for Further Study

Further information about Judicious Discipline and resources for its use in the classroom can be found by contacting

Forrest Gathercoal
Caddo Gap Press
3145 Geary Boulevard
Suite 275
San Francisco, CA 94118
Telephone 415-666-3012
Fax 415-666-3552

## Chapter References

Busse, N. (2008). Deliberately building the culture for students with severe emotional/behavioral disabilities. In B. Landau (Ed.), *Practicing Judicious Discipline: An educator's guide to a democratic classroom* (4th ed.). San Francisco: Caddo Gap Press.

Gathercoal, F. (2001). *Judicious discipline* (5th ed.). San Francisco: Caddo Gap Press.

Gathercoal, F. (2004). *Judicious discipline* (6th ed.). San Francisco: Caddo Gap Press.

Gathercoal, P. (2000). *Conducting democratic class meetings: School violence and conflict.* New Orleans, LA: Annual Meeting of the American Educational Research Association. (ERIC Document Reproduction Service No. ED442736.)

Gathercoal, P., & Nimmo, V. (2001). *Judicious (character education) discipline programs.* Seattle, WA: Annual Meeting of the American Educational Research Association. (ERIC Document Reproduction Service No. ED453124.)

Gathercoal, P., & Nimmo, V. (2002). *Judicious Discipline: 5 years later.* New Orleans, LA: Annual Meeting of the American Educational Research Association. (ERIC Document Reproduction Service No. ED467234.)

Grandmont, R. P. (2003). Judicious Discipline: A constitutional approach for public high schools. *American Secondary Education, 31,* 97–117.

Landau, B. (2008a). Introduction. In B. Landau (Ed.), *Practicing Judicious Discipline: An educator's guide to a democratic classroom* (4th ed.). San Francisco: Caddo Gap Press.

Landau, B. (2008b). Using consequences judiciously. In B. Landau (Ed.), *Practicing Judicious Discipline: An educator's guide to a democratic classroom* (4th ed.). San Francisco: Caddo Gap Press.

Landau, B. M., & Gathercoal, P. (2000). Creating peaceful classrooms. *Phi Delta Kappa, 81,* 450–455.

Larson, C. (1998). *Judicious discipline.* Beijing, China: Annual China–U.S. Conference on Education. (ERIC Document Reproduction Service No. ED427395.)

McEwan, B. (1991). *Practicing Judicious Discipline: An educator's guide to a democratic classroom.* Davis, CA: Caddo Gap Press.

McEwan, B. (2000). *The art of classroom management: Effective practices for building equitable learning communities.* Upper Saddle River, NJ: Merrill/Prentice Hall.

McEwan, B., Gathercoal, P., & Nimmo, V. (1999). Application of Judicious Discipline: A common language for classroom management. In H. Jerome Freiberg (Ed.), *Beyond behaviorism: Changing the classroom management paradigm.* Boston: Allyn & Bacon.

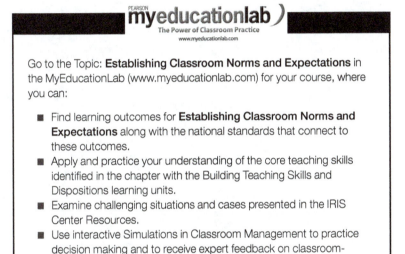

PEARSON
**myeducationlab )**
The Power of Classroom Practice
www.myeducationlab.com

Go to the Topic: **Establishing Classroom Norms and Expectations** in the MyEducationLab (www.myeducationlab.com) for your course, where you can:

- Find learning outcomes for **Establishing Classroom Norms and Expectations** along with the national standards that connect to these outcomes.
- Apply and practice your understanding of the core teaching skills identified in the chapter with the Building Teaching Skills and Dispositions learning units.
- Examine challenging situations and cases presented in the IRIS Center Resources.
- Use interactive Simulations in Classroom Management to practice decision making and to receive expert feedback on classroom-management choices.

# PART IV
# Developing a Personal System

The final two chapters of this text provide information to assist teachers in designing a personal system of classroom management. Chapter 14 provides best practices in classroom management. The best practices identified are the result of over forty years of research in the field. Chapter 15 helps the individual teacher put together all elements of classroom management into a comprehensive program.

# Research-Based Best Practices in Classroom Management

## Objectives

Chapter 14 prepares preservice teachers to meet INTASC standards #2 (Student Development), #5 (Motivation and Management), #6 (Communication), #7 (Planning), #9 (Reflective Practitioner), and #10 (School and Community) by helping them to

- use research on effective classroom management to select strategies and methods for managing the classroom.

- evaluate research concerning the impact of reinforcement on learning and behavior.

- evaluate classroom arrangement in maintaining appropriate classroom control.

- determine appropriate instructional strategies to be used in teaching classroom rules and procedures.

- determine the characteristics and actions of effective classroom managers.

- plan for an effective beginning of the school year.

- evaluate the impact of teacher–student interactions on the learning environment.

**253**

## Scenario

Gently tapping on the door, Rebecca Choi sticks her head into the office of her classroom management professor, David Libertore. "Dr. Libertore, do you have a minute to talk to me?"

Smiling, Dr. Libertore puts down the papers he is grading and points to the empty chair in the corner. "I always have time for you. What's on your mind?"

"I'm frustrated. The more classroom models we review, the more confused I get. They all seem so different, and yet, each theorist seems to think he or she has the answer." Rebecca leans in a little closer. "So, Dr. Libertore, what is the answer? Which one is right?"

Smiling, he says, "Wow, I wish it were that simple. What might be the 'right' answer for you," he says, making imaginary quotation marks with his fingers, "might not be the answer for another teacher. Each classroom is different, each school is different, and each teacher is different."

Seeing her confusion, he quickly adds, "But there are some strategies that the majority of theorists agree upon because research has shown them to be effective. Take rule development for example. Don't most theorists say we should create classroom rules in order to have a well-ordered classroom?"

"Of course, but they certainly don't agree about how those rules should be written or even who should develop them," Rebecca argues.

"Ah, you have discovered the great rule development debate. I'm glad you noticed the conflict. While most everyone agrees that rules are important, there are philosophical differences about who should develop the rules or how the rules should be written. For example, Coloroso thinks the rules should be based on what students will be asked to do once they leave school."

"And Gathercoal thinks they should be based on compelling state interests," Rebecca adds.

"Exactly, and probably both are right. If a particular theory fits your personal philosophy, then it will work well for you. But if there is not a theory that speaks to you personally, the best plan might be to identify the strategies that seem to cut across all theories and then determine how you will implement those strategies into your classroom. And remember, you want to pick strategies that have a proven research base."

Preparing to leave, Rebecca says, "That makes a lot of sense. I've really learned a lot this semester, but sometimes it is so much, it's overwhelming. Thanks for your time."

"Oh, I enjoyed it. I needed a break from all this grading," Dr. Libertore says, putting on his reading glasses. "But now, I guess it's back to work. I'll see you in class."

# INTRODUCTION

When Rebecca begins her search for research on classroom management, she may struggle to find useful research. This might seem surprising, but classroom-management researchers Carolyn Evertson and Carol Weinstein (2006) note that despite the concern of faculty, administrators, parents, and the public about discipline and classroom management, few researchers focus explicitly on classroom management or identify themselves with this field. They suggest that too often, classroom management is seen as a "bag of tricks" rather than a set of research-based principles, concepts, and skills that warrant serious professional study. Brophy (2006) agrees and notes that classroom management has an orphaned status and has never been established as a true part of the teacher education curriculum. Because classroom management cuts across disciplines, it has never been adequately addressed.

Brophy (2006) stresses that one reason for the lack of research in classroom management is that it is not feasible to use classical experimental methods to examine management strategies. Classroom teachers can control only a portion of what happens in the class-room, and much of good management involves reacting to unforeseen situations. The inability to control the environment makes traditional experimental design difficult. Therefore, investigators are forced to use interviewing, observing, and surveying as the principal methods of researching classroom management.

Much of the research that has been in classroom management was actually conducted by professionals outside the field of education. For example, research on behavioral theory has applications for classrooms. Much of the research on the application of reinforcers to influence the behavior of animals and individual students also can be used to control groups. The body of research on the effective use of reinforcers, modeling, extinction, and punishment has found its way into the classrooms (Landrum and Kauffman, 2006).

Beginning in the 1960s and continuing through the 1980s, several research teams explored relationships between classroom processes and subsequent outcomes (Brophy, 2006). Gettinger and Kohler (2006) identify this search for a relation between classroom processes (teaching) and outcomes (how students behave) as **process-outcome research.**

Important instructional advancements for both improving classroom behavior and promoting student achievement have come from this research. Process-outcome research has been successful in identifying management and instructional variables associated with high student performance. As a result, process-outcome research has moved the field of classroom-management research closer to that of being a science through evidence-based teaching practices derived from credible data.

Since the 1990s, studies of classroom management have used a different method of research known as meta-analysis to analyze the effectiveness of management strategies. Meta-analysis is the statistical procedure for combining data from multiple studies. When the treatment effect (or effect size) is consistent from one study to the next, meta-analysis can be used to identify this common effect. Two groups of researchers have used **meta-analysis** to research effective classroom-management methods. Wang, Haertel, and Walberg (1993) conducted a comprehensive study of hundreds of research reviews, journal articles, and government reports to determine what elements most related to student achievement. Marzano, Marzano, and Pickering (2003) analyzed the research of over 100 separate reports on effective schools. Their research clearly indicates that classroom management is one of the critical ingredients of effective teaching.

From nearly fifty years of research in classroom management has come a significant discovery—there is a direct correlation between effective management and student achievement. Brophy and Evertson (1976) found that teachers whose students consistently gained in achievement had organized classrooms that ran smoothly with a minimum of disruptions. Wang et al. (1993) found that effective classroom management has been shown to increase student engagement, decrease disruptive behaviors, and enhance use of instructional time. In their analysis, classroom management was rated first in terms of its impact on student achievement.

Marzano et al. (2003) agree as their findings show that effective classroom management has been seen as a critical element in teaching. They found that poor management results in wasted time, reduction of time on-task, and distractions from the learning environment. When these factors were eliminated, student achievement increased. Brophy

---

### Tips from the Field

I teach behavior modification to elementary school students at an alternative school in South Mississippi. I have found that art therapy is an extremely successful behavior modification tool. I use the arts to give students an opportunity to express their feelings, to evaluate their own behavior, and to facilitate the development of healthy peer relationships. I use arts throughout all areas of academic instruction. I teach math with drumming and dance. I teach social studies with drama and visual arts. I teach science through digital photography. By teaching the arts, I am able to meet the learning needs of students with unique and different learning styles.

My students have been referred to as the "ing" children (jumping, shouting, screaming, cursing, fighting, failing). Through participation in arts-infused programs, they have been transformed! They are still "ing" children . . . they are singing, dancing, painting, acting, sculpting, smiling, learning children.

> Christina Ross Daniels
> Center for Alternative Education
> Picayune, Mississippi
> 2005 Mississippi Teacher of the Year

---

(2006) agrees and notes that teachers who have withitness, who can overlap, and who can pace lessons, are better classroom managers. Therefore, when an individual teacher uses the techniques and strategies found to be effective in managing a classroom, the payoff is increased student achievement.

> When Alexander McNeese became the principal of Whitaker High School, he had been given the charge by the local school board to change the learning environment of the campus. Whitaker had earned the reputation of being the worst school in the district, and parents complained about the lack of classroom management by teachers. Mr. McNeese immediately pulled his faculty together and created a schoolwide management system that provided consistent expectations for the entire campus. During the next year, the climate at Whitaker slowly changed as students responded to the changes in the learning environment. The most surprising result, however, was that for the first time Whitaker was removed from the list of poor performing schools because the percentage of students making significant gains on achievement increased.

## BEST PRACTICES IN CLASSROOM MANAGEMENT

For over forty years, researchers such as Carolyn Evertson, Edmund Emmer, Linda Anderson, Barbara Clements, Jere Brophy, and Carolyn Weinstein have researched effective classroom-management practices. Some sought to verify the results of Jacob Kounin's pivotal study (see Chapter 1), and others have sought to determine the impact of effective classroom management on student achievement. These studies involve large numbers of teachers and students from all grade levels. More recently, meta-analysis studies by Robert Marzano, Margaret Wang, Geneva Haertel, and Herbert Walberg have reviewed hundreds of studies in classroom management.

Both types of research have identified eight specific strategies that represent the best practices in classroom management. These strategies were evaluated using sound experimental design and methodology and have been demonstrated to be effective as reported by numerous studies. Although most theorists agree that these strategies are essential to good management, the application of these strategies continues to cause debate.

## Creating Classroom Rules

Research by Gettinger and Kohler (2006) and Marzano et al. (2003) found that classroom rules are an integral part of effective classroom management. Classroom rules refer to the general expectations or standards for classroom conduct for all students. Clearly the research supports the notion that designing and implementing rules has a profound influence on student behavior and learning.

In his research on effective classroom rules, Thornberg (2008) identified the following types of classroom rules:

- relational rules—rules that provide students the standards for how to relate to other students.
- structuring rules—rules for participating in the activities of the classroom.
- protecting rules—rules that are created to provide safety for students.
- personal rules—rules that require self-reflection on a student's personal behavior.
- etiquette rules—rules that relate to how students should behave in social situations.

His research found that students felt relational rules to be the most critical for classroom. Older students are highly critical of "etiquette rules" and feel they are treated as little kids. Thornberg's research also found that if students do not see the point of a rule, they will have negative feelings toward it. Research by Brophy and McCaslin (1992) supports this finding because they found that effective teachers not only articulate and enforce rules, but they make sure that students understand why the rules are needed.

Cotton (1995) noted that rules should set standards that are consistent with or identical to the schoolwide code of conduct. Rules should be stated in positive terms rather than as a list of things that cannot be done. Once written, these rules are posted and/or provided to students and their parents.

Once rules are created, effective classroom managers teach the rules in the same way that they teach academic content (Marzano et al., 2003). Effective teachers explain, practice, and review classroom rules until students have mastered them. Simonsen, Fairbanks, Briesch, Myers, and Sugai (2008) found that pairing rule instruction with feedback and reinforcement leads to greater gains.

However, creating rules and teaching them to students is the beginning of the process. Effective teachers act when rules are broken. Effective teachers inform students of the consequences of breaking rules and then monitor compliance and enforce consequences.

### Tips from the Field

"The idle brain is the devil's playground" is an infamous saying that is quite good advice for classroom management. The key to keeping students focused on learning is to have them constantly engaged in some way of thinking about ideas or practicing skills from the moment they step in the classroom to the moment they leave. Students in my classroom understand that I expect all of them to be actively participating at all times. It eliminates the need to use methods to "fairly" call on students. The only fair way to assess learning is for all students to be participating at all times. Receiving feedback from one student randomly does not help. Each student in my classroom is provided a whiteboard, so all students are responding simultaneously. Teachers who want more effective classroom management learn to keep all learners thinking and engaged at all times.

Michael Fryda
Westside High School
Ninth-Grade Science
Omaha, Nebraska
2010 Nebraska Teacher of the Year

Consistency is critical as Thornberg (2008) discovered that students judge how their teachers handle rule violation and are critical of disrespectful and unfair treatment. Students want consistencies in the rule system.

> Kindergarten teacher Ericka Diamond begins her discussion of classroom rules to her class by reading *Never Spit on Your Shoes*. The book tells the story of a kindergarten class of animals who help their teacher create the class rules. The students love the book and find the rules the students create hysterical. Building on the experiences of the animals, she has her students suggest rules for their classrooms. Typically, by the end of the first day, her class has created a set of rules in which the students feel ownership.

## Creating Classroom Procedures

Along with establishing rules, creating classroom procedures has been proven to be an effective classroom-management strategy. Marzano et al. (2003) define classroom procedures as expectations for specific behaviors. Though rules might be general in nature, procedures are very specific. The importance of establishing procedures was first investigated in the late 1970s. In a study of third-grade classrooms that recorded behaviors of teachers and students from the first day of school and throughout the school year, Emmer, Evertson, and Anderson (1980) found that better classroom managers analyzed the classroom tasks. Their research found that effective managers were able to analyze in precise detail the procedures and expectations required for students to function well in a classroom.

This reserach was confirmed more recently when Emmer et al. (2006) and Cotton (1995) found that ineffecnt procedures and the absense of routines for common aspects of the classroom resulted in lost instructional time and caused students to lose focus. As classrooms become more learning centered, more complex procedures are needed due to the variety of activities, the movement of students around the room, and simultaneous activities by multiple students (Evertson and Neal, 2006).

Needed procedures for all classrooms include the following:

- a process for distributing and collecting materials

- a procedure for the storage of common materials

- specific procedures for the use of equipment such as computers

- procedures for entering and exiting the classrooms

- specific procedures for handling emergency situations such as fire alarms, weather alerts, and security issues

Just as rules need to be taught and practiced, procedures also must be taught and practiced. Practicing is especially essential for complex tasks so that students will have a thorough understanding of procedures. Gettinger and Kohler (2006) found that practicing procedures makes classroom activities less suscepible to breakdowns during interruptions to the normal school day.

> The first fifteen minutes of twelfth-grade history teacher Shavonna Pulley's class are always chaotic. She has trouble quieting the class as she is bombarded with students who need notes signed, who are turning in late assignments, or who are asking for missing papers. By the time the class is finally settled, her nerves are frayed and she is screaming at the students to be quiet. Her students enjoy the drama and are reinforced by the chaos to be even more disruptive.

> Across the hallway, Brittney Trice's class is an example of organization. As students arrive to class, they pick up a folder that contains their graded work or assignments they might have missed if they have been absent. While they complete the bell ringer assignment, Brittney moves through the room signing any paperwork that is needed and answering individual questions. Five minutes after class starts, bell work is completed and the day's lesson begins.

## Managing Classroom Transitions

Transitions are a constant in classrooms and have been a favorite topic of researchers in classroom management. In 1970, Jacob Kounin found that effective classroom managers possessed "transition smoothness." Kounin defined transition smoothness as the ability to manage various activities throughout the day and noted that the typical teacher must initiate, sustain, and terminate many activities during school time. Thirty years later, Gettinger and Kohler (2006) confirm Kounin's finding. They estimate that 15 percent of classroom time is spent in transition. Minor transitions occur between speaking turns, and major transitions occur between activities or phases of a lesson, between lessons, or as students move from one location to another. Therefore, the successful management of transitions is critical for maximizing learning time and minimizing misbehavior.

Effective classroom managers have the ability to make such transitions in a smooth and orderly fashion. The quality of transitions sets the pace and tone of the subsequent segment (Doyle, 2006). Successful managers have the ability to prevent problems before they occur and clearly signal the onset of transitions to prevent confusion. Effective teachers actively structure and orchestrate transitions, and they minimize the loss of momentum during these changes in activities. As with rules and procedures, effective teachers provide students with beginning-of-year instruction and practice transitions in the classroom.

> Beginning teacher Brandon Long was amazed when he realized he would have approximately 90 students in each of his physical education classes. He wondered how he would be able to manage that large number of students. It seemed that just checking the roll would take up a large portion of the class time. Fortunately, Brandon was not alone in teaching these students and found his co-teacher, Dedrick Parsons, a master in managing the classroom. What impressed Brandon most was the skill Dedrick used in having the students transition from one class to another. On the gym floor were the numbers 1 through 100. Each student had been assigned a number. During the change of class, Dedrick played several songs that had been suggested by the students. By the time the music ended, each student was to be sitting on his or her assigned number. In the minutes following the ending of the music, Brandon checked the roll for students numbered 1 through 45 by walking by the students and noting who was not sitting on his or her number. Dedrick checked numbers 46 through 90. In less than a minute, roll was taken and the list of those who were absent recorded. As soon as roll is completed, students are divided into groups and class begins.

## Creating an Effective Classroom Design

Marzano et al. (2003) found that the way a teacher arranges and decorates the classroom sends a message to students. As students enter the classroom on the first day, judgments are made about the teacher and how the teacher will manage the classroom. However, they stress to teachers that "it is not your job to create a 'pretty environment'; it is your job to create a 'learning' environment" (p. 98).

Creating a learning environment requires designing a classroom that supports the learning activities and the management of students that is desired. Teachers must consider the physical characteristics of a classroom, the number and needs of the students who will occupy the space, the arrangements of the desks, and restraints of the physical design of the room. Simonsen et al. (2008) note that additional attention must be given to traffic flows, teacher–student areas, and visual displays on the walls. Marzano et al. (2003) found that effective classroom arrangements allow

- all students to be seen by the teacher.
- all students to be reached by the teacher in moments.
- students to see all presentations.
- materials to be accessible to students and teachers.
- clear traffic flow for students.
- students to be easily organized into learning groups.
- no distractions in the learning process.

Simonsen et al. (2008) found that the physical arrangement of the classroom influences behavior. Effective planning and arrangement of the learning environment can prevent inappropriate and disruptive behavior.

> When new teacher Kawana Hughes saw her third-grade classroom for the first time, she thought she would cry. During her student teaching, she had been in bright, colorful classrooms. Now, facing her blank walls, she feared she didn't have the time, energy, or money to transform the dull room into what she had envisioned her classroom to be. Her principal suggested she contact the retired teacher association to see if anyone had materials they might donate to her. To her delight, she was given bean bags, boxes of books, a bookcase, curtains, and bulletin board materials. Within days, she had filled her room with materials that had been donated to her and transformed what had been an empty dull room into a bright learning environment for her students.

## Planning for the Beginning of the Year

Over thirty years ago, Emmer et al. (1980) found that classrooms that ran smoothly had set the stage by thorough preparation and organization at the beginning of the school year. In 2003, Marzano et al. agreed when they stated that "virtually all research points to the beginning of the year as the 'linchpin' for effective classroom management" (p. 92). During the first days of class, teachers convey powerful messages about who they are and how they will manage their classrooms. If during the beginning weeks of school, rules, procedures, and transitions are established, taught, and reinforced, teachers find the rest of the year tends to go smoothly. Therefore, planning how one manages the classroom during the first weeks of school is as critical as planning instruction.

Doyle (2006) notes that from the perspective of order, the early class sessions of the school year are of utmost importance. Relationships are established during these critical weeks, and Brophy (2006) found that at the beginning of the year, the best teachers conveyed more personal acceptance of students. Brophy (2006) notes that the consensus of the research in effective classroom management shows that from the first day of school, teachers should be friendly, personable, and businesslike while they take charge and establish a positive classroom atmosphere. Effective teachers reinforced good behavior and praised students more than less effective teachers. They provided critical cues for the behavior that is desired. These teachers watched student behavior carefully and corrected behavior quickly.

Clearly, there is a difference during the first weeks of school in an elementary classroom versus a middle or secondary classroom. Evertson and Emmer (1982) found that elementary students must learn "going to school" behaviors. Middle school and high school students have been taught these skills and, therefore, need to spend their time learning their responsibility for engaging in and completing work.

> As a veteran eighth-grade science teacher of over thirty years, Melissa Webb understands the importance of establishing procedures for her classroom during the first week of classes. The first day of class is spent going over her classroom rules and getting to know her students. The second day is devoted to safety. As Melissa introduces the procedures for using the science equipment in the classroom, she stresses that the purpose of the procedures is to keep students safe. At the end of the first week, her

students put on skits showing the correct and incorrect ways to use the equipment. Her students have a great deal of fun showing the tragic things that can happen when science equipment is used incorrectly.

## Providing Individual and Group Reinforcements

The use of positive reinforcement as a classroom-management strategy has been well established (Landrum and Kauffman, 2006). This research cuts across all age groups, ability levels, and a variety of settings. In the past forty years, literally thousands of studies have shown that teacher's delivery of social reinforcement can result in improved academic performance, rule following, and good school behavior.

Simonsen et al. (2008) identify a continuum of strategies to acknowledge appropriate behavior. The following strategies have been supported by research as effective in changing and controlling student behavior:

1. Specific contingent praise. Simonsen et al. (2008) state that praise has the strongest evidence base as being an effective strategy.

2. Group reinforcements. This strategy is used to create common expectations for a group of students, and the group is rewarded when all engage in expected behaviors.

3. Behavior contracts. Used with individual students, behavior contracts have been effective in changing unacceptable behaviors.

4. Token economies. Students earn tokens individually or as a group when they display desired behaviors. These tokens are then cashed in for a desired award.

The four types of reinforcers above have all been proven to be effective in changing behaviors. Group reinforcement and token economies are often used together. These reinforcers have been found to

- increase positive and decrease negative verbal interactions.
- decrease transition time.
- increase achievement.
- increase appropriate classroom behavior.
- promote peer social acceptance.
- increase student attendance.
- decrease inappropriate behavior.
- decrease talk-outs and out-of-seat behavior.
- increase student preparedness for class and assignment completion.

Although research clearly shows the effectiveness of reinforcers, many educators disagree with their use. They argue that these reinforcers only change behavior for a short period and do nothing to create lifelong learners (Kohn, 1996). Reeve (2006) agrees that if reinforcers are administered in controlling ways, they can undermine a student's autonomy, intrinsic motivation, self-regulation, and engagement. Therefore, it is critical that teachers who provide

*Often teachers must research the most effective interventions to reach challenging students.*

reinforcers to their students study research on extinction so that the reinforcers can be withdrawn as students learn to take responsibility for their learning and their behaviors.

> Heather Collins was known for her popcorn in a jar. Each day she determines the overall behavior of the class. If they have had a good day, a scoop of unpopped popcorn is placed in a large gallon jar. Sometimes, a scoop is put in the jar when the students get a good report from another teacher or when they are especially well behaved. When students perform a procedure accurately and quickly (such as lining up in the class), Heather gives them a scoop. This encourages them to perform the task the same way each time. When the jar is full, they pop the popcorn and have a popcorn party. Heather's students love watching the jar fill.

## Monitoring Student Performance

Gettinger and Kohler (2006) found that monitoring student performance is a critical aspect of classroom management. Research by Doyle (2006) agrees with this finding and adds that effective teachers constantly monitor the classroom and are able to juggle many tasks at once. Effective teachers monitor student behavior in one of the following ways:

1. They monitor the entire class. The teacher constantly circulates around the room and sees that the class is functioning as a whole.

2. They observe individual students. Effective teachers watch for verbal and physical cues that students are stressed or having difficulty. Therefore, they are able to prevent situations from escalating. They respond to incidents of student misbehavior promptly and consistently. Because of this constant monitoring, effective teachers know who is off-task and redirects the corrected student.

3. They monitor their own teaching. Effective teachers read their students' nonverbal behaviors and adjust the pace, rhythm, and duration of classroom activities and assignments to meet student needs. They use feedback from students and their assessment of their students to provide clear instructions. Most important, they consider this adjustment as a natural part of the teaching process rather than a failure on their part or on the part of their students.

4. They monitor their thoughts. Marzano et al. (2003) stress that it is critical for teachers to self-monitor their attitudes about specific students because negative attitudes get in the way of helping students who are most in need of interventions.

> Kindergarten teacher Melinda Parsons noticed that her students had spent a lot of time during recess pointing at her and staring at her head. Unable to suppress her curiosity any longer, she calls a group of students over to her. "I noticed that you have been watching me. What's going on?"
>
> Two of her little girls giggled. "Can we feel the back of your head?"
>
> Surprised, Melinda responded, "Well, I guess so. Why do you want to feel my head?"
>
> "Cody's daddy said you must have eyes in the back of your head because you always know when Cody is bad even when you aren't looking at him. We told Cody that you can't have eyes in the back of your head. You don't, do you?"
>
> Laughing, Melinda parted her hair so the girls could take a closer look. "See, there are no eyes in the back of my head. I don't need eyes in the back of my head to know when you are being bad or good."
>
> Giggling, the girls ran to tell Cody that Mrs. Parsons didn't have eyes in the back of her head.

## Building Positive Relations with Students

Marzano et al. (2003) note that a quality student–teacher relationship is critical for a positive learning experience. Wang et al. (1993) agree and found that just as positive student–teacher academic interactions foster learning, positive student–teacher interactions foster a positive classroom environment. They found that effective teachers express personal warmth and encouragement and use humor to hold students' interest and defuse classroom tensions.

---

### Tips from the Field

Some unruly students suffer from family discord and divorce, parents with drug and alcohol problems, neglect or abuse, serious lack of self-confidence and self-esteem, and personal emotional problems. Sometimes having a personal talk early in the year can uncover what is bothering a student. Take the time early in the year to develop a relationship with your students—get to know them.

Alison Standing
Behaviour Management Teacher
Churchill State School
Churchill, Ipswich
Australia

Because of these positive relationships, there are fewer disruptions, more acceptance of rules, fewer disciplinary actions, and more tolerance toward divergent points of view.

Often behavioral problems are the result of a breakdown in teacher–student relationships. Teachers who want total control in the classroom will find that students rebel against that control. Teachers who are too lax will lose control of the classroom as students take over the running of the class. What students want is a benevolent dictatorship in which the teacher is in charge of the classroom. Marzano et al. (2003) found that the optimal teacher–student relationship consists of equal parts of dominance and cooperation. Students want the teacher to be in control but to be fair in that control. Effective managers do not treat all students the same, particularly in situations involving behavioral problems. They recognize that some students need encouragement, others need a gentle reprimand, and still others might need another consequence. It is important that teachers convey the message that they are concerned about their students as individuals and the class as a whole.

Though effective teachers maintain control of the classroom, Cotton (1990) found that they share the responsibility for managing the classroom with students. Their goal is that students develop a sense of belonging, ownership of their own behavior, and responsibility for each other.

> For-sixth grade teacher Natasha Brown, building a positive relationship with students begins before the first day of class. As soon as Natasha receives her class list, she begins making calls to her students' parents. After introducing herself, she asks several questions about the student's family, pets, and interests. She uses this information on the first day of class. As she greets each student, she makes a point of mentioning something she knows about the students. This acknowledgment is the start of the positive relationship she has with her students.

## Selecting Appropriate Interventions

When teachers talk of the interventions they use in their classroom, the idea of punishment comes to mind. However, the majority of interventions in classroom settings are not punitive. Most interventions fall into two categories—preventive or reactive (Clunies-Ross, Little, & Kiehuis, 2008). In general, preventive strategies are those behaviors that a teacher uses to prevent the likelihood of behavior problems. Reactive strategies occur following a student's behavior. Figure 14.1 provides examples of both types of interventions.

Preventive interventions include rule development, the creation of procedures and transitions, the development of positive relationships with students, the monitoring of students, and the arrangement of the classroom. These strategies have been discussed extensively in this chapter. When these interventions are in place, the need for reactive interventions diminishes.

Reactive interventions also fall into two categories, and the guiding principle for reactive interventions is that that there should be a healthy balance between negative interventions for inappropriate behavior and positive interventions for appropriate behavior (Marzano et al., 2003). Therefore, it is important that teachers recognize when their students display good behavior. This recognition can be provided through praise, tangible rewards, group rewards, or through a token economy. If appropriate behavior is never recognized, the students will decide that they can never please the teacher and will eventually stop trying.

**Figure 14.1**

Effective Interventions

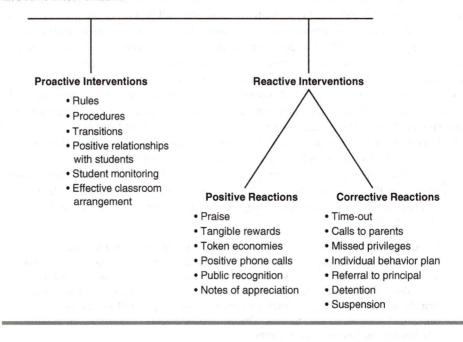

**Proactive Interventions**

- Rules
- Procedures
- Transitions
- Positive relationships with students
- Student monitoring
- Effective classroom arrangement

**Reactive Interventions**

**Positive Reactions**

- Praise
- Tangible rewards
- Token economies
- Positive phone calls
- Public recognition
- Notes of appreciation

**Corrective Reactions**

- Time-out
- Calls to parents
- Missed privileges
- Individual behavior plan
- Referral to principal
- Detention
- Suspension

Eventually all teachers will be forced to provide a corrective intervention when students display undesirable behavior. Teachers dread these types of interactions because as Clunies-Ross et al. (2008) found, student misbehavior affects teacher stress, well-being, and confidence. It also impacts negatively on student learning and academic achievements.

Care is needed when corrective interventions are used because they call attention to potentially disruptive behavior. Doyle (2006) states that corrective interventions are risky because the teacher must determine if stopping instruction is necessary. The decision to intervene requires complex judgments concerning the behavior, the student, and the circumstances at a particular moment in classroom time. In some cases, interventions can pull the class farther away. Some teacher responses to disruptive behavior can backfire and actually increase disruptive behavior.

Some investigators suggest that corrective interventions are not effective, but Marzano et al. (2003) found that the categorical rejection of corrective interventions is simply not supported by research. Their findings strongly support a balanced approach that employs a variety of techniques. Research by Stage and Quiroz (1997) confirms this, and they learned that corrective interventions resulted in a decrease in disruptive behavior among almost 80 percent of the subjects in the studies they analyzed. In addition, Nelson, Martella, and Galand (1999) found that a systemic response to disruptive behavior was a key role in reducing office referrals.

Therefore, corrective interventions are needed in order to maintain classroom control and to help individual students become more responsible. More effective teachers tried to develop long-term solutions to address the causes of problems rather than simply trying to control the students (Brophy & McCaslin, 1992). Teachers who got the most effective results used minimally intrusive yet prescriptive techniques. Often the technique was as simple as gaining attention by touching or moving closer to misbehaving students. These teachers provided specific cues concerning the desired behavior. Effective teachers remained professional in their interactions and maintained control of their own emotions.

In contrast, teachers who were nonintrusive but less prescriptive appeared to be ineffectual. Teachers who relied on loud and disruptive interventions were reported to be less successful in achieving student compliance. Other ineffective techniques included yelling, blaming, threatening, and punitive actions. When students did comply, they did so grudgingly and often returned to the previous behavior as soon as the teacher was not present.

Brophy and McCaslin (1992) found that effective teachers and ineffective teachers often used the same interventions. What differed was the way the strategies were used. Effective teachers catch disruptive behavior early (Nelson et al., 1999). They don't let the situation escalate and get out of control.

## Scenario

Principal Jorge Hernandez stared at two stacks of office referrals on his desk. Looking up at his two assistant principals, he said, "Can you explain what we have here? This stack," he said as he motioned to the stack, "comes from ten faculty members. These ten teachers have had less than thirty referrals this semester." He waved his hand over the second stack. "And this stack is from ten faculty members. There are over three hundred referrals here. These teachers are averaging one referral a day. I want to know why. I want you"—he nodded toward the two assistant principals—"to find out the difference. If the first group has some magic formula that we don't know about, I want us to all know it."

Two weeks later, his assistant principals return to give Mr. Hernandez a report of what they had found. Bill Lawson leans back in his chair. "I have to tell you that before I did this research I was convinced that the first group of teachers just had better kids. However, what I found was that some of the students are in the classes with teachers with the low number of referrals and also in the classes of teachers with the high numbers of referrals. The number of referrals seems to have nothing to do with the students."

"I agree," Rebecca Ramsey says. "And there's not any magic. The teachers with low referrals have extremely organized classes. The students come in to class, and they know what is expected. If there is a disruption, they take care of it quickly and everyone gets back to work. When I observed the other teachers, however, I found classes in chaos. It takes the teachers half the class time to get the attention of the students. I saw no rules posted and no rules enforced. They let the class run wild until they are frustrated and send students to the office. I didn't see them even try to correct behavior. They simply sent students to the office. If we want this to change, the second group must use the same tactics as the first group. It seems simple, but I doubt it is."

**Table 14.1**   Summary of Research in Classroom Management

- Group behaviors differ from individual behavior.
- Effective classroom management starts with careful planning for the school year and each school day. The order created during the first few days of school reliably predicts the degree of student engagement and disruption for the rest of the year.
- Effective classroom management prevents disruptions from occurring rather than merely reacting to situations.
- Effective teachers weave instructional and disciplinary strategies together.
- Better managers provide instruction in classroom rules and procedures as part of the curriculum.
- Academic achievement and effective classroom management are tied together.
- Effective classroom management enables teachers to spend more time on instruction, resulting in greater academic gains for students.
- Effective managers begin by identifying the goals of instruction. They then consider the student behaviors needed to achieve these goals. As they plan instruction, they also plan for the management necessary to accomplish their objectives.

## Summary

In the past fifty years, researchers have spent thousands of hours observing the behaviors of teachers who successfully and unsuccessfully managed their classrooms. The findings from these fifty years of research appear in Table 14.1. The good news is that research verifies that good managers aren't born; they are made by using research-based practices (Marzano et al., 2003).

## Key Terminology

Definitions for these terms appear in the glossary.

Meta-analysis research    255                              Process-outcome research    255

## Chapter Activities

### Reflecting on the Theory

1. Consider a class you attended that had a successful beginning. What activities established the learning environment in that class? What activities made you feel welcome and part of the learning environment?

2. Where do you stand in the great rule debate? Will you create the rules for your classroom or will you involve your students in the creation of the rules?

3. Robert Marzano said, "It is not your job to create a 'pretty environment'; it is your job to create a 'learning' environment." What did he mean? How do you create a "learning environment"?

4. Research on effective classroom management points to the importance of having a positive relationship with students. What strategies will you use to establish effective relationships with your students?

## Developing Artifacts for Your Portfolio

1. Find a research article related to the topic of classroom management. Critique the article by providing a brief analysis of the research and your evaluation of the research.

2. Review a lesson plan you have created. Evaluate the lesson plan to determine what procedures will be needed for the lesson to be effective.

## Developing Your Personal Philosophy of Classroom Management

1. This text has presented twelve models of classroom management. Which of these models do you feel best utilizes the effective strategies identified in this chapter?

# Chapter References

Brophy, J. (2006). History of research. In C. Evertson & C. Weinstein (Eds.), *Handbook of classroom management: Research, practice, and contemporary issues.* Mahwah, NJ: Lawrence Erlbaum Associates.

Brophy, J. E., & Evertson, C. M. (1976). *Learning from teaching: A developmental perspective.* Boston: Allyn & Bacon.

Brophy, J. E., & McCaslin, M. (1992). Teachers' reports of how they perceive and cope with problem students. *The Elementary School Journal, 93,* 3–68.

Clunies-Ross, P., Little, E., & Kiehuis, M. (2008). Self-reported and actual use of proactive and reactive classroom management strategies and their relationship with teacher stress and student behaviour. *Educational Psychology, 28,* 693–710. DOI: 10.1080/01443410802206700.

Cotton, K. (1990). *Schoolwide and classroom discipline.* School Improvement Research Series. Portland, OR: Northwest Regional Educational Laboratory.

Cotton, K. (1995). *Effective schooling practices: A research synthesis 1995 update.* Portland, OR: Northwest Regional Educational Laboratory. Retrieved May 15, 2010, from http://home.comcast.net/~reasoned/4410/PDFonCRM/Effective%20School%20Prac.pdf.

Doyle, W. (2006). Ecological approaches to classroom management. In C. Evertson & C. Weinstein (Eds.), *Handbook of classroom management: Research, practice, and contemporary issues.* Mahwah, NJ: Lawrence Erlbaum Associates.

Emmer, E., Evertson, C., & Anderson, L. (1980). Effective management at the beginning of the school year. *Elementary School Journal, 80,* 219–231.

Emmer, E. T., Evertson, C. M., & Worsham, M. E. (2006). *Classroom management for middle and high school teachers* (7th ed.). Boston: Allyn & Bacon.

Evertson, C., & Emmer, E. (1982). Effective management at the beginning of the school year in junior high classes. *Journal of Educational Psychology, 74,* 485–498.

Evertson, C. M., & Neal, K. W. (2006). *Looking into learning-centered classrooms: Implications for classroom management. Working paper.* Washington, DC: National Education Association.

Evertson, C. M., & Weinstein, C. S. (2006). Classroom management as a field of study. In C. Evertson & C. Weinstein (Eds.), *Handbook of classroom management: Research, practice, and contemporary issues.* Mahwah, NJ: Lawrence Erlbaum Associates.

Gettinger, M., & Kohler, K. M. (2006). Process-outcome approaches to classroom management and effective teaching. In C. Evertson & C. Weinstein (Eds.), *Handbook of classroom management: Research, practice, and contemporary issues.* Mahwah, NJ: Lawrence Erlbaum Associates.

Kohn, A. (1996). *Beyond discipline: From compliance to community.* Alexandria, VA: Association for Supervision and Curriculum Development.

Kounin, J. S. (1970). *Discipline and group management in classrooms.* New York: Holt, Rinehart & Winston.

Landrum, T. J., & Kauffman, J. M. (2006). Behavioral approaches to classroom management. In C. Evertson & C. Weinstein (Eds.), *Handbook of classroom management: Research, practice, and contemporary issues.* Mahwah, NJ: Lawrence Erlbaum Associates.

Marzano, R. J., Marzano, J. S., & Pickering, D. J. (2003). Classroom management that works: Research-based strategies for every teacher. Alexandria, VA: Association for Supervision and Curriculum Development.

Nelson, J., Martella, R., & Galand, B. (1999). The effects of teaching school expectations and establishing a consistent consequence on formal office disciplinary actions. *Journal of Emotional and Behavioral Disorders, 6,* 53–61.

Reeve, J. (2006). Extrinsic rewards and inner motivation. In C. Evertson & C. Weinstein (Eds.), *Handbook of classroom management: Research, practice, and contemporary issues.* Mahwah, NJ: Lawrence Erlbaum Associates.

Simonsen, B., Fairbanks, S., Briesch, A., Myers, D., & Sugai, G. (2008). Evidence-based practices in classroom management: Considerations for research to practice. *Education and Treatment of Children, 31,* 351–380.

Stage, S. A., & Quiroz, D. R. (1997). A meta-analysis of interventions to decrease disruptive classroom behavior in public education settings. *School Psychology Review, 26,* 333–368.

Thornberg, R. (2008). School children's reasoning about school rules. *Research Papers in Education, 23,* 37–52.

Wang, M. C., Haertel, G. D., & Walberg, H. J. (1993). Toward a knowledge base for school learning. *Review of Educational Research, 63,* 249–294.

# Creating Your Own System

## Objectives

Chapter 15 prepares preservice teachers to meet INTASC standards #1 (Content Pedagogy), #3 (Diverse Learners), #4 (Instructional Strategies), #5 (Motivation and Management), #9 (Reflective Practitioner), and #10 (School and Community) by helping them to

- evaluate the impact of a teacher's philosophy, personality, and teaching style on the selection of a classroom-management plan.

- evaluate the impact of teaching strategies on the selection of a classroom-management plan.

- determine whether they will use a teacher-centered or student-centered approach to classroom management.

- develop a personal classroom-management plan.

- select specific classroom-management strategies they will use in their individual classrooms.

**271**

- determine ways to prevent student misbehavior.

- select methods for dealing with inappropriate behavior.

- evaluate how subject-area content impacts classroom-management strategies.

- determine how the school environment impacts individual management plans.

## Scenario

As part of the recruitment process for the Denton School District, a team of principals interviews all candidates using a predetermined list of questions. Two of the questions deal with classroom management, and candidates are asked to provide a personal definition of effective classroom management and to describe the classroom-management plan they intend to use in their classrooms. Today, recent graduates Denise Sowell, Martin Segovia, and Brianne Kraeske are being interviewed.

Denise hesitates only a moment before answering the two questions. She had anticipated the questions and says, "I think that effective classroom management is having sufficient control of your classroom so that everyone can learn. To do this, I plan to use Assertive Discipline. I studied Assertive Discipline when I was in college, and my cooperating teacher was using Assertive Discipline as her management plan when I student-taught. So, I've had a lot of opportunity to see its application. I think I will feel comfortable using this model."

Martin is visibly nervous when he is being interviewed, and his hands shake as he responds to the questions. "I see classroom management as managing all the elements of the classroom so that learning can occur. That means I have to carefully plan how my room is arranged, my class rules, and the procedures for how we will do our activities. I don't have a specific plan in mind. I hope to follow the plan the school has adopted or to use what the majority of the teachers in the school use, because I think there should be consistency within a school."

Brianne is pleased when she is asked the question. She has spent a lot of time thinking about the management plan she would adopt. She has even brought diagrams of how she hopes to arrange her classroom. "I want to use a very student-centered approach with my students. That means I want them to help me create our rules and our consequences. I plan to have a student-centered classroom with lots of activities, so I will need to carefully plan the procedures I will use for group management. I guess I would define effective classroom management as helping students learn to be responsible for their own behavior. That will be my ultimate goal: to help students learn to manage themselves."

## INTRODUCTION

The panel of principals may have a difficult time selecting from the three candidates, because none of their answers were incorrect. Their answers represented the philosophy, personality, and teaching style of each candidate. Therefore, any of the three candidates would be an appropriate choice if the teacher's plan fits into the principal's philosophy and management style.

Ultimately, the most effective classroom-management plan is one that meets the needs of the individual teacher, the teacher's students, and the school environment. In many cases, an existing model will be the best choice. In other cases, the teacher will find it best to merge parts of several models to meet the requirements of the classroom and school environment. Often, the teacher is more comfortable creating a plan that meets the teacher's unique needs. Swick (1985) suggests that the selection of the appropriate classroom-management plan requires teachers to give careful consideration to their own philosophies, personalities, teaching styles, and teaching experiences, and to carefully evaluate the mission and environment of their school and community.

## THE PHILOSOPHY OF THE TEACHER

Gathercoal (2001) notes that the basis of a teacher's philosophy is generally formed from fundamental beliefs concerning the basic nature of students, the way students learn, the amount of control or freedom students need, and the way students should respond to the authority of the teacher. This philosophy will provide the foundation for the classroom-management plan selected and used by the teacher.

Martin and Baldwin (1993) suggest that there is an ideological continuum along which a teacher's philosophy will fall. At one end of the continuum is the belief that a student must learn appropriate behaviors and that one of the functions of the teacher is to maintain classroom control while this learning process occurs. At the other end of the continuum is the belief that it is a student's nature to "be good" and that a student will behave appropriately if given the freedom and responsibility to do so.

Gathercoal (2001) also argues that two different educational philosophies exist regarding the nature of students. One philosophy contends that students are evil from birth and that this evil nature can be corrected only by a strong teacher who uses authoritarian methods. The other philosophy views students as innately good and the teacher's role as nurturing the growth of this goodness through positive interactions.

Teachers like Denise, who consider it the responsibility of teachers to maintain control in the classroom, are considered **teacher-centered** in their approach. In the past few years, teacher-centered approaches have been viewed negatively by educators as new research on teaching has focused on the effectiveness of student-centered approaches. However, many teachers think students need guidance by a trained teacher as they move through various stages of cognitive, social, and moral development. Often, it is not their view of students as "evil" that causes teachers to support a teacher-centered approach, but rather their belief that the student's environment influences behavior and that student behavior can be changed by reward, reinforcement, and punishment (Martin & Baldwin, 1993). In the teacher-centered classroom, rules begin with student responsibilities. The breaking of rules requires interventions in the form of punishments or consequences to help students make mental connections between behavior and the consequences of behavior. Privileges in a teacher-centered classroom are earned through appropriate behavior.

At the opposite end of the continuum are teachers like Brianne, who propose a **student-centered approach** to teaching and classroom management. The student-centered teacher presupposes that the student has an inner drive to do what is right and learn responsibility through interactions and experiences in a safe, welcoming environment. Gathercoal (2001) notes that student-centered teachers think of students as inherently good and believe they can trust students. Therefore, they are quite comfortable putting into practice methods designed to help students learn and develop attitudes of respect and responsibility. When behavior problems occur, the student-centered teacher is concerned with which strategies will be most effective in bringing about a reasonable resolution to the problem. Every interaction with misbehaving students centers on the resolution of the problem by creating learning experiences that allow them to grow and recover from mistakes. This growth results in students learning responsibility. Choice is important in a student-centered classroom because of the belief that students are active, positive, motivated, and unique problem solvers.

Few teachers act totally according to either of these extreme philosophies or are either totally teacher- or student-centered. Most teachers weigh their basic philosophies about students with educational research and their own experiences to provide a more balanced approach in their teaching practices and management strategies.

## THE PERSONALITY OF THE TEACHER

Martin and Baldwin (1993) propose that the personality of the teacher is the most significant variable in classroom success. They found no real research, however, that defines the ideal personality for a teacher. Students, too, would have difficulty describing the ideal personality for a teacher. During their twelve years of school, students will encounter teachers with a variety of personalities. Some teachers can tolerate a great deal of noise in their classrooms, whereas others want their classrooms to be a quiet place. Some teachers joke and kid with their students, whereas others maintain a serious, businesslike demeanor. A look into classrooms will find some that are messy, with materials scattered around the room, and others that are neat, with everything carefully organized and in its place. Some teachers allow students to leave their seats to sharpen their pencils and retrieve materials, whereas others will allow students to leave their seats only with permission. Teachers vary in a thousand ways, and amazingly, most students manage to deal relatively effectively with this variety of personalities.

---

### Tips from the Field

Fellow teachers can be your best resource. Don't try to reinvent the wheel. New teachers think they have to come up with some snappy original idea for every concept they teach. Let me dispel the myth. I haven't had an original idea in twenty years. I've learned to sponge off others' ideas and weave them into my own to make magical lessons. However, it is important to give credit where credit is due. Use the Internet, professional magazines, and colleagues to gain great ideas. Go to professional meetings (a potpourri of great ideas) and absorb. Don't burn out. Bone up on what others can teach you.

Cynthia H. Lynch
Fourth-Grade Teacher
C.E. Hanna Elementary School
Oxford, Alabama

Perhaps, then, it is not a specific teacher personality that creates a successful classroom, but the congruence between the teacher's personality and the teacher's actions. Teachers often adopt a particular instructional or discipline technique because research shows it is effective or there is a mandate from the administration. If that technique does not fit the teacher's personality, however, the technique will fail, students will be frustrated, and problems will occur.

Martin found this to be true during his student teaching experience. Both Martin's cooperating teacher and his university supervisor encouraged him to use cooperative learning as a part of his teaching strategies. However, Martin found that he was constantly telling students to lower their voices. Although his cooperating teacher thought the noise level appropriate, Martin felt the class was constantly out of control, and he often resorted to shouting at students to lower their voices. Brianne had the opposite experience. Observing a very traditional classroom, Brianne found the activities boring and wondered what kept the students from falling asleep. She vowed that when she had her own classroom, students would move, talk, and work together.

A second key to finding the balance between teaching personality and classroom management lies with the teacher's expectations. Students can and do deal effectively with a variety of teaching styles, management styles, and teacher personalities as long as they understand what the teacher expects and the teacher is consistent in those expectations. When expectations are not clearly defined, however, students may feel they are treated unfairly and conflicts may develop between students and the teacher. It is important, therefore, that the management plan selected fit the personality of the teacher, and that all components of the plan, including rules, consequences, and procedures, are clearly defined for students from the first day of school.

*Collaborating with fellow teachers will enhance your classroom-management plan.*

## THE TEACHING STYLE OF THE TEACHER

Brianne's answer about her classroom-management plan showed an unusual understanding of the connections between teaching style and classroom management. Having given careful consideration to how she wanted to provide instruction, she used her approach to teaching as the springboard for selecting the plan she would use. Swick (1985) agrees that room size, seating arrangements, time spent in various activities, available learning resources, subject-area transitions, and group interactions are typical management issues that teachers need to work out in advance of actual teaching and in conjunction with the teaching strategies they plan to use.

Brophy (2006) emphasizes that well-established classroom-management techniques often have to be adapted or elaborated to fit a particular classroom. Strategies used for managing small groups might not be effective for large groups. Therefore, the teacher will be required to adjust based on the teaching strategies used. Classroom-management practices must be aligned to support the teacher's intended goals and activities. Brophy suggests that teachers work backward from the goals they hope to achieve to the strategies that will make these goals possible.

Many classroom-management instructional issues are dictated by the subject area taught. Lab classes, vocational classes, and fine arts classes require differing approaches to classroom management because of the physical design of the classroom, the activities involved, group interactions, transitions, procedures, and safety requirements. However, these same issues must be considered with regard to the learning environment in traditional classrooms. Therefore, classroom-management plans must be developed with consideration given to both the subject area taught and the teaching style of the classroom teacher.

Brianne plans to use a student-centered approach to her teaching. As she noted in her response to the panel of principals, this approach requires that she give careful thought to the grouping of students, the management of transitions, and procedures for working in cooperative groups. She may find it helpful to adopt a model such as Marshall's Discipline without Stress® Punishments or Rewards, Curwin and Mendler's Discipline with Dignity and Kohn's Building Community, or Evertson's Classroom Organization and Management Program (COMP), because these models support student-centered teaching strategies. She may find elements from several of these models helpful and create a model that combines many of the ideas and strategies presented in these existing models.

Teachers who plan to use teacher-centered approaches have other issues to consider and must develop a classroom-management plan that supports the instructional practices they intend to use. Lectures, tutorials, drills, demonstrations, and other forms of teacher-controlled teaching tend to be the focus of instruction in teacher-centered classrooms. Such activities require that the seating arrangement allow all students to see and hear the teacher. In classrooms where students respond to teacher-directed questions, the teacher must develop clear rules for engaging in the discussion process. Because teacher-centered classrooms tend to use distinct time periods for each subject area, it is important that students progress through the day in an orderly fashion. Teachers using a teacher-centered approach to teaching may want to adopt Skinner's *Behavioral Management,* Canter's

## Tips from the Field

My most effective classroom-management "trick" is always to have fast-paced lessons and to keep students focused on the task at all times. I must know my lesson so well that I can constantly run and work the class while being aware of potential issues and problems before they appear. If students are actively engaged in their own education, they will not have time to stray from the purpose of the class. I have found, in many classes I observe, that time is wasted by the teacher preparing class mate-

rial during instructional time. Thus students know that their time is being wasted, and they act out. To prevent this, teachers must be prepared with all materials ready when instruction begins.

David Neves
Music Teacher and Band Director
Scituate High School–Middle School
2002 Rhode Island Teacher of the Year
North Scituate, Rhode Island

*Assertive Discipline,* Jones's *Positive Classroom Discipline,* or Albert's *Logical Consequences,* because all of these models work well in teacher-centered classrooms.

The establishment and maintenance of an effective classroom-management plan is derived not only from knowledge about management theory and strategies, but also from the teacher's content and procedural knowledge of the subject matter. Daily planning by the teacher must include thoughtful consideration about both classroom management and instruction.

## THE TEACHER'S EVALUATION OF THE SCHOOL ENVIRONMENT

Martin looked to the school and its administration for guidance in developing his classroom-management plan. To create his plan, Martin will assess the school environment because he understands that a knowledge of the mission of the school; the policies of the school, district, and state; and the management style of the administration will impact his plans for classroom management. Martin must also consider the size of the school and the cultural, gender, and socioeconomic makeup of the student body as he develops his plan.

Swick (1985) recommends that a teacher's classroom-management approach evolve from the total school setting and reflect the ecology of the school. He advises that classroom management should be proactive and related to all the factors that influence the functioning of teachers, students, parents, and administrators in the classroom and the school. Swick identifies six elements of a school ecology that directly influence classroom management:

1. *Behavior of School Personnel:* A visit to any school immediately gives a view of the interactions between school personnel and the student body. Often overlooked are the interactions of the office staff, custodians, and other support people. If these personnel see their jobs as important to the functioning of the school and understand that their interactions

contribute to the overall climate of the school, the atmosphere will be one of mutual respect among staff, faculty, students, and administrators.

2. *The Campus:* The physical layout of the campus contributes to the overall feeling of safety and security felt by students and teachers. Classrooms that are isolated or that are housed in portable facilities present unique management issues. The neighborhood bordering the campus must also be evaluated for additional security issues.

3. *Existing Discipline Practice:* Many schools have a schoolwide discipline plan. As Martin pointed out in his interview, confusion develops when teachers fail to follow the schoolwide plan. It is important that teachers understand the school's plan for discipline before accepting a position. The three candidates should also question the principals about their individual school's discipline policies, so they can determine whether their philosophies will fit into the existing discipline policies.

4. *Parental Involvement:* Parents will not be supportive if they do not think that the school and its personnel have their students' best interest at heart. Parents must feel comfortable coming to teachers and administrators with their concerns. When parents feel part of the school community, they will support teachers and administrators as they make difficult management decisions.

5. *Current Student Behavior Pattern:* A walk down any school hallway reveals much about the existing behavior pattern of a school. The noise level, degree of student engagement, amount of movement within the classrooms, and room arrangements speak volumes about how students behave. Change in existing behavior patterns comes slowly and requires all faculty to make a commitment to new patterns.

6. *School Administrators:* The amount of administrative support provided to teachers will determine how successful they will be in carrying out their discipline plans. Therefore, it is important that teachers share their plans with their administrators before implementing them. Denise wants to use Assertive Discipline as her classroom-management plan. However, if her principal doesn't value or agree with the principles of Assertive Discipline, Denise will find it difficult to carry out her plan.

## THE TEACHER'S EXPERIENCES IN THE CLASSROOM

Gathercoal (2001) notes that there is often a difference between what a teacher considers philosophically to be an appropriate action and what the teacher actually does when a problem occurs.

This is because actual classroom situations are complicated by the need for quick action, unforeseen situational factors, and emotions that are not present when a teacher abstractly plans for classroom management. Gettinger and Kohler (2006) stress that the key to effective teaching rests on the teacher's ability to make decisions about the appropriate classroom-management techniques within the context of their particular classroom. As a result, until teachers are put under pressure to act, they are never really sure how they will behave. Such will be the case for Denise, Martin, and Brianne. Although they all think they

## Tips from the Field

As teachers, we often fall into habits of communication with our children. In order to keep myself accountable for positive praise, I use a $+/-$ system for tracking interactions. On my clipboard I place a list of the names of all my students. For each positive comment I make I will add a $+$ sign, and for each redirection I add a $-$ sign. At the end of the data-gathering week, I will analyze the trends in my interactions. Not only do I see data on how I communicate with my class, but also how often I am talking to individuals. For students who receive frequent positive praise, I look for opportunities to push them to be more independent and rely on intrinsic satisfaction. For students who receive frequent redirection, I determine whether I need to review classroom rules and procedures with my whole class or if just a few individuals require a review of expectations. This also helps to determine the necessity of

a Functional Behavior Assessment for additional behavior support. For students who are often off-task, I also make sure that the first and last interaction of the day is a smile. I let them know I am happy to have them in my class, because they are the most high risk for additional problems such as depression, withdrawal, and lack of school success. In addition, I measure the frequency of interactions to ensure that I am fair in how often I talk to students to make sure that everyone is an equal partner in our classroom environment.

Stephanie Day
PK–Second-Grade Special Education
  Resource Teacher
Friendship Public Charter School
Chamberlain Campus
Washington, DC
2010 Washington, DC, Teacher of the Year

know the classroom-management plan they will use, ultimately what they do will be determined by a multitude of factors, many of which cannot be planned for in advance.

Each year teachers are required to revise their plans as they evaluate their experiences, learn about new research about classroom management, deal with changing school and district policies, and strive to meet the changing needs of students. Therefore, few teachers will use a single classroom-management plan throughout their careers; instead, over the years they will modify their plans and develop new ones as they reflect on their teaching and their students and as they learn from experience.

## PUTTING IT ALL TOGETHER

This textbook has reviewed twelve classroom-management models. These models fit into one of three distinct categories: classroom management as discipline, classroom management as a system, classroom management as instruction. Teachers may find that the models for one category might best meet their needs. Others may find that they will choose to pick aspects of various models to create a unique classroom management plan. One way to determine which category fits a particular teacher's personality traits, teaching styles, and personal philosophies is to complete the quiz found in Table 15.1.

**Table 15.1**  Classroom-Management Quiz

| Classroom-Management Item | Personal Agreement Score | | | | |
| --- | --- | --- | --- | --- | --- |
| | Strongly Disagree | | Agree | | Strongly Agree |
| 1. Effective classroom management includes the teaching of appropriate behavior and social skills. | 1 | 2 | 3 | 4 | 5 |
| 2. The teacher is in control and responsible for all decisions concerning classroom management. | 1 | 2 | 3 | 4 | 5 |
| 3. Planning for rules, instruction, classroom design, and procedures is essential to effective classroom management. | 1 | 2 | 3 | 4 | 5 |
| 4. Students must be taught morals and personal responsibility. | 1 | 2 | 3 | 4 | 5 |
| 5. Discipline must come before instruction. | 1 | 2 | 3 | 4 | 5 |
| 6. Consequences must exist for inappropriate behavior and for consistency should be the same for all students. | 1 | 2 | 3 | 4 | 5 |
| 7. Teachers must assure that students' rights are honored and respected. | 1 | 2 | 3 | 4 | 5 |
| 8. Students choose to misbehave and must face the consequences of their decisions. | 1 | 2 | 3 | 4 | 5 |
| 9. Students must be taught appropriate behavior. | 1 | 2 | 3 | 4 | 5 |
| 10. Effective classroom management is providing sufficient control so that all students can learn. | 1 | 2 | 3 | 4 | 5 |
| 11. Classroom management and instruction are interwoven and not two separate jobs of the teacher. | 1 | 2 | 3 | 4 | 5 |
| 12. Effective classroom management does not focus on behavior at a particular moment but on helping students develop positive interactions throughout their lifetime. | 1 | 2 | 3 | 4 | 5 |
| 13. Rules should be developed by the teacher and must be clearly defined. | 1 | 2 | 3 | 4 | 5 |
| 14. Teachers should teach the rules and procedures of the classroom rather than assuming that students understand their meaning. | 1 | 2 | 3 | 4 | 5 |
| 15. Teachers must help students make ethical judgments and decisions. | 1 | 2 | 3 | 4 | 5 |

*(continued)*

| Classroom-Management Item | Personal Agreement Score | | | | |
|---|---|---|---|---|---|
| | *Strongly Disagree* | | *Agree* | | *Strongly Agree* |
| 16. Students must share in classroom responsibilities. | 1 | 2 | 3 | 4 | 5 |
| 17. Rule development is a joint effort between students and teachers. | 1 | 2 | 3 | 4 | 5 |
| 18. Consequences should be based on the motivation and nature of the offense and designed to meet the individual needs of students. | 1 | 2 | 3 | 4 | 5 |

Calculate your score below. Determine which category in which you had your highest score. Based on the score you have below, consider the following:

■ *If you scored highest in category A, you may wish to consider the following classroom models:* Skinner's Behavioral Management, Canter's Assertive Discipline, Jones's Positive Classroom Discipline, and Albert's Logical Consequence.

■ *If you scored highest in category B, you may wish to consider the following classroom models:* Curwin and Mendler's Discipline with Dignity, Evertson's Classroom Organization and Management Program (COMP), Kohn's Building Community, and Marshall's Discipline without Stress® Punishments or Rewards.

■ *If you scored highest in category C, you may wish to consider the following classroom models:* Coloroso's Inner Discipline, Positive Behavior Support, Bodine and Crawford's Conflict Resolution and Peer Mediation, and Gathercoal's Judicious Discipline.

Place a score for each number beside the number of item.

| Category A | Category B | Category C |
|---|---|---|
| 2. _____ | 3. _____ | 1. _____ |
| 5. _____ | 9. _____ | 4. _____ |
| 6. _____ | 11. _____ | 7. _____ |
| 8. _____ | 14. _____ | 12. _____ |
| 10. _____ | 17. _____ | 15. _____ |
| 13. _____ | 18. _____ | 16. _____ |
| Total _____ | Total _____ | Total _____ |

# Key Terminology

Definitions for these terms appear in the glossary.

## Chapter Activities

### Reflecting on the Theory

1. Imagine that the same panel of principals that interviewed Denise, Martin, and Brianne is interviewing you. How would you define classroom management?

2. Take the quiz found in Table 15.1. What did the results of the quiz reveal about the classroom management you should select?

### Developing Your Personal Classroom Plan

1. State your philosophy of classroom management. In developing your philosophy, consider the following:

   - How do you view students? Must they learn appropriate behaviors because their basic nature is to be "bad," or do you consider that most students are "good" and want to behave appropriately?
   - How much freedom are you prepared to give students?
   - Do you want a teacher-centered or student-centered classroom?
   - Is your goal to prepare students for your classroom or for the world beyond your classroom?

2. How will your personality impact your classroom management? Evaluate your personality by considering the following with regard to your classroom-management plan:

   - What is your tolerance for noise?
   - What will be your tolerance level for student movement within the classroom?
   - What, if any, place is there in your classroom for joking and humor?
   - Do you consider yourself organized and structured?

3. What will be your instructional style? What teaching strategies will you use? How will your teaching style impact your classroom-management plan?

4. What will your classroom look like? Draw the floor plan and design your classroom. Explain in writing why you have designed the room as you have. How did you deal with issues of visibility, distractibility, and accessibility?

5. What will you do to prevent behavioral problems in your classroom?

6. What rules will you have? Who will develop the rules—you or you and your students working together? How will you share your rules with your students? How will you share your rules with parents?

7. How will you correct behavioral problems in your classroom? What will be the consequences for inappropriate behavior?

8. How will you use rewards or reinforcers in your classroom? What rewards will you give? Will they be individual or group rewards? What is your personal belief about giving rewards?

9. Describe three procedures you will use in your classroom.

## Chapter References

Brophy, J. (2006). History of research. In C. Evertson & C. Weinstein (Eds.), *Handbook of classroom management: Research, practice, and contemporary issues.* Mahwah, NJ: Lawrence Erlbaum Associates.

Gathercoal, F. (2001). *Judicious discipline.* San Francisco: Caddo Gap Press.

Gettinger, M., & Kohler, K. M. (2006). Process-outcome approaches to classroom management and effective teaching. In C. Evertson & C. Weinstein (Eds.), *Handbook of classroom management: Research, practice, and contemporary issues.* Mahwah, NJ: Lawrence Erlbaum Associates.

Martin, N. K., & Baldwin, B. (1993). *Validation of an inventory of classroom management style: Difference between novice and experienced teachers.* Atlanta, GA: American Educational Research Association. (ERIC Document Reproduction Service No. ED359240.)

Swick, K. J. (1985). *A proactive approach to discipline: Six professional development modules for educators.* Washington, DC: National Education Association. (ERIC Document Reproduction Service No. ED267027.)

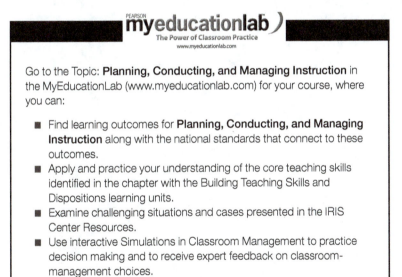

Go to the Topic: **Planning, Conducting, and Managing Instruction** in the MyEducationLab (www.myeducationlab.com) for your course, where you can:

- Find learning outcomes for **Planning, Conducting, and Managing Instruction** along with the national standards that connect to these outcomes.
- Apply and practice your understanding of the core teaching skills identified in the chapter with the Building Teaching Skills and Dispositions learning units.
- Examine challenging situations and cases presented in the IRIS Center Resources.
- Use interactive Simulations in Classroom Management to practice decision making and to receive expert feedback on classroom-management choices.

# Glossary

**70-20-10 Principle:** concept proposed by Richard Curwin and Allen Mendler that suggests that 70 percent of students rarely break rules or violate principles, 10 percent of students break rules on a somewhat regular basis, and 10 percent of students are chronic rule breakers and out of control most of the time.

**Accessibility:** a classroom arrangement that allows teachers to maintain on-task behavior by proximity control and to reach every student in the classroom quickly and without disturbing other students.

**Acquisition phase:** the time of the school year when students are first learning classroom rules.

**Active supervision:** the control of behavior by the physical presence of faculty and administrators in all areas of the school.

**Activity reinforcers:** participation in a preferred activity that is earned after completion of a required activity.

**Anarchy:** the lowest level of behavior identified by Marvin Marshall. Anarchy is the least desirable level of social behavior and classrooms operating at this level are without social order or are in chaos.

**Apology of action:** actions following an apology designed to repair the relationship between the offender and the person who was hurt.

**Applied behavior analysis:** a systematic approach to changing undesired behaviors; sometimes used as an alternative term for behavior modification.

**Appreciative praise:** praise that describes a student's work, action, or accomplishments.

**Assertive Discipline:** a classroom-management program developed by Lee and Marlene Canter in the early 1970s.

**Assertive teachers:** teachers who clearly and firmly express their requirements.

**Attention seeking:** one of the four reasons students misbehave.

**Backbone classroom:** a term developed by Barbara Coloroso to describe a classroom that is a consistent structure in which students are listened to and learn to respect themselves and others.

**Backup system:** a systematic, hierarchic organization of negative sanctions for misbehavior.

**Behavior modification:** a systematic program developed to change the behavior of individual students.

**Behavioral techniques:** classroom practices that use reinforcement and punishment to modify behaviors.

**Bothering:** term that is used interchangeably with bullying in Marvin Marshall's social development hierarchy.

**Brick-wall classroom:** a term developed by Barbara Coloroso to describe a classroom that is a dictatorship and in which rules are rigid and unbending.

**Bullying:** the second level of Marvin Marshall's social development hierarchy. Students who operate at this level of social development bully other students and, in some cases, the teacher as well.

**Checking for Understanding:** the second step in implementing Discipline without Stress® Punishments or Rewards in a classroom.

**Classroom community:** a classroom in which communities are built upon a foundation of cooperation throughout the day, with students continually being allowed to work together.

**Classroom Organization and Management Program (COMP):** a classroom-management program developed by Carolyn Evertson.

**Classroom principles:** statements that represent the value system of the classroom that define attitudes and expectations for long-term behavioral growth.

**Classroom universals:** organizational and teacher instructional practices that are essential to prevent the occurrence of problem behaviors while simultaneously increasing academic achievement.

**Compelling state interests:** four time-tested public-interest arguments crafted in the courts for the precise purpose of limiting constitutionally protected freedoms. The Judicious Discipline model uses four arguments as the basis for rule development.

**Conflict Curriculum approach:** an approach to conflict resolution in which students receive instruction in a separate course, distinct curriculum, or daily or weekly lesson plan.

**Conflict resolution:** a viable alternative to traditional classroom-management programs, in which students are taught alternatives for resolving personal conflict.

**Consensus decision making:** a group problem-solving strategy in which all parties affected by the conflict collaborate to resolve the conflict.

**Consequences:** the results of a student's behavior. When the behavior is inappropriate, the consequences are typically punitive in nature. This can be a synonym for punishment.

**Continuous schedule of reinforcement:** the reinforcement of behavior every time it occurs.

**Cooperation/Conformity:** the third level of Marvin Marshall's hierarchy of behaviors. This level of behavior is acceptable and desired because cooperation/conformity is as essential for a classroom to function as it is for a society to exist.

**Corrective consequences:** specific strategies for helping students manage their own behavior.

**Cyberbullying:** the use of technology to intimidate, threaten, stalk, ridicule, humiliate, taunt, and spread rumors about those being bullied.

**Democracy:** the highest level of Marvin Marshall's hierarchy of behaviors. It is at this level that students take responsibility for their own behaviors.

**Desists:** the actions and words used to stop misbehavior.

**Direct bullying:** bullying that involves face-to-face confrontation, open attacks (including physical aggression), and threatening and intimidating gestures.

**Discipline hierarchy:** a listing of consequences for misbehavior that begins with a warning and increases in severity with each infraction of a class or school rule.

**Discipline with Dignity:** a classroom-management theory developed by Richard Curwin and Allen Mendler that has as a fundamental principle the idea that everyone in the school setting is to be treated with dignity.

**Discipline without Stress® Punishments or Rewards:** a classroom management model developed by Marvin Marshall that promotes the internal motivation to develop responsibly—both individually and socially.

**Distractibility:** a classroom arrangement containing things or people in the room that compete for the teacher's attention or encourage off-task behavior.

**Evaluative praise:**   praise that evaluates personality or judges student character.

**Exclusionary time-out:**   the removal of a disruptive child from the immediate instructional area to another part of the room for a specified amount of time.

**Extinction:**   the weakening or elimination of behavior by withdrawing reinforcement.

**Failure-avoiding:**   one of the four reasons students misbehave.

**Flag rules:**   rules developed by the teacher that are nonnegotiable.

**Functional behavioral assessment:**   a process which seeks to identify the problem behavior a child or adolescent may exhibit, particularly in school, to determine the function or purpose of the behavior, and to develop interventions to teach acceptable alternatives to the behavior.

**Grandmama's rule:**   the concept that students must complete a required task before participating in a preferred activity.

**Guided Choices:**   the last part of Marvin Marshall's three-part strategy and designed to provide choice to students and to foster responsible behavior. By using guided choices, the teacher maintains authority without being confrontational.

**Hard response:**   a reaction to conflict in which adversaries compete until one is victorious.

**Hostile teacher:**   a teacher who responds to students in a manner that disregards the needs and feelings of students and in many cases violates students' rights.

**Indirect bullying:**   bullying that is psychological in nature and includes name calling, making faces, teasing, taunting, and making threats.

**Individual contract:**   a plan developed with an individual student when the social contract in the classroom fails to work.

**In loco parentis:**   a legal stance that grants to educators the same legal authority over students as that of parents.

**Inner Discipline:**   a classroom-management model developed by Barbara Coloroso.

**Integrated curriculum approach:**   a technique for teaching conflict resolution by using conflict in stories and literature as an example of positive and negative conflict resolution.

**Intermittent schedule of reinforcement:**   the reinforcing of behavior on some occasions but not each time the behavior occurs.

**Interval schedule of reinforcement:**   the distribution of reinforcements based on the passage of time.

**Intervention strategies:**   strategies used to redirect emerging student misbehavior.

**Jellyfish classroom:**   a term developed by Barbara Coloroso to describe a classroom that has no structure and in which the teacher's expectations are constantly changing.

**Judicious Discipline:**   a classroom-management system developed by Forrest Gathercoal that is based on the synthesis of professional ethics, good educational practice, and students' constitutional rights and responsibilities.

**Law of Effect:**   the concept that if behavior is rewarded it will be repeated, and if behavior is not rewarded it will cease.

**Limit Setting:**   a technique from Fredric Jones's Positive Classroom Discipline through which teachers systematically teach students to obey the classroom rules.

**Logical Consequences:**   a classroom-management program developed by Rudolf Dreikurs that suggests that the consequences of behavior should be natural, or logically tied to the behavior. Also, teacher-arranged consequences that are logically tied to the misbehavior.

**Mediation:** an approach to conflict resolution that uses trained selected individuals (adults or students) to act as neutral third parties who help conflicting students resolve their differences.

**Meta-analysis research:** a research method that combines the results of several studies that address a set of related research hypotheses.

**Natural consequences:** the results of ill-advised acts by students that are not imposed by the teacher or administrators but are the natural result of the behavior.

**Negative consequences:** undesired consequences that follow a behavior that are used to decrease the unwanted behavior.

**Negative reinforcement:** the removal or avoidance of an aversive stimulus following a desired behavior, which strengthens the likelihood that the desired behavior will be repeated in the future.

**Negotiation:** a process that allows conflicting students to work together to solve their dispute.

**Nonassertive teacher:** a teacher who does not make his or her needs or wants known and allows students to take advantage of him or her.

**Nonseclusionary time-out:** punishment of a student by excluding him or her from participation in classroom activities for a specified amount of time.

**Omission Training:** the name given to an incentive system that rewards the omission of unwanted behavior. In Omission Training, the teacher rewards the individual student for behaving appropriately for a certain period of time.

**Overlapping:** the teacher's ability to manage two issues simultaneously.

**Peaceable classroom:** an approach to conflict resolution in which the classroom becomes a warm and caring community.

**Peaceable school:** an approach to conflict resolution that applies the peaceable-classroom approach to managing the entire school.

**Perspective taking:** a strategy that teaches students to look at the world from another person's point of view.

**Positive Behavior Support:** a classroom management plan that uses a set of behavioral strategies to decrease problem behavior by teaching new skills and making changes in the environment.

**Positive Classroom Discipline:** a classroom-management model developed by Fredric Jones.

**Positive consequences:** the presentation of extrinsic incentives or rewards following behavior to increase or maintain behavior.

**Positive reinforcement:** the presentation of a reinforcer desired by the student after he or she has exhibited desired behavior.

**Power seeking:** one of the goals of misbehavior, in which the students try to control the teacher.

**Precorrection:** reminders given to students before students misbehave to remind students of the expected behavior and provide reinforcement for correct behavior.

**Preferred Activity Time (PAT):** activities students enjoy are earned by completing required work.

**Premack Principle:** a concept developed by David Premack suggesting that participation in a preferred activity can be used to reinforce a less-desired activity.

**Presentation punishment:** the presentation of an aversive stimulus in order to decrease inappropriate behavior.

**Primary prevention:** first level of a three-tier approach to managing behavior, which focuses on preventing the development and frequency of behavior problems.

**Primary reinforcements:** reinforcers that satisfy the biological needs or drives of a student.

**Principled response:** a response to conflict in which students use conflict-resolution skills.

**Procedures:** the specific "how-tos" that show students step by step how to successfully follow the rules.

**Process-outcome research:** research that seeks to identify a relation between class-room processes (teaching) and outcomes (how students behave).

**Proximity control:** the management of classroom behavior by moving throughout the classroom and being physically close to students.

**Punishment:** the application of an unpleasant stimulus or the withdrawal of a pleasant reward in an attempt to weaken a response.

**Punishment lite:** a term used by Alfie Kohn to describe consequences.

**Range of consequences:** an element of Discipline with Dignity that suggests that a consequence for misbehavior be selected, based on the needs of the individual student, from an established list.

**Ratio schedule of reinforcement:** the distribution of reinforcements based on the number of responses given.

**Real-world consequences:** a concept developed by Barbara Coloroso suggesting that consequences for misbehavior should either happen naturally or be reasonable consequences that are intrinsically related to a student's actions.

**Reconciliatory Justice:** a three-step process through which students are taught to fix problems they create, to prevent similar situations from recurring, and to heal their relationships with people they have harmed.

**Reinforcement:** the presentation of a desired reward to increase the likelihood that the desired behavior will be repeated under the same or similar circumstances.

**Removal punishment:** the removal of a pleasant stimulus or the eligibility to receive a positive reinforcement as a consequence for inappropriate behavior.

**Responsibility Training:** a group incentive program in which students are accountable for each other.

**Revenge-seeking behavior:** the result of a long series of discouragements in which the student has decided that there is no way to acquire the attention or power desired, and that only revenge will compensate for the lack of belonging.

**Ripple effect:** the concept that the teacher's method of handling misbehavior by one student influences the behavior of other students in the classroom.

**Seclusionary time-out:** the removal of a disruptive child for a specified period of time.

**Secondary prevention:** second level of a three-tier approach to managing behavior, which includes individualized behavior management programs and targeted group interventions.

**Secondary reinforcement:** a stimulus that is not reinforcing in itself but that becomes a reinforcer as a result of the connections students make to it.

**Severity plan:** the immediate removal from the classroom of a student whose severe misbehavior places students or the teacher in danger or prevents instruction from taking place.

**Shaping:**   the process of teaching new behaviors and new skills through the reinforcement of successive approximations of a terminal behavior.

**Social contract:**   a system for managing the classroom designed to enhance human interaction in the classroom.

**Social reinforcer:**   a behavior by teachers, parents, peers, or administrators that reinforces students and therefore increases desired behaviors.

**Soft responses:**   a reaction by students to conflict in which they give in as a way to keep peace in the classroom, school, or neighborhood.

**Student-centered approach:**   an approach to classroom management that focuses on helping students learn responsibility through interactions and experiences in a safe, welcoming environment.

**Teacher-centered approach:**   an approach to classroom management that places the total responsibility for maintaining control with the teacher.

**Teaching the Concepts:**   the first step in implementing Discipline without Stress® Punishments or Rewards in a classroom.

**Tertiary prevention:**   third level of a three-tier approach to managing behavior, which focuses on students who exhibit patterns of behaviors that are dangerous, highly disruptive, and/or impede learning interventions.

**Three-tier approach:**   the three levels of intervention in Positive Behavior Support.

**Token reinforcer:**   a reinforcer that has no intrinsic reinforcing properties; it obtains its value because it can be exchanged for something tangible or a desired activity.

**Transition smoothness:**   the teacher's management of the transition from one activity to another throughout the day.

**Variable schedule of reinforcement:**   the distribution of reinforcers in such a way that no pattern can be established, and the students cannot predict when they will be reinforced.

**Visibility:**   a classroom arrangement that allows every student to see teacher-led instruction, demonstrations, and presentations.

**Withitness:**   the teacher's ability to know everything that is happening in the classroom and an awareness of the verbal and nonverbal interactions of students with the teacher and classmates.

# Author Index

# Subject Index